COUPLE STORIES

The Library of Couple and Family Psychoanalysis

Series Editors: Susanna Abse, Christopher Clulow, Brett Kahr, and David E. Scharff

Other titles in the series:

Sex, Attachment, and Couple Psychotherapy: Psychoanalytic Perspectives
    edited by Christopher Clulow

How Couple Relationships Shape Our World: Clinical Practice, Research, and Policy Perspectives
    edited by Andrew Balfour, Mary Morgan, and Christopher Vincent

What Makes Us Stay Together? Attachment and the Outcomes of Couple Relationships
    Rosetta Castellano, Patrizia Velotti, and Giulio Cesare Zavattini

Psychoanalytic Couple Therapy: Foundations of Theory and Practice
    edited by David E. Scharff and Jill Savege Scharff

Family and Couple Psychoanalysis: A Global Perspective
    edited by David E. Scharff and Elizabeth Palacios

Clinical Dialogues on Psychoanalysis with Families and Couples
    edited by David E. Scharff and Monica Vorchheimer

COUPLE STORIES

Application of Psychoanalytic Ideas in Thinking about Couple Interaction

edited by

*Aleksandra Novakovic
and Marguerite Reid*

From the Committee on Family and Couple Psychoanalysis of
the International Psychoanalytical Association

LONDON AND NEW YORK

First published 2018
by Routledge
2 Park Square, Milton Park, Abingdon, Oxon OX14 4RN

and by Routledge
711 Third Avenue, New York, NY 10017

Routledge is an imprint of the Taylor & Francis Group, an informa business

Copyright © 2018 to Aleksandra Novakovic and Marguerite Reid for the edited collection and to the individual authors for their contributions..

The rights of the contributors to be identified as the authors of this work have been asserted in accordance with sections 77 and 78 of the Copyright, Design and Patents Act 1988.

All rights reserved. No part of this book may be reprinted or reproduced or utilised in any form or by any electronic, mechanical, or other means, now known or hereafter invented, including photocopying and recording, or in any information storage or retrieval system, without permission in writing from the publishers.

Trademark notice: Product or corporate names may be trademarks or registered trademarks, and are used only for identification and explanation without intent to infringe.

British Library Cataloguing-in-Publication Data
A catalogue record for this book is available from the British Library

Library of Congress Cataloging-in-Publication Data
A catalog record has been requested for this book

ISBN: 9781782206088 (pbk)

Typeset in Palatino
by The Studio Publishing Services Ltd
www.publishingservicesuk.co.uk
email: studio@publishingservicesuk.co.uk

CONTENTS

ACKNOWLEDGEMENTS ix

ABOUT THE EDITORS AND CONTRIBUTORS xi

SERIES EDITOR'S FOREWORD by David Scharff xix

INTRODUCTION xxiii

PART I
MAINLY THEORY

CHAPTER ONE
"As my shrivelled heart expanded": the dynamics of love, hate, and generosity in the couple 3
Aleksandra Novakovic

CHAPTER TWO
Oedipus killed the couple: murder on the Thebes highway 25
Viveka Nyberg

CHAPTER THREE
Projective identification processes in the couple relationship 47
Mary Morgan

CHAPTER FOUR
On container–contained dynamics in the couple relationship   65
David Hewison

PART II
COUPLE STORIES AND CLINICAL COMMENTARIES

CHAPTER FIVE
Marco and Rosa   85
   Co-therapy, containment, and the couple   91
   A clinical commentary for Marco and Rosa
      Christopher Clulow
   Finding a story   96
   A clinical commentary for Marco and Rosa
      Joanna Rosenthall
   Projective identification: rivalry, competition,   101
   and exclusion
   A clinical commentary for Marco and Rosa
      Stanley Ruszczynski
   Narcissism and loss of a shared ideal, oedipal exclusion,   107
   and sibling transference affecting a couple state of mind
   A clinical commentary for Marco and Rosa
      Jill Savege Scharff

CHAPTER SIX
Peter and Helen   113
   Over the hill to Oedipus   120
   A clinical commentary for Peter and Helen
      Andrew Balfour
   Facing death: mourning and reparation in a late   125
   middle-aged couple
   A clinical commentary for Peter and Helen
      Warren Colman
   Therapy: anxieties, defences, and the couple   129
   A clinical commentary for Peter and Helen
      Susan Irving
   Couples come in twos and threes: an oedipal perspective   135
   A clinical commentary for Peter and Helen
      Molly Ludlam

CHAPTER SEVEN
Daniel and Caroline — 141
- Containment and the couple — 147
  - A clinical commentary for Daniel and Caroline
    Eve Ashley
- Oedipal dynamics and the "white heat" of the session — 152
  - A clinical commentary for Daniel and Caroline
    Brett Kahr
- Shared couple defences against anxiety — 158
  - A clinical commentary for Daniel and Caroline
    Monica Lanman
- Trauma, the first born, and the oedipal situation — 163
  - A clinical commentary for Daniel and Caroline
    Sara Leon

CHAPTER EIGHT
Greg and Lottie — 169
- Anxieties and defences — 175
  - A clinical commentary for Greg and Lottie
    Susanna Abse
- The fog and the shadows of the past — 180
  - A clinical commentary for Greg and Lottie
    Pierre Benghozi
- Oedipal dynamics and the couple — 185
  - A clinical commentary for Greg and Lottie
    Peter Griffiths
- Containment and the couple — 190
  - A clinical commentary for Greg and Lottie
    Patsy Ryz

EPILOGUE — 195

REFERENCES — 197

INDEX — 207

To Miomir and Nicholas

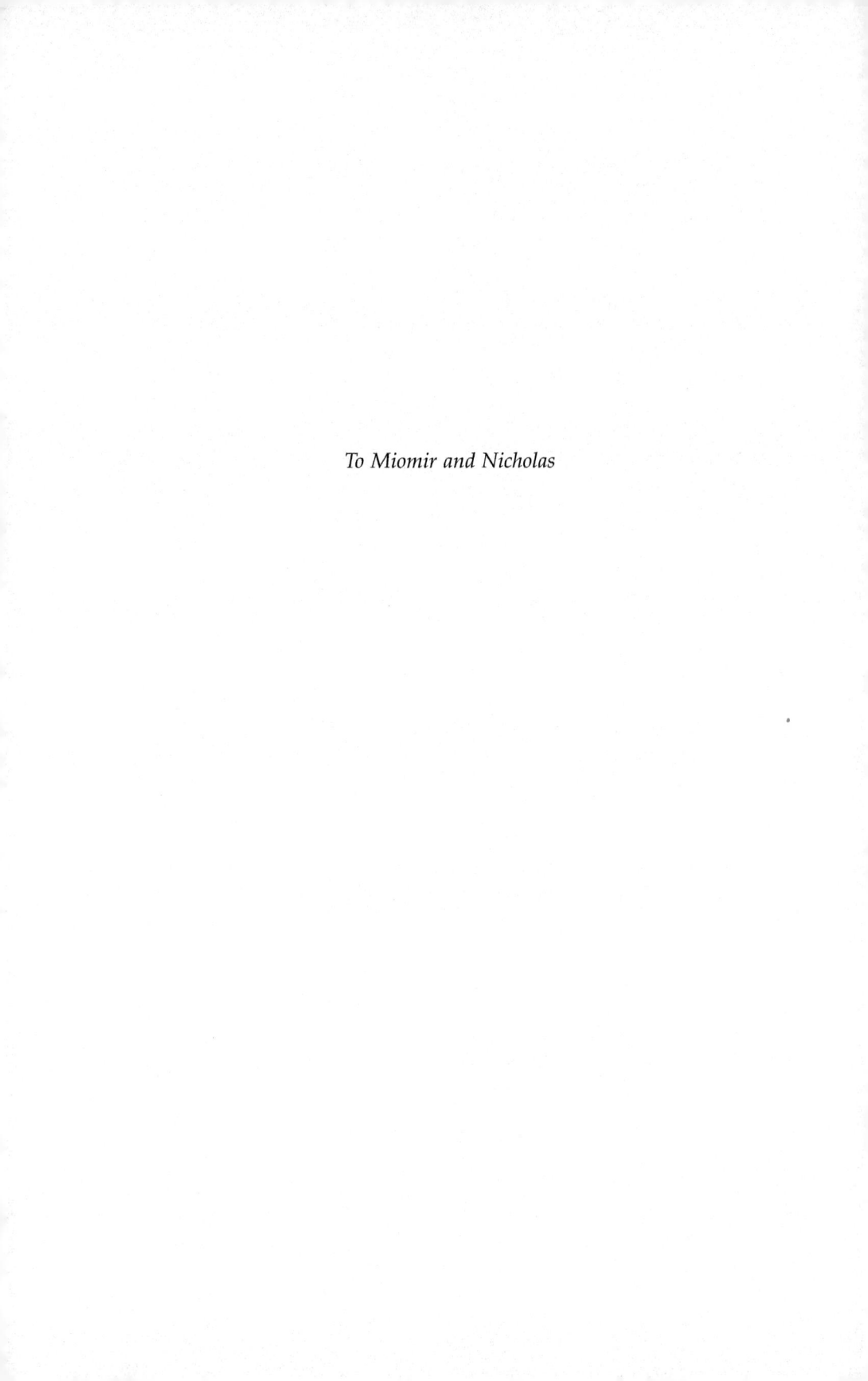

ACKNOWLEDGEMENTS

We would like to express our deep gratitude to all contributors to this book. Our thanks to Susanna Abse, Christopher Clulow, Brett Kharr, and David Scharff, Editors of The Library of Couple and Family Psychoanalysis Series, and Rod Tweedy, Karnac Editor, for their kind support of this project.

We are very grateful to Shirin Patel for her invaluable help editing this book, and to our friends John Rhodes and Colleen Gardener for their generous support.

ABOUT THE EDITORS AND CONTRIBUTORS

Susanna Abse is a couple psychoanalytic psychotherapist who has worked in private practice since 1991. She was CEO of the charity, Tavistock Relationships (2006–2016), and now also works as an organizational consultant and executive coach. She is a member of the British Psychoanalytic Council, and serves on its Executive Board. Susanna is a Fellow of the Centre for Social Policy at Dartington, a Leadership Fellow at St George's House, Windsor Castle, as well as a Member of the Editorial Board of *Couple and Family Psychoanalysis*, and Series Co-Editor of "The Library of Couple and Family Psychoanalysis" for Karnac Books.

Eve Ashley trained as an art teacher, and then as a child and adolescent psychotherapist at the Tavistock Clinic, qualifying in 2001. She continues to work in the NHS, with children, young people, and parents, alongside training and supervising child psychotherapists. In 2013, she completed a further training in couple psychotherapy at the Tavistock Centre for Couple Relationships (TCCR), now Tavistock Relations (TR). Eve has a private practice in Hastings, and is an online therapist at Tavistock Relations. She has contributed a commentary to the *ACP Journal*, and to Annalisa Barbieri's regular column in the

Guardian. A particular interest is how early childhood experiences are reworked in couple relationships.

Andrew Balfour studied English Literature before training in clinical psychology at University College London. He went on to train as an adult psychoanalytic psychotherapist at the Tavistock & Portman NHS Trust, while working in a staff post there. He subsequently trained as a couple psychotherapist at Tavistock Relationships (formerly Tavistock Centre for Couple Relationships). For more than ten years, he was Clinical Director, and he is now Chief Executive, there. He has published widely, and teaches both in the UK and abroad. With Mary Morgan and Christopher Vincent, he co-edited *How Couple Relationships Shape Our World: Clinical Practice, Research, and Policy Perspectives* (Karnac, 2012).

Pierre Benghozi is a child psychiatrist, psychoanalyst, and training analyst for group therapy training and for couple and family therapy training. He is President of the Research Institute for Couple and Family Psychoanalysis, Board Member of the European Federation for Psychoanalytic Psychotherapy (EFPP), Chair Founder of the EFPP Section for Psychoanalytic Couple and Family Psychotherapy, Member of the International Association of Couple and Family Psychoanalysis, and the French Society of Psychoanalytic Family Psychotherapy. He writes, lectures, and supervises internationally. His publications include "Adolescence and sexuality, links and network meshing" (in Benghozi, P., 1999), and "Families in transformation: a psychoanalytic approach" (in Nicolo, A., Benghozi, P., Lucarelli, D., 2014).

Christopher Clulow is a consultant couple psychoanalytic psychotherapist, registered with the British Psychoanalytic Council, and a Senior Fellow of Tavistock Relationships. He has published extensively on marriage, partnerships, parenthood, and couple psychotherapy, most recently from an attachment perspective. He is a Fellow of the Centre for Social Policy, Dartington, a member of the editorial board of *Couple and Family Psychoanalysis,* and an international editorial consultant for sexual and relationship therapy. He maintains a clinical and training practice from his home in St Albans and through the Balint Consultancy in London.

Warren Colman is a Jungian psychoanalyst and couple psychoanalytic psychotherapist, whose work has developed an experience-based relational style, rooted in the Jungian and psychoanalytic traditions. From 1982–1997, he worked at the Tavistock Marital Studies Institute. He is now a training and supervising analyst for the Society of Analytical Psychology, and Consultant Editor of the *Journal of Analytical Psychology*. He teaches, lectures, and supervises internationally, and has published many papers on diverse topics, including couple interaction, sexuality, the self, synchronicity, symbolic meaning, and the therapeutic process. His book, *Act and Image: The Emergence of Symbolic Imagination*, was published in 2016.

Peter Griffiths is a nurse consultant in child and family mental health, and therapist at the Tavistock and Portman NHS Foundation Trust working in both the child, young adults and families directorate (CYAF) and within the national workforce skills development unit (NWSDU). Regionally and nationally, he has developed training for a range of professionals in the child and adolescent mental health workforce. He is interested in all forms of experiential learning, in particular, Group Relations Conferences, which he has both designed and directed. Within the Family Mental Health Team at the Tavistock, he undertakes interpersonal therapy with parents, couple work, and parents as partners groups, and, at Tavistock Relationships, is completing training as a couple psychoanalytic psychotherapist.

David Hewison is a consultant couple psychoanalytic psychotherapist and Head of Research at Tavistock Relationships. He is the co-author (with Christopher Clulow and Harriet Drake) of *Couple Therapy for Depression: A Clinician's Guide to Integrative Practice* (2014), based on the model of couple therapy he developed as an evidence based treatment for depression in the National Health Service (NHS). He is a Jungian training analyst at the Society of Analytical Psychology, and he teaches internationally and publishes widely on individual and couple therapy and research. He has a particular interest in links between psychoanalysis and Jungian analysis, and in understanding creativity and imagination.

Susan Irving is a psychoanalyst, member of the British Psychoanalytic Association, and couple psychoanalytic psychotherapist, and qualified at TCCR, now Tavistock Relations. Her professional background was in psychiatric social work, in which she worked in London teaching hospitals until retraining as a psychotherapist with the British Association of Psychotherapy. She worked part-time in the public sector for many years, and is now in private practice in both London and Cornwall. She was a visiting lecturer at Tavistock Relations and facilitated clinical seminars for trainees in psychoanalytic couple psychotherapy. She is particularly interested in how primitive anxiety and trauma affect later couple relationships.

Brett Kahr is Senior Fellow at Tavistock Relationships at the Tavistock Institute of Medical Psychology in London, and also Senior Clinical Research Fellow in Psychotherapy and Mental Health at the Centre for Child Mental Health. He is a consultant psychotherapist at The Balint Consultancy, and former Chair of the British Society of Couple Psychotherapists and Counsellors. He is a Trustee of the Freud Museum, London, and author or editor of nine books, including, *Forensic Psychotherapy and Psychopathology: Winnicottian Perspectives*, and *Exhibitionism*, as well as *Sex and the Psyche*, *Tea with Winnicott*, and *Coffee with Freud*. He works with individuals and couples in Hampstead, North London.

Monica Lanman started out as a social worker, and then trained at the Tavistock Centre as an individual adult psychoanalytic psychotherapist, qualifying in 1980. She later trained as a couple psychoanalytic psychotherapist at the Tavistock Centre for Couple Relationships, now Tavistock Relationships (TR). Although semi-retired now, she still supervises at TR. She has written a number of papers on couple psychotherapy, published in various professional journals, including two papers reporting a research project she undertook on the outcome of couple psychotherapy, published in the *British Journal of Psychiatry*, and in *Psychology and Psychotherapy*.

Sara Leon trained at the Tavistock Clinic. She is a senior child and adolescent psychotherapist working in the East London NHS Trust. She works in the trauma and attachment pathway in the CAMHS Disability team at Hackney Ark, and has a particular interest in psychoanalytic interventions and attachment relationships that are complicated by disabilities and adoption. She also trained at Tavistock

Relationships as a psychoanalytic couple psychotherapist, and works as a visiting clinician in the generic and adopting together teams. She is a training supervisor for the Independent Psychoanalytic Child & Adolescent Psychotherapy Association, and teaches infant observation at the British Psychotherapy Foundation.

Molly Ludlam has worked as a teacher and social worker, before becoming a psychoanalytic psychotherapist with couples, individuals, and parents. Now focusing on teaching, writing, and editing (she is the founding editor, from 2011, of *Couple and Family Psychoanalysis*), her recent publications include "The perinatally depressed couple and the imperative of mourning" (2014), in: K. Cullen, E. Bondi, J. Fewell, E. Francis, & M. Ludlam (Eds.), *Making Spaces*; and "Lost—and found —in translation: do Ronald Fairbairn's ideas still speak usefully to 21st century couple therapists?" *fort da*, 22(2), 12–26 (2016).

Mary Morgan is a psychoanalyst and couple psychoanalytic psychotherapist. She is a Fellow of the British Psychoanalytical Society and at Tavistock Relationships, is the Reader in Couple Psychoanalysis and Head of the Couple Psychoanalytic Training. She has published many papers in the field of couple psychoanalysis, and is currently completing a book, entitled *A Couple State of Mind*. She is a member of the IPA's Couple and Family Psychoanalysis Committee, and on the board of the International Association for Couple and Family Psychoanalysis. She has developed and led couple psychotherapy trainings in several countries, lectures internationally, and has a private individual and couple analytic practice.

Aleksandra Novakovic is a psychoanalyst and couple psychoanalytic psychotherapist. She was a consultant clinical psychologist in the Adult Psychology Service, and Joint Head of the Inpatient & Community Psychology Service. She worked at Tavistock Relationships, taught and supervised on couple psychoanalytic psychotherapy training, and she supervised on the IGA Diploma Course in Reflective Practice in Organisations. Currently she teaches for the British Psychoanalytic Association, and is a Consultant Visiting Lecturer at Tavisock Relationships. She co-edited, with David Bell, a book on psychotic processes (Karnac, 2013), and edited *Couple Dynamics: Psychoanalytic Perspectives in Work with the Individual, the Couple, and the Group* (Karnac, 2016).

Viveka Nyberg is a lecturer and visiting clinician at Tavistock Relationships, where she was on the faculty staff. She is a Graduate Member of the Tavistock Institute of Medical Psychology, and a Senior Member of the British Psychotherapy Foundation. She has lectured in the UK, and internationally, and has a private practice in London. She is on the editorial board of the *Journal of Couple and Family Psychoanalysis*. Her writings include *Couple Attachments: Theoretical and Clinical Studies*, Karnac (2007), with Molly Ludlam, and "Developing a mentalization-based treatment (MBT) for therapeutic intervention with couples (MBT-CT)", with Leezah Hertzmann, in *Couple and Family Psychonalysis*, 2(4), 2014.

Marguerite Reid is a consultant child and adolescent psychotherapist who has more recently trained as a couple psychoanalytic psychotherapist. She co-founded the Perinatal Service at Chelsea and Westminster Hospital, where she specialised in perinatal mental health problems. Her doctoral research was in the area of perinatal loss and the mother's experience when she gives birth to the next baby. She is a visiting clinician at Tavistock Relationships. She has taught in the UK and abroad, and co-founded the Infant Observation Course in Izmir, Turkey where she has taught for many years. She has published in the area of perinatal mental health, and now works in private practice in London.

Joanna Rosenthall is a psychoanalyst (BPA) and psychoanalytic couple psychotherapist. She is Clinical Lead of the Couples Unit in Adult & Forensic Services of the Tavistock & Portman NHS Foundation Trust. She was senior staff for over twenty years at Tavistock Relationships, where she ran the Professional Doctorate in couple psychoanalytic psychotherapy. She teaches and lectures in the UK and abroad, on the psychoanalytic theory and practice of working with couples. She has published papers in this area—recently on violent couples, and working in the transference with couples. She also works in private practice, and is writing a novel.

Stanley Ruszczynski is a psychoanalyst and couple psychoanalytic psychotherapist, a Full Member of BPA, IPA, BPF, and the BSCPC. He is Consultant Adult Psychotherapist (and past Clinical Director, 2005–2016) at the Portman Clinic (Tavistock and Portman NHS Foundation

Trust, London), which offers psychotherapeutic treatment to patients presenting with criminality, violence, or damaging sexual behaviours. He was Deputy Director of Tavistock Centre for Couple Relationships, now Tavistock Relationships, 1987–1993. He has a private clinical practice, authored many book chapters and articles, and edited and co-edited five books, including *Psychotherapy with Couples* (Karnac, 1993), and, with James Fisher, *Intrusiveness and Intimacy in the Couple* (Karnac, 1995).

Patsy Ryz is a child and adolescent psychotherapist and a psychoanalytic couple psychotherapist. She has worked for a number of years in a wide variety of NHS settings and also in the voluntary sector, where she headed a Child and Family Consultation Service. She currently works in private practice in North London, seeing children, adolescents, parents, and couples. She is also a visiting clinician at Tavistock Relationships, where she has undertaken assessments, supervision, and long-term work with couples. Patsy has been involved in the Parenting Together and Parents in Dispute Services, and is part of the MA training team.

Jill Savege Scharff, MD, is co-founder of the International Psychotherapy Institute www.theipi.org; Faculty Member of its Couple, Child, and Family Program; Founding Chair and Supervising Analyst at its International Institute for Psychoanalytic Training and its Child Analytic and Psychotherapy Training Program; Clinical Professor of Psychiatry, Georgetown University, Washington, DC, USA. She is the co-author of books and chapters on object relations, and individual, couple, and family therapy, including *Object Relations Couple Therapy* and *The Interpersonal Unconscious*; co-editor of *New Paradigms in Treating Relationships* and *Psychoanalytic Couple Therapy, Psychoanalysis Online 1, 2 and 3*; and an analyst, child, couple, and family therapist in private practice in Chevy Chase, MD, USA.

SERIES EDITOR'S FOREWORD

As the pace of change in our world accelerates, as social forces impinge on the privacy and wellbeing of family and marital life, societies around the world face crises concerning the viability of marriage and adult intimate partnerships as containers of healthy development, as crucibles for the growth of future generations. In consequence, our skills as professionals who support the inevitable vulnerabilities that impinge on marital, couple, and family life need constant development, re-examination and renewal. The Library of Couple and Family Psychoanalysis, the series in which this book is published, is dedicated to that task. The Series Editors have invited colleagues who share our dedication to these tasks to report on their work, on the questions that confront them as they strive to help people all over the world and from all walks of life, and to join in strengthening our abilities to help when help is needed. No one finds this an easy task, and it is rare that we are fully satisfied with our ability or with the completeness of our work. Instead, we take comfort and satisfaction from our own continuing learning about how to do our work better, how to formulate ways of thinking that guide us and our colleagues and students as we all learn, and how to adjust our skills to the evolving forms of relationships and the changing problems that couples and families bring us.

I come to this role as one of the series editors with a deep conviction about the importance of analytic work with couples. Those who practise this difficult craft need devotion, a depth of training, continuing renewal, and a community of colleagues with whom to share the work. I have always thought it was pretty much the most difficult mode of psychotherapy I do, because couples so often come to us with locked-in systems constructed over many years. Although the design of their partnerships is built to keep them going, they come to us because they have woven in compromises they can no longer tolerate. When we see such partners as a couple, we are on the outside. While they hope we can help them fashion something fundamentally different, they are all too often devoted to keeping their partnership going as it has been, a devotion crafted out of fear that change will only make things worse. So, the partners often share the effort to keep us on the outside, perhaps putting up with what we have to say while unconsciously ignoring us almost completely.

Because this work is often—although not always—so difficult, it requires that we be part of a community of fellow travellers who are also committed to persisting, to improving our skills. It is not easy to stay on the alert for subtle openings in the bastions couples present. While we are staying alert to do so, at the same time we have to move with the times in order to understand the changing face of marriage, the changing conditions that couples face in their own worlds, and the changing contours of marriage and intimate partnerships in the wider world that bring both new opportunities and new challenges. We can no longer assume that we will be doing marital therapy with a couple comprising a man and a woman with traditional views about marriage, sex, and family. Mores and patterns are changing so fast that keeping up clinically and theoretically is a continuing challenge. Nevertheless, even while we face the need to understand same-sex couples, affairs, and open marriages, changing gender issues and sexual practices, the widening structure of the families in which the couples live, and the cultural assumptions that couples from widely varying worlds bring to us—all enough to make our heads swirl—we still need to hone our basic analytical tools. We need to sharpen our focus on the unconscious organisation of the couple in the room with us, to look for transference and countertransference interaction as our basic guide to where we are at any given moment, and to where the couple needs to go in treatment. We need these skills because, across the widening variety of situations we meet in the modern world, fundamental skills and our basic compasses are needed more than ever.

The editors of this book have assembled a "Who's Who" of eminent contributors in the field of couple and child therapy in order to provide a much-needed collection of clinical studies that aims to support us in our work. They have produced a book that does two main things. In the first part of the book, they summarise the principle ideas that form the foundation of our work: first, the understanding of development with special emphasis on the early shifts in capacity of mind to move from black-and-white sorting of experience, to nuance, understanding, empathy, and the ability to forgive and repair; second the central psychoanalytic formulation of the Oedipus complex as the foundation of triangular thinking that lifts each of us towards an ability to see ourselves and our relationships from an outside perspective; third, the mechanism of unconscious communication that uses projective and introjective identification; fourth, the necessity of a personal mind to form a containing crucible for the growth and repair of another person's mind. Although there are many differences of psychoanalytic theory and varying approaches to analytic couple therapy, these four areas constitute a shared framework on to which we can then graft other contributions from disparate parts of our field. This first section of the book, therefore, constitutes a reliable foundation for relatively new students of our craft, and, at the same time, an opportunity for veteran colleagues to update and validate their foundational ideas.

The second section of the book does something quite different. It offers a rich addition to the library of a basic resource in our field: the clinical case report. The four cases, given anonymously and generously by students and colleagues, allow the examination of basic ideas in our work, as each is discussed by several eminent colleagues. Each discussion is unique, not only for the particular case, but within the collection as a whole. These discussions can be taken as examples of the many valuable perspectives that formal discussants bring, each illuminating from its own particular vector of examination. The discussions demonstrate the variety of ideas that seem to each discussant to be most relevant to the cases, even as these colleagues can be seen to share an overall basic orientation that views clinical experience through a psychoanalytic lens. For these reasons, the cases and their discussions are valuable both to those of us who have been doing this work for a long time, and to new students of couple psychotherapy. They let us compare the lens we use ourselves with those of valued colleagues, even while showing our younger colleagues how we, as a group, think about the large variety of issues relevant to our work with any given couple.

This collection is not a monograph that tells us how to do our work; it does something more important. It leads the way in establishing our common foundation, and then in demonstrating a variety of ways these foundational ideas can be applied in order to serve our understanding and empower the therapy we offer. This book, a treasure trove of clinical wisdom, is a resource well worth examining and re-examining as each of us strives to improve our own clinical thinking and our clinical work.

David Scharff
International Psychotherapy Institute,
Chair of the International Psychoanalytic Association
Committee on Family and Couple Psychoanalysis,
The Library of Couple and Family Psychoanalysis
Series Co-Editor

Introduction

The aim of this book is to present the application of some key psychoanalytic concepts in thinking about the couple relationship. The contributors to the first part of the book, "Mainly theory", discuss how psychoanalytic ideas can be used in conceptualising the nature of the couple relationship. They draw on different models, and discuss couple interaction in the paranoid–schizoid and depressive positions, oedipal dynamics in the couple relationship, and the processes of projective identification and containment in the couple.

In the second part of the book, "Couple stories and clinical commentaries", four couples tell a "couple story" during their clinical session. There are several clinical commentaries for each couple story, presenting different ways of thinking about a particular couple. The couple stories are brief, perhaps dreamlike or poetic, not in terms of their *content*, as they are neither a direct expression of the unconscious nor artistic, but in *form*, since each story is one of the "condensed" narratives of the couple's conscious and unconscious relations. It would be unrealistic to analyse in greater depth a couple relationship based on the one therapy session presented in a couple story. It is possible, however, to reflect on the feelings that the partners evoke in each other in the course of a session, and on the partners' experience of their relationship.

The clinical commentaries present the contributors' analytic attitude and the models that they draw upon in their imaginative interpretations of the couple stories. The clinical commentaries provide an insight into how psychoanalytic couple therapists think about the themes that couples bring to their session, what they might select as a focus, how they might go about developing a hypothesis about the nature of the relationship between the partners, and the links they make between the clinical material and theory. The contributors bring some convergent, complementary, as well as different, ideas about "what is going on" in a particular session with a particular couple. Different clinical commentaries present different perspectives on the same clinical material, and this complexity perhaps approximates the plurality of a couple or a group. The reader is not presented with a single point of view or a defined and specific understanding of a case, but with multiple layers and different and complementary ideas and stories.

We wish here to emphasise that for any given event or experience in the life of a person or couple, many meanings can be discerned, and that there are different ways of understanding the phenomena as they emerge in the consulting room. Interpretation is never quite "finished" or definitive, and each interpretation is an opportunity to develop a deeper understanding, or search for another way of conceptualising the meaning. Different interpretations in this book address various aspects and levels, and highlight the reality of the diverse manifestations and meanings in the couple interactions. Multiple interpretations can, of course, be in contradiction to each other, but they can also be harmonious and resonant. In the spirit of collaboration, all contributors jointly create the content of this book on the application of psychoanalytic concepts in the exploration of couple dynamics, and each author contributes to the group of ideas their particular interpretation and point of view. We hope that this book will stimulate further dialogues and thoughts about couple relations.

All the authors in these chapters share a view that psychoanalytic concepts can yield a greater understanding of the sometimes baffling complexity and suffering, but also fulfilment, of life as a couple. We believe that there have been significant developments in conceptualisation and practice in this field, and hope that detailed thinking and clinical examples will be of interest to experienced therapists, and of use to those who are learning psychoanalytic ways of working. We also believe that the texts here will be of interest to any who seek to understand the life of the couple, professionals who are not directly involved in clinical work, and members of the general public with an academic interest.

PART I
MAINLY THEORY

CHAPTER ONE

"As my shrivelled heart expanded": the dynamics of love, hate, and generosity in the couple

Aleksandra Novakovic

In this chapter, I present the object relations theory of the paranoid–schizoid and depressive positions and discuss the couple interactions within these two positions. I summarise Klein's (1975c,f,g[1940, 1946, 1957]) and some post-Kleinian ideas[1] about the two basic positions, or states of mind—the paranoid–schizoid and depressive positions—and present concepts that are, in my view, most relevant to the topic of this chapter. The paranoid–schizoid and depressive positions are characterised by different anxieties and defences that most, and perhaps all, individuals and couples alike, experience to some extent and at some points in their lives. I found that Proust's (2002[1919]) metaphors imaginatively capture and bring to life, so to speak, the fantastical aspects and complexity of emotional life described by Klein, and resonate with the dynamics in these two positions, and I discuss a few segments from *In the Shadow of Young Girls in Flower* (*In Search of Lost Time*, Volume 2). Finally, I consider the fused, warring, differentiated, benign, creative, and generous couple relations within these different positions.

Paranoid–schizoid and depressive positions

In her work with small children, Klein developed the play technique. She found that children's unconscious phantasies,[2] that is, their wishes, anxieties, and feelings about the relationship between the parents, and feelings about parents, siblings, and family, were represented in children's play. Klein observed in children's play a split between how the parents are unconsciously represented, and that the "parental imagos are separately endowed ... with wholly good and benign qualities and intentions, or else with wholly bad ones" (Hinshelwood, 1989, pp. 417–418). Klein used the term "splitting" to describe this process of separating the "good" from the "bad" and the splitting into "only good" and "only bad" figures.

By using mental mechanisms of splitting, projection, and introjection, children, and individuals in all stages of life, project good and bad parts of themselves, that is, their phantasies, into the world and they also take in—introject—aspects of external reality. Segal (1988a) points out the difference between the processes of projection and introjection, and the unconscious mental representation in phantasy:

> For instance, it is possible to say that an individual at a given moment is using the processes of projection and introjection as mechanisms of defence. But the processes themselves will be experienced by him in terms of phantasies which express what he feels himself to be taking in or putting out, the way in which he does this and the results which he feels these actions to have. (Segal, 1988a, p. 16)

The child's experiences stem from the continuous interaction between the child's internal world and the environment, and it is on the basis of these interactions that the child's complex internal world develops. Klein emphasised that from the beginning of life love and hate coexist. It is of crucial significance in early development, and also in later life, how feelings of love and hate are experienced or denied, introjected or projected, integrated or split.

Klein discovered that there were two kinds of anxieties that children expressed in their play, the paranoid–schizoid anxiety, which is about the survival of the self, and the depressive anxiety, which is about the survival of the other. Although, the paranoid–schizoid position is established first, and the depressive position subsequently, Spillius (2007a) points out that Klein refers to "positions" and not to "phases", since "throughout childhood and indeed also in later life there can be fluctuation between the two positions" (p. 35).

The paranoid–schizoid position refers to a particular state of mind, when the individual perceives himself or herself, as well as people with whom he or she has a close relationship, as either completely good or wholly bad. In this split universe, the relationship with a "good" person is experienced as good, loving, or valuable, while with a "bad" person, it is akin to being at war, hateful, or just devoid of any meaning or goodness. It is not only that the subject or external figure[3] is felt to be all "good" or all "bad", but the whole world and life itself can be perceived in this idealised or devaluing tone, without many nuances in between.

The main anxieties in this position are persecutory or paranoid.[4] Persecutory anxieties concerning the survival of the self are, essentially, a fear of being destroyed, annihilated, or fragmented, and, similarly, there might be related anxieties of being attacked, controlled, hurt, tormented, etc. In order to cope with, or rather survive, these anxiety situations, the subject uses defences, usually referred to as paranoid or primitive defences: projective identification, idealisation, omnipotence, and splitting.

Klein describes a process she terms projective identification that involves splitting and projection (in phantasy) of parts of the self, or internal figures, into the other person, who might then identify with these projections. Projective identification is based on the schizoid mechanism of splitting "good" from "bad" parts of the self. The subject can project and get rid of a "bad" part of the self, or project a "good" part of the self into the external figure. Conversely, by introjection, "good" and "bad" external figures are taken in.

Projective identification as a defence mechanism can be employed for attacking a "bad" figure, or for atoning feelings of envy by attacking and spoiling the goodness of a "good" figure. Projective identification is also used for evasion of a frightening or painful experience of separation. Thus, by projecting a part of the self into the other, the other can be omnipotently possessed and controlled in phantasy. In reality, these processes are much more interdependent and fluid.

Grotstein (2009) describes Klein's view of projective identification as a defensive mechanism that is basically an unconscious, omnipotent, and intrapsychic phantasy. He emphasises the significance of Bion's finding that projective identification could also be a "communicative phenomenon in which the unconscious of the subject actually influences the unconscious of the object" (p. 301). The concept of projective identification is discussed by Morgan in Chapter Three, while the communicative aspects of projective identification and containment are discussed by Hewison in Chapter Four.

Segal (1988b) highlights the significance of the paranoid–schizoid position, not only in child development, but also the important protective function some defences provide, in a modified form, for adults:

> With splitting are connected persecutory anxiety and idealisation. Of course both, if retained in their original form in adulthood, distort judgment, but some elements of persecutory anxiety and idealisation are always present and play a rôle in adult emotions. Some degree of persecutory anxiety is a precondition for being able to recognise, appreciate and react to actual situations of danger in external conditions. Idealisation is the basis of the belief in goodness of objects and of oneself, and is a precursor of the good object–relationships. (Segal, 1988b, p. 36)

When an individual is in the paranoid–schizoid position, the picture of oneself and the other is clear-cut, or, rather, it is black or white, but, on an unconscious level, the subject can experience different internal figures, or parts of the self, in various relationships or in conflict with each other. For example, in a couple relationship, both he and she are convinced that they "know" what is going on. The situation is clear—the other is "doing" something "wrong" or "bad". They both "know" that they are "right" in feeling that they have to protect themselves or retaliate for the undeserved, unprovoked, and hurtful act or sentiment that the other makes them suffer.

On an unconscious level, both he and she project their own feelings into their partner, for instance, a fear of abandonment, and then provoke and attack in the other this disavowed part of themselves. She feels he makes her suffer, because she cannot rely on him and trust him to want to commit to the relationship. She then retreats in silence and withdraws emotionally. Faced with her retreat, he sees her as deliberately withholding, and this makes him angry. While she ignores him, he feels unwanted, hurt, and enraged, because he cannot "get through" to her. He becomes insulting, shouts, and threatens to leave. His rage, hurtful comments, and threat to leave convince her, yet again, that she is "right" in not trusting him. The hurtful, enraging, or frightening experience of abandonment is enacted in the couple relationship, since they both feel rejected. Yet, in their different ways, they both also "force", or induce, the other by projective identification to experience their own fear of being abandoned. In this instance, both partners share this anxiety. Perhaps the hope in coming together was that the other would "give" them that "belief" that they were "wanted". However, by projecting their anxieties and making the other identify with feeling "unwanted", they recreate the hurtful experience in the other. While both feel rejected, they each also become a rejecting and abandoning figure for the other. Both feel hurt and on another, less conscious level, perhaps avenged for being "rejected".

This would be a more ordinary occurrence of a heated and possibly repetitive couple conflict, while in psychosis, when the subject regresses or predominantly functions on a pathological paranoid–schizoid level, the boundaries between the subject and the external reality can become extremely blurred. In very disturbed states of mind, due to the relentless and massive employment of projective identification, the subject can be delusional and experience a profound confusion between self and other. It is also relevant to note, however, that when children, and individuals in general, feel disturbed in their internal or external reality by an event that provokes fear about their safety or survival, they can regress to a more infantile paranoid–schizoid level, although, subsequently, they regain a more balanced outlook.

Envy and jealousy are significant in early development, as in life in general, and can have a profound impact on the capacity to love, work, and relate with others, depending on how these feelings are experienced, worked through, or defended against. Likierman (2015) summarises the distinction between the two:

> Klein suggested that jealousy is experienced in relation to a twosome or a couple, and triggered by possessive desires for a loved object when it is out of reach and seen to belong to another . . . Unlike jealousy, which focuses on the rivalry for a good object, envy does not place value on the object at all. On the contrary, it focuses direct aggression not on rivals for the object, but on the object itself, and represents a malign resentment of its goodness. (Likierman, 2015, p. 175)

The envied figure is attacked, and its good qualities can be diminished and spoiled in different ways. Spillius (2007b) adds a dimension in considering the dynamic interaction between two people, the giver and receiver, in stirring up or containing the experience of envy. She finds that factors that can mitigate or exacerbate the envy depend on how the person who gives is perceived by the person who receives, and how, in turn, the giver perceives the receiver.

In the depressive position, the subject is able to bring together different and diverging feelings about the other person, to experience the *otherness* of the other, and to feel that he or she is *separate* from the other person and *different*. Therefore, the subject can experience the other in a more realistic way. Instead of an either black or white picture of the other, of the world, and, indeed, of oneself, which is a characteristic experience in the paranoid–schizoid position, the other is perceived as having both helpful, caring, loving attributes, as well as, a number of weaknesses. When the subject is in a depressive position state of mind, he or she is aware that the other can, at times, be inconsiderate, withholding, envious, or hostile, but, on the whole, the subject is able to maintain an awareness of both good and bad aspects of the other person, and contain different ambivalent feelings about people and life in general.

For instance, in a couple relationship, one partner becomes angry with the other, and, in the grip of a disturbing emotional experience, feels hurt or resentful. In the heat of the moment, he or she sees, or, rather, feels, only the "badness" of the other. This "badness" could be anything that gave rise to the annoyance or upset with the partner. However, there is a capacity to eventually move out of the paranoid–schizoid state and regain the experience of the other as a "whole" person, as both "good" and "bad". This ability to recapture the "whole" person, despite still feeling some declining reverberations of hurt or anger evoked when the other was experienced only as "bad", is enabled by recapturing the "whole" person within oneself, both the "good" and the "bad" parts of the self. Hence, one is no longer in the grip of a paranoid–schizoid state type of illusion of being completely "right", solely "good" or morally justified.

The paranoid–schizoid and depressive positions are never fixed. The shifts between these two positions can reflect and can also be reflected in the different oedipal phantasies pertaining to these two different positions. Hinshelwood (1994) points out that Klein modified Freud's theory of the Oedipus complex in emphasising the importance of the early stages of development, and that, in her theory of the early Oedipus complex, she shifts the focus from the idea of actual parents to the phantasy world of the child.

The infant's increasing capacity to come to terms with the oedipal situation is linked with the establishment of the depressive position. Britton (1989) made a significant contribution in conceptualising the link between the depressive position, mental development, and the oedipal situation. He found that the development is enhanced when the child is able to envisage a benign parental intercourse from a different position, in a space outside the self. It is this awareness of the space outside the self, that furthers the development of the child's capacity to observe and think, the capacity to be a witness, and not a participant in, the parental relationship, and, in turn, to work through the oedipal situation. The theories about the Oedipus complex are discussed by Nyberg in Chapter Two.

A capacity to experience guilt in the depressive position and concern about the effects of one's actions on another person is a fundamentally different experience from the persecutory guilt in the paranoid–schizoid position. The latter is marked by the subject feeling threatened and having a nagging feeling of being "bad" for having done something "wrong". Persecutory guilt is a disturbing experience, and, essentially, it is a fear of punishment and retribution for one's misdeeds. In psychotic depression, the subject might feel he or she is utterly despicable, doomed to be hated, or unworthy for having caused some unforgivable and irremediable damage. In a very disturbed state of mind, the subject can feel compelled to atone and expiate the persecuting guilt by some violent self-destructive act, or, if the phantasies about being persecuted for the irremediable damage are projected on the other, then by attacking this "other".

In the depressive position, the subject's guilt is felt as sorrow, pain, and sadness about the injustice, harm, or injury they believe that they inflicted on the other, either in their thought or deed. Since the main anxiety in this position is not about a threat or damage to oneself, but about the damage one has caused in phantasy or reality to the other, the person feels concern for the other, a need to repair, to put right the harm that one feels one has caused. There is a capacity for gratitude and appreciation of the other, and also for generosity manifest in the ability to forgive the other and oneself. Klein emphasises the importance of mourning in the depressive position, and Steiner (1992) points to the intensely conflicting experiences of mourning when the subject has a realisation of the hurt and harm inflicted on the internal or external figure, and feels that his or her love was not sufficient to protect and prevent the damage that was done.

Jaques (1988[1965]) links the depressive position with a capacity, in mid life (and in later life), to experience and re-experience the feelings of loss and grief, and "to love and mourn what has been lost and what is past, rather than to hate and feel persecuted by it" (p. 245). If the subject can mourn the losses and past grievances, he can then begin to mourn his own eventual death, while his capacity for creativity "takes on new depths and shades of feeling".

If, in the depressive position, the recognition of dependence and need for the other person provokes too much anxiety or envy, or if the pain about the perceived damage in phantasy is too great, the subject can resort to manic defences. By employing these defences, one avoids awareness of these disturbing feelings: the guilt is evaded by denying the damage that the subject feels he has caused, and by denying the goodness and importance of the other person, the need for the other is evaded and denied. The other person is then perceived as having nothing good, desirable, or valuable, and, in this act of disparaging the other, the subject feels triumphant and superior.

The focus of this chapter is on the paranoid–schizoid and depressive positions and how the different states of mind within these positions manifest in couple interaction; however, there are innumerable and myriad possible experiences within each of these two positions. Steiner (1988) reminds us that: "The distinction between the two positions has an impressive quality but does sometimes makes us forget that, within the positions, mental states with very different qualities exist. (p. 325)

The two positions fluctuate, and the shifts between the positions can be regressive or developmental. Britton (1988a) develops further Bion's idea of the alternating movements between the two positions, and distinguishes a regression to the pathological paranoid–schizoid position from the movement to a non-pathological, or normal, paranoid–schizoid position. He points out the developmental aspects of shifts between reintegration in the depressive position and a disintegration in the non-pathological paranoid–schizoid position that occur in the encounter with a "new" idea that shatters the stability of "knowing".

The fears and grievances, as well as the capacity to mourn, love, and bear the turmoil of "new" ideas, are reworked over and over again in phantasy and reality, with past and present figures, in repetitive or in new ways:

> Although love-relationships in adult life are founded upon early emotional situations in connection with parents, brothers and sisters, the new relationships are not necessarily mere repetitions of early family situations . . . Normal adult relationships always contain fresh elements which are derived from the new situation—from circumstances and the personalities of people we come in contact with . . . (Klein, 1975b[1937], p. 325)

Segments from Proust and reflections on the shifting states of mind

I now turn to Proust and consider several sections from his work where he ingeniously and in detail describes the protagonist's imaginings, associations, and feelings, and the subtle changes that occur from moment to moment. I chose these passages since they vividly convey the vicissitudes of feelings, and capture the flow of conscious and unconscious preoccupations in the shifts between the paranoid–schizoid and depressive states of mind. As in any reflections on a work of art, my interpretation is but one of many.

Proust describes some unsettling feelings that the protagonist of his novel had when he separated from his parents, and went with his grandmother on a holiday to the seaside resort of Balbec. He was critical of his new surroundings, and felt disconcerted when they checked into the Grand Hotel. By the time he found himself alone in an unfamiliar hotel room, and was just about to rest, he was in a state of turmoil:

> I would have liked at least to lie down for a moment on the bed: but that would have done me no good, since I would have been incapable of granting any rest to that bundle of sensations that the waking body, even the material body, is for each of us, and also because the unknown objects which surrounded it, by forcing it to keep its perceptions in a permanent state of defensive alertness, would have held my eyes and ears, all my senses, in a posture as cramped and uncomfortable, even if I had stretched out my legs, as the one Louis XI inflicted on Cardinal La Balue by having him locked in a cage which made it impossible either to sit or stand. (Proust, 2002[1919], p. 245)

I find Proust's description of the persecutory experience of having no secure place, internally and externally, to be a striking description of a paranoid–schizoid state of mind. He, the protagonist, was unable to control and arrest "that bundle of sensations", the "bundle" suggesting a bunch of raw unprocessed "sensations" or nonsensical, frightening, and unintegrated bits of experiences. He was shackled and tormented by his own phantasies that he projected into the room, and, by projecting, he invested his feelings and parts of himself into the "unknown objects" that "surrounded" him.

Consequently, the room became a disturbing place that cruelly caged him. He was trapped, and there was no escape. He was helpless, without any control, unable to "sit or stand", let alone move and save himself from the dreadful situation. There is also a sense of some confusion, as, on the one hand, he was feeling "cramped" within himself, stuck in having incessantly to keep his "perceptions in a permanent state of defensive alertness", and, on the other hand, the objects in the room were confining and tormenting him.

His phantasies about the cruel control could reflect the unconscious dynamic relationship between his internal figures, the punishing "Louis XI" and the suffering "Cardinal La Balue". One can speculate whether the figure of "Louis XI" unconsciously represents his mother or his father, or the parental couple jointly attacking him, the helpless "Cardinal La Balue", or whether he identified with "Louis XI" in wanting to control, trap, and punish "Cardinal La Balue" (his mother, his father, or both parents). Or, perhaps, the situation reflects another split within him, the "Louis XI" part of him feels the impossible persecutory guilt for his cruelty and desire to revenge himself on, and torment, his mother or his father, or both parents for banishing him to Balbec, while another part of him, "Cardinal La Balue", must suffer in equal measure the deserved punishment for his horrendous cruelty.

In the paragraph below, Proust depicts both persecutory phantasies and vacillating oedipal preoccupations:

> As our attentiveness furnishes the room, so habit unfurnishes it, making space in it for us. In that room of mine at Balbec, "mine" in name only, there was no space for me: it was crammed with things which did not know me, which glared my distrust of them back at me, noting my existence only to the extent of letting me know they resented me for disturbing theirs. Without let-up, in some unfamiliar

tongue, the clock, which at home I would have never heard for more than a few seconds a week, on surfacing from a long reverie, went on making comments about me, which must have sounded offensive to the tall violet curtains, for they stood there without a word in a listening posture, looking like the sort of people who will shrug their shoulders to show they are irked by the mere sight of someone. (p. 245)

In the context of the focus here on anxieties and defences, the "attentiveness" that "furnishes the room" can represent processes of projective identification in operation. He is in a paranoid–schizoid state of "furnishing" the external reality by projecting and adorning the objects in the room.

In the depressive position, the subject feels sufficiently safe to reduce, or even relinquish the urge to control, and will, thus, withdraw his projections and "unfurnish" the room. "Unfurnishing" enables "making space in it", to feel less confined and more free, within oneself and in the relationship with another, and one could add that, consequently, one is also making space for the other person to feel less confined and more free in the "room" of the relationship.

The thought that one can "furnish" and "unfurnish" is followed by a surge of anxieties about the clock's menacing attitude and the possible ominous turn of events, as "things which [do] not know" him "glared" or projected his "distrust" back at him. There are forebodings about the remaining "unknown objects" in the still "unfurnished" parts of the room.

His "furnishing", that is, his phantasies, coalesce into a different constellation. The binding of the scattered sensations into the "clock" and the "curtains", mirrors a change in his internal situation, in that he becomes less split and fragmented, although he is still in the paranoid–schizoid state of mind. The nature of the oedipal struggle at this moment differs in quality from the more unsettling paranoid experience that he suffered when he felt cruelly trapped, unsafe, and persecuted by various scattered raw impressions and "bundle of sensations".

He felt "resented" by the father/clock and mother/curtains for "disturbing" their "existence", as if, at that point, he held a belief that his intrusion would have a *consequence* and affect his parents. He wanted to get *into* the parents' relationship, to be *in* with them, or perhaps *between* them and keep them separate. He was not able to come to terms with the painful fact of his parents' separate existence, not only in that they *could close their bedroom door*, but that they would *desire* to do so. These two objects, now representing his parents in relationship with each other and in relationship with him, do not appear to be extremely persecuting, although he was troubled and taken aback in being made to feel like an unwelcome intruder and looked down upon.

The father/clock is in dialogue with the mother/curtains. He cannot grasp the "unfamiliar tongue", the language of parents' sexuality. The curtains with disdain—or perhaps just standing aloof—point out to the clock the intruder in "their" room. Then with a "shrug" of her "shoulders", the curtains casually gesture to the clock that this newcomer is not worth noticing. He is dismissed and left to feel he is inconsequential. He has nothing of value or substance in any way that is either good or bad, desirable or disturbing, to offer. Actually, to his parents, who are engaged with each other, he is *a nothing*. He felt shut out, small, and irrelevant. In his phantasy, he was no longer intruding, and thus "resented" for "disturbing" them, because, at that moment, he was positioned outside the parental relationship, or, rather, his parents' relationship was *outside* him. He suffered an oedipal disillusionment of a kind, a shock and woe for his utter insignificance to his parents as a sexual couple, and that the parental couple's relationship does not include him in a space *with* them or *between* them.

The following paragraph shows movement between different states of mind. He regresses from the state he was in just a few moments ago in the previous passage to an even more persecuted state of mind, but then there is an oscillation towards the depressive position, as his grandmother comes into his room and attends to him:

> Deprived of my universe, evicted from my room, with my very tenancy of my body jeopardised by the enemies about me, infiltrated to the bone by fever, I was alone and wished I could die. It was then that my grandmother entered the room and, as my shrivelled heart expanded, broad vistas of hope opened to me . . . I fell into my grandmother's arms and pressed my lips to her face as though that were how to take refuge in the greatness of heart she offered to me. Whenever my mouth was on her cheeks or her forehead, I drew from them something so nourishing, so beneficent, that I had all the immobility, gravity, and placid gluttony of an infant on the breast. (pp. 246–247)

As if with a vengeance, feelings of persecution were resurrected, and he was even more frightened than before. Just prior to the emergence of these persecuting anxieties, he had a glimpse of his *parents as a couple who had a life of their own, in a space outside him*, and the illusion of his importance for the couple was fundamentally shaken. He had a transient, but shockingly painful realisation, that his parents were separate from him, and he from them. It was a glimpse of something momentous that he had just lost.

The pain of this understanding, albeit transitory, that he was *outside* his parents' relationship, pierced his heart. This provoked such hatred towards them for causing him this pain that he became murderously angry. And, as he projected his hate into his parents, they changed into persecuting figures who wanted to abolish his existence. Being "evicted" was equal to exclusion from life itself. He was horrified, in a "fever" and frenzy of anxieties that "infiltrated" his core "to the bone", and his existence was "jeopardised". He was so frightened of the dangerous "enemies" that his parents had turned into, that he only wished to be delivered from this torment and "to die".

The "shrivelled heart" can be seen as a metaphor for the loss of good internal figures, a withered internal presence, or, rather, an absence of love. When he saw his grandmother, his "heart expanded", hope in life and trust in goodness prevailed over persecution. His "vistas" changed into a gentler, kinder, and broader view of the world. He found safety, "refuge" in his grandmother's "greatness of heart". It was her generosity that he experienced, as she freely "offered" him her heart. Yet, it was also significant that he had the capacity to take what she "offered", to feel gratified, and, I think, grateful, as he felt she saved him. She comforted him and gave him something "so beneficent", that, while he "drew" that "something so nourishing", he became content like "an infant on the breast".

She was able to contain his feelings, absorb and process his distress. In turn, he experienced her as a good external and internal figure that he had regained. I think that his trust in his grandmother, and appreciation of the "greatness of [her] heart", and his contentment and containment while he "drew" upon her goodness, reflect his belief in her ability to repair him, and also his capacity to take in her goodness.

There is a kernel of idealisation in the experience of the goodness of internal and external figures, and, as Segal (1998b) points out, some features of idealisation play a role in adult emotional life and are always present. Here, he clearly idealises his grandmother, and her "goodness" is not just one aspect of her being, although an immensely significant and defining element in his experience of her. However, I think there is a shift here towards the depressive position, in that he felt a genuine appreciation for "the greatness of her heart", and experienced her to a degree as a separate person. She "offered", that is, from her own volition, gave freely her heart.

In the following sequence, his grandmother is depicted as concretely separated from him in another "room", but also in another space in his mind, where he feels he has somewhat less control over her. He and his grandmother agreed that if he felt unwell, he would knock three times on the wall of her room, which was next to his:

> . . . so that evening I did give three knocks; and a week later, when I felt unwell for a few days, I did the same thing each morning . . . As soon as I thought I could hear she was awake . . . I would try giving my three little knocks, gently and tentatively, but quite clearly, since, though I was reluctant to interrupt her sleep when it was possible I might have been mistaken and she was not awake, I would not have wanted her to lie there expecting a renewal of summons which it was possible she might not have heard distinctly, but which I did not dare repeat. (Proust, 2002[1919], p. 247)

I think his worry about waking up his grandmother or keeping her waiting does not stem from paranoid anxieties, that is, having to keep her well disposed towards him, since, otherwise, she would become a vengeful figure. It seems that he sincerely cares for her wellbeing, yet, on the other hand, he is also fearful about being alone in his "room". It was as if he was standing on two boats, with one foot on each.

His concern for her wellbeing, for either waking her up and so depriving her of sleep, or for keeping her waiting and thus worried about him, is a genuine feeling of concern for her fate. He was troubled about exhausting and depleting her. Yet, he also had doubts about whether she was holding him in mind and would she hear the "knocks" of his distress. He said to his grandmother that he was worried that if he did not knock loudly, she might not hear him, or that she might think it was someone else and not recognise his knocking. She said with a "laugh",

"What! How could I mistake my dear little chap's knocking for someone else's? I'd know it a mile away. Do you really think there's anyone else in the whole world who's as silly and anxious and torn between the fear of waking me up and not being heard?" (p. 248)

He is anxious that his need and demands could damage and drain his grandmother, and he wanted to look after her, not to wake her too often or keep her waiting too long. However, in looking after her and knocking gently, so as not to wake her up if she was asleep, he was worried that she might not hear him. That would expose him to the dangers of being left alone with frightful persecutions. Thus, either way, he might do something harmful, either to her or to himself. This is such a fitting analogy for something that is so difficult to capture in the nuances of relationships, the fluctuations so pervasive and never quite resolved of being torn between the "paranoid" fear for the fate of oneself and the "depressive" concern for the fate of the other.

The concern for the other and the wish to put things right is a mark of the depressive position. The dynamic of reparation in a couple relationship is, at the same time, an intrapsychic event and an intersubjective process that involves two people. Partners can consciously try to put things right and unconsciously engage with each other in reparation. Since partners relate at the same time on conscious and unconscious levels, I refer to the latter as *the couple's unconscious relations*. The couple's unconscious relations are the partners' phantasies about the nature of *relations* between them, about what they are *doing* to the other and what the other is *doing* to them.

> Therefore, what "connects" the partners in a "couple" are unconscious objects, internal figures, *contents* of the mind, and the *processes*, functions, or relations between the objects . . . I refer to these complex unconscious dynamics as *the couple's unconscious relations*. This formulation puts an emphasis on the *processes*, on the object relations, or on the relations between the internal figures in the individuals and the relations between them. (Novakovic, 2016, p. 97)

The phantasies about what the partners are *doing* to each other derive not only from the partners' previous relationships and from the early experience of their parents' relationships, but also from how partners have an impact on each other and the changes they effect in the unconscious of each other. The freedom or desire to give and to take in the "beneficence", or the compulsion to provoke hurt and to suffer it, or any other shared emotional experience or joint enactment in the couple interaction, has an impact and makes a conscious and an unconscious impression. It is these continuous impressions, interactions between the internal and external reality, interactions between the partners' internal worlds and the external "other", just as in the development of a child, and, indeed, in the course of any relationship, that shape the nature of the experience that partners have about themselves and the other.

I shall use Proust's description about the grandson's experience of his grandmother to exemplify the dynamic of reparation and generosity in a couple interaction. After a disturbing event and interchange, the partners held themselves close to each other. As they embraced, and as he "drew" in the "beneficence" she gave him, he was also restoring her, since, while he was *taking in,* he was also *giving her* the beneficent experience that she can restore and repair him, because she is good and loved. Furthermore, in being able to take from her "something so nourishing", he took in her "beneficence", and, on some level, he unconsciously identified with her in *how* she gave—*freely and generously*—and with *what* she gave—*the beneficence and nourishing love.* She, too, unconsciously identified with him in *how* he took—*with trust in her*—and with *what* he took—*her beneficence, and her nourishing love for him.*

> Whenever we can admire and love somebody—or hate and despise somebody—we also take something of them into ourselves and our deepest attitudes are shaped by such experiences. (Klein, 1975h[1959], p. 256)

The fused, warring, differeiated, benign, creative, and generous couple

I refer here to a very interesting finding by Halton and Sprince (2016) of four distinct groupings of phantasies of a parental couple that reflect different experiences of the oedipal situation in the paranoid–schizoid and depressive positions. They consider primitive perceptions of a couple that Klein observed in her work with children, and the various phantasies of the parental couple that children expressed and enacted in their play, and formulate a typology of four specific images of the couple: the fused attacking couple, the warring couple, the differentiated couple, and the benign couple.[5]

This typology can be applied in conceptualising the nature of the couple interaction. What kind of "couple" phantasy are the partners enacting in their couple relationship, and in their relationship with their children, family, or any third party? These four distinct phantasies range from the persecuting phantasies and idealisation in the paranoid–schizoid position to more differentiated images in the depressive position. I briefly describe four specific images, or phantasies, that Halton and Sprince discerned, and illustrate the images from a "couple" perspective, with a brief example of the couple enactment in the paranoid–schizoid and depressive positions.

The fused attacking couple is a primitive and frightening phantasy of the parental couple united in mutual feeding or fused in continuous intercourse. The persecutory anxiety derives from phantasies that this fused attacking couple will attack the child in revenge for his murderous feelings towards the fused parental figure.

Example 1: Partners in a couple are fused in their denigrating attack against a third party. In their "ganged up" stance they feel wronged, outraged, and justified to pass certain judgements, uncover deceits, or concretely maltreat a third. In these preoccupations and activities, they experience themselves, and are also experienced by others, as a united and impenetrable "front". They jointly and viciously criticise, control, or punish a third party.

Example 2: A couple presents in social situations as an ideal unity. Their relationship appears to be special, seamless, blessed, without any frictions or struggles, as if they were perpetually gratifying each other sexually, emotionally, or intellectually, and they evoke idealisation or envy in others. The difference between a couple in love and the fused couple discussed here lies in the need of the latter to exhibit their relationship and provoke envy.

The warring couple is a phantasy of a couple trapped in hurtful warfare and in destroying each other in different ways. These phantasies arise from the child's projection of its aggression into the parental couple, and evoke persecutory guilt for attacking the parents and fear that the warring couple will take revenge.

Example 3: The partners are locked in a hurtful and hateful struggle that is both persecuting and exciting. In their conflicts, they treat each other in a contemptuous way, each undermining the other in their need to denigrate and triumph over the other. In this way, they manage their own intolerable feelings; they project the "badness", whatever it might be, and then attack and expose this "badness" in the other. There is a harsh and ruthless quality in the couple's relationship.

The differentiated couple is an image of the parents as two separate and differentiated individuals in a couple relationship. Experience of the parents as separate beings gives rise to the hope of uniting with one of the parents, and anxieties that the excluded parent will retaliate. This is what is usually termed classical Oedipus complex. Alternatively, the child is excluded and idealises, denigrates, or attacks the parental couple.

Example 4: A couple lacks the capacity to sustain the separateness of their relationship from the third, and they allow their family to interfere in their affairs, or they are unable to put their child to sleep in his bedroom. This is linked to their own inability to tolerate feeling excluded. They are often in competition, trying to get someone to side with their point of view. However, there is also an anxiety and guilt about being "included". Both partners have a strong unconscious motivation to collude with being "left out". In their different ways and at different times, both partners invariably end up feeling upset or angry about being excluded, although, at the same time, in colluding with being left out, they, in phantasy, "atone" one excluded parent for their unconscious belief that they "possess" the other.

The benign couple is a perception of a parental couple in the depressive position when the oedipal dynamics are worked through. This parental couple phantasy is not persecutory, and parents are experienced to be united by love. The couple actualising this phantasy in their relationship would be less destructive, and more generous and differentiated. They would also have a capacity to relate more creatively. I shall consider the experience of generosity in a couple, but will, first, briefly refer to the concept of the "creative couple".

Morgan (2005) develops the idea of the "creative couple" as an internal "psychic object", and a "primarily psychic development" that allows the subject to make links, that is, have different thoughts and feelings that can come together in his or her mind. If a person can "allow this kind of mating within oneself, it becomes more likely that one can allow it to occur between oneself and one's partner (p. 22)".

Morgan refers to this kind of interaction in a couple as "creative couple state of mind". She defines the creative and containing nature of the couple relationship as "something they both have in mind, and they can imagine the relationship as something that has them in mind" (p. 29).

> In a creative couple, the relationship itself is continually being created by the couple's intercourse of every kind and at every level, as the different, or sometimes opposing, perspective of the other can be taken in to one's psyche and allowed to reside there where it mates with one's own experience to create something new. (Morgan, 2014a, p. 117)

Morgan points out that a creative couple can tolerate some degree of disintegration in the shifts between the paranoid–schizoid and depressive positions, without resorting to primitive defence mechanisms.

The generosity in a couple can be expressed in situations when partners resort to primitive defence mechanisms that are hurtful, but are subsequently able to mourn and repair the injury inflicted in thought or deed. Klein's view is that the creative impulses stem from a need to repair the damage caused by the subject's aggressive or envious attacks and that "generosity underlies creativeness, and this applies to the infant's most primitive constructive activities as well as to the creativeness of the adult" (Klein, 1975i[1963], p. 310). I think generosity and creativity are different concepts and describe different dimensions of the personality or relationship, but that sometimes there can be a connection when the creative impulse arises from feelings of generosity, or when the latter is represented in a creative act.

I pointed out earlier in this chapter that the generosity in a couple is apparent in their desire to give something "beneficent" and "nourishing" to each other, and to take this in with trust, enjoyment, and gratitude. The capacity to forgive and come to terms with the hurts and disappointments is another feature of the generosity in a relationship. Jaques describes this state of mind in relation to the mid life crisis and creativity: the unconscious feelings of hate that are mitigated by love, the envious spoiling mitigated by admiration, the injury of good things mitigated by the healing grief, destruction mitigated by the desire to live and repair.

As Klein (1975b[1937]) put it, if we "became able, deep in our unconscious minds, to clear our feelings to some extent towards our parents of grievances, and have forgiven them for the frustrations we had to bear", it may be possible to have an experience of being "at peace with ourselves" and "able to love others in the true sense of the word". (Klein, 1975b[1937], p. 343)

In a couple, it is the injury caused by the other, the hate or betrayal that can be mourned and forgiven or not. Kernberg (1995b) succinctly describes this:

> To be able to attack one's partner sadistically yet witness the survival of his or her love; to be able to experience in oneself the transition from relentless rage and devaluation to guilt, mourning, and repair – these are invaluable experiences for the couple. (Kernberg, 1995b, p. 93)

In forgiving, there is an encounter with the "badness", the tormenting, rejecting, or hating, and, in the moment of injury, the hated other. The feelings of pain or hate are evoked by the partner's "badness", yet, in forgiving, love and generosity prevail in *allowing the lost goodness to be found*. Forgiveness entails mourning the loss of the goodness in the other, in the relationship, and in oneself. There is an internal process of integration, and while the "badness" of the other is experienced and the pain and anger about this loss felt, the subject can, nevertheless, recapture the lost "goodness", and regain a more integrated or "whole" experience of the other and oneself, with both "good" and "bad" parts. The goodness and the badness are felt in different degrees, and not in an all-encompassing and mutually exclusive way.

Forgiveness can be conceptualised as a process of reparation both within the individual and between the individuals in a couple relationship. The subject is putting right the injury inflicted by another person by repairing the *damage caused by the other to oneself*, and the *damaging other within oneself*. The reparation in forgiving does not stem from depressive guilt, but from compassion for the other in a moment when love predominates over hate, and in the identification with both "good" and "bad" aspects of the other. One might add that the generosity is in forgiving, not in forgetting, since the injustices, hurts, and fears reside "somewhere" in the heart, dormant or aroused, depending on whether one is in the paranoid–schizoid or depressive position state of mind. However, "If the meaning of the past is changed by forgiveness, its influence on the future is also changed" (Westcott, 2017).

The gratitude and love in the depressive position in taking and giving something nourishing is but one feature of the generosity in the couple. The process of *finding* the lost goodness and *giving it back* to the other is a different kind of *giving*. A "generous couple" would be able to be more forgiving and mourn the hate and hurts, both endured and evoked, in the encounter with the other; regain the lost "goodness", as just good enough and not ideal; bear the disturbing confrontations with new ideas and situations that rupture the stability of what is known about the other and oneself; "unfurnish" projections, and so allow the space for the other to feel less confined and more free in the "room" of the relationship; and manage the inevitable shifts between the more paranoid fear for the fate of oneself and the depressive concern for the fate of the other.

Conclusion

In this chapter the anxieties and defences in the individuals and couples are presented as clusters of feelings and phantasies within paranoid–schizoid and depressive positions. The two positions can be envisaged as two dynamically opposing and interdependent constellations, of love versus hate, generosity versus grievance, trust versus fear, that reflect essential and fundamental aspects of existence.

Notes

1. Following Klein's original work, there have been a number of developments that are often described as post–Kleinian.
2. The term phantasy is employed to denote unconscious mental representation in order to differentiate the unconscious nature of phantasy from fantasy or conscious imaginings.
3. I shall use the term "external figure" to mean a person, an aspect of a person, or a thing in the external world, and "internal figure" to mean self or a part of self as a mental representation in phantasy. "Figure" here, signifies "object" a term used in object relations theory. In the paranoid–schizoid position, the infant has no awareness of a whole person, hence its relationships are with internal and external "part-objects", while in the depressive position, for example,

the mother is experienced in a more integrated way, as a "whole object" or "whole" person.
4. These paranoid anxieties are universal and should not be confused with a diagnosis of paranoia.
5. In the course of the consultancy work in different organisations, Halton and Sprince observed employees' experiences of a couple working in the same organisation. They found that employees' experiences of the couple in a group could change and that these experiences resonated with the four discrete images.

CHAPTER TWO

Oedipus killed the couple: murder on the Thebes highway

Viveka Nyberg

Introduction

The myth of Oedipus has been retold in many different versions over the centuries. Freud first referred to the narrative in a letter to Fliess on 15 October 1897 (Masson, 1985). He described how, in the course of self-analysis, he reached the momentous conclusion that falling in love with the mother and jealousy of the father seemed to represent a "universal event of childhood" (Freud, 1897, p. 265). This became the foundation of what Freud called the Oedipus complex. In classical psychoanalytic theory it stands as a shorthand expression to denote a son's or daughter's love for the parent of the opposite gender, while experiencing the parent of the same gender as a rival. Correspondingly, the term, "Electra complex", is used to denote a girl's love for her father, and her experience of the mother as a rival. The notion of the Electra complex has not been incorporated into psychoanalytic parlance to the same extent as the male variant of the oedipal triangle.

This chapter presents Freud's original theory and the post-Freudian development of the psychoanalytic understanding of the Oedipus complex. It explores the impact of oedipal dilemmas and conflicts upon the adult couple relationship. It offers a brief, critical appraisal of the Oedipus theory in traditional and contemporary contexts and examines whether the concept represents a hetero-normative and/or Eurocentric approach to theorising family dynamics.

The Oedipus myth

Sophocles' *Oedipus Rex* centres on the tragic child of King Laius and Queen Jocasta of Thebes. The infant is prophesied to end up killing his father. However, the servant tasked with leaving the baby Oedipus to die of exposure delivers him to the care of a shepherd. Oedipus grows to adulthood in Corinth, supposedly as son of its King and Queen. He later learns from the oracle that he is destined to marry his mother and murder his father. Fleeing this curse, Oedipus returns to Thebes. En route, he unknowingly kills his father, King Laius. In Thebes, he defeats the Sphinx, who has terrorised the city, and wins the kingship and the hand of the widowed Queen Jocasta. However, the gods will not allow this state of affairs to continue without retribution: pestilence and plague falls on the city of Thebes. Oedipus consults the oracle in Apollo's temple in Delphi, wishing to establish why his city suffers in this way. At last, Oedipus finally learns that he has killed his father and married his mother, exactly as prophesied. Jocasta is so horrified by this knowledge that she hangs herself. When Oedipus learns of her suicide, he seizes two pins from her dress and blinds himself. Henceforth, he will wander the world sightless and outcast from mankind.

Freud identifies in the ancient Oedipus story a powerful representation of universal human phantasies that are embedded in the unconscious and preconscious, of wishing to possess the parent of the opposite sex and wishing to kill off the rival parent (1900a).

> Like Oedipus, we live in ignorance of these wishes, repugnant to morality, which have been forced upon us by Nature, and after their revelation we may all of us seek to close our eyes to the scenes of our childhood. (Freud, 1900a, p. 263)

Freud regarded the Oedipus complex as a central finding, and its significance remained pivotal throughout his life's work. It is now recognised as a fundamental conflict in the human psyche, and represents a cornerstone in the theory and practice of psychoanalysis. The universality of the Oedipus complex is considered by some to be the greatest of Freud's discoveries (Jones, 1961). However, when Freud first published his revolutionary theory identifying a boy's loving, erotic feelings for his mother and his hateful, rivalrous feelings for his father, the suggestion was met with widespread hostility and disbelief. It was, and perhaps still is, a shocking thought that small children could harbour such feelings, let alone incestuous impulses. As psychoanalytic theory has evolved over the past century, there has been an increasingly profound understanding of the compelling psychic needs and phantasies associated with the Oedipal complex.

The repercussions of this conflict are particularly relevant to the adult couple relationship. Couples often discover that, within the intense intimacy of the relationship, they receive more than they consciously bargained for. They might become embroiled in a passionate, or even passionless relationship, where they experience the other as a profound disappointment or a figure of hatred, rather than the supportive, loving partner of their dreams. When an unhappy couple come for help with their relationship, the therapy will often uncover traces of unresolved Oedipal conflict and dissonant feelings associated with a sense of exclusion and rejection. One could say that an unfolding Oedipal drama is always present in human relationships, whether consciously or deeply embedded in the unconscious.

The third man, or woman

The symbolic representations that psychoanalysis derives from Freud's theory of the Oedipus myth are a way to understand a set of dilemmas that are focal to the construction of our internal world and the way our minds are structured through particular experiences. Freud's theory refers to the earliest experience of the nuclear family threesome, which incorporates themes of jealousy, rivalry, and the longing for exclusive relationships. A universal aspect is the recognition that these psychic experiences underpin all relationships, both in phantasy and in external reality. This is equally relevant, whether the family constellation is a lone parent family or an extended family with siblings, step-relationships, and other complex social configurations.

A young mother presents an illustrative episode. She described how she was reading a book on child development when she came to the chapter on oedipal feelings. She found herself metaphorically rolling her eyes in disbelief when reading of the child's capacity to feel possessive towards one parent and the wish to exclude the other parent. She felt that this kind of "classical Freudian theory" was now outmoded and irrelevant. A couple of days later, she was out walking with her one-year-old baby and her partner. The father was carrying the baby, and at one point she affectionately placed her hand on his arm, only for the baby to push her hand firmly away. It was as if her daughter had said, "Hands off! He's mine. Leave him alone!" This is no doubt one of many experiences where a child's omnipotent wishes might have to be rebutted and disillusioned. It cannot be overstated how agonisingly hard and emotionally painful this developmental process is. The infant will gradually realise that she is not "Her Majesty the Baby" but that there are demands upon the carer or parent from other people. Although, at twelve months old, the baby had not yet developed verbal language, she was, none the less, expressing a clear point of view, which presumably relates to an internal conflict about who was to be included/excluded in the threesome at a given moment.

The manner in which this development is negotiated by the infant and the family is highly significant. For example, is one of the parents able to tolerate feelings of being excluded, to be temporarily placed on the outside, looking in? Or is there a persistent need for that person to avoid feelings of unfairness and envy by constantly seeking to be included, to be in the middle, to be the centre of attention? It is often commented on in psychoanalytic literature that the reverberations of the Oedipus complex are continuously being reworked throughout a person's lifespan, through conflicts around inclusion and exclusion that reappear in different disguises at different developmental "trigger" points throughout life. For the adult intimate couple, such triggers can include the birth of a first child, an extra-marital affair, or the loss of a partner (Balfour, 2005, 2016; Morgan, 2005; Nathans, 2012).

Since Freud

Since Freud, psychoanalytic thinking has widened the understanding of oedipal feelings to include more complex psychological longings shared by both genders, with increasing understanding of the way that primitive anxieties can develop around experiences of intrusion and abandonment. While Freud thought the child's oedipal feelings were at their strongest from the ages of three to five, Klein (1975d[1945]) revised and extended Freud's ideas in her conception of an earlier Oedipus complex, what she called the early "oedipal situation". She widened the psychoanalytic understanding of the child's deepest fears and anxieties and the psychic defences used to resist them.

Klein's ideas have become the foundation for later developments in psychoanalytic theory, in particular the British psychoanalytic school of post-Kleinian thinking. This body of work has widened our understanding of the individual's capacity to tolerate bonds between people, as well as the psychic capacity to make emotional connections and allow ideas to interact with each other in the process of thinking (Britton, 1989; Feldman, 1989). Klein argued that the manner in which a child comes to terms with the reality of a parental couple, the fact that the relationship includes a sexual expression, and the reality of being excluded from this relationship, will be fundamental to the child's psychological and emotional functioning. Although Klein and other psychoanalytic writers regularly refer to the experience of two parents (usually a heterosexual couple), it is recognised in contemporary literature (Berkowitz, 2011; McCann, 2014; Nathans, 2012; Shenkman, 2016) that such ideas are equally applicable to families with parents of the same gender, and to one-parent families where the other parent is absent. Someone growing up in a single parent family will, nevertheless, have an imaginary representation of the other parent. This might be an unrealistic phantasy of an idealised parent, or it might be the exact reverse, the idea of a useless, neglectful, and hostile parent. The child's internal representation of the absent parent and the parental couple will, to a large extent, be influenced by the carer/single parent's own internal idea of the "missing" partner or person. This could relate to the kind of couple the parents once were when they first met and when the child was conceived, or the relationship could be coloured by hateful feelings towards a partner who is felt to have failed them.

Klein used the term "depressive position" to describe the capacity to function and achieve mature emotional activity (1975d[1945]). If the child can accept the reality of the parental couple and tolerate being excluded from this dyad, it will lead to a more flexible type of triangulation, where feelings of rivalry are experienced as less destructive and the sense of exclusion will not be felt as catastrophic. The oedipal situation requires a gradual letting go of the phantasy of exclusive possession of the desired parent and an acceptance of the reality of the parents' relationship, and this difficult process can help create a capacity to share psychic space (Britton, 1998b).

The child then comes to realise that he or she benefits from a more united parental couple, and learns to contain possessive and hostile feelings. "Together with the awareness of exclusion goes the experience of finding out, of learning. This process of change and growth always involves pain, but it also opens up the potential for warmer and more generous relationships" (Boswell, 2001, p. 79). This speaks to the importance of containment of the child's experience provided by an emotional environment where carers/parental figures have a "good–enough" capacity to contain and manage the child's primitive feelings and anxieties.

The capacity to distinguish between phantasy and fact depends on the person finding a "third position", enabling him to reflect on his subjective belief about the object concerned. This process, in turn, depends on tolerance of an internal version of the early Oedipus situation. Defensive phantasies are meant to obscure psychic realities in order for oedipal illusions to be maintained. An example might be the way Oedipus shares his throne with his wife/mother, while the court turns a blind eye to something they "half-know" but choose to ignore. In a situation where the illusion reigns, it is difficult to be curious, because it would mean having to discover something disastrous. In a similar vein, depending on the early emotional environment, the child may get caught up in an oedipal illusion, where the parents' relationship is known, but its full significance can be evaded and left unacknowledged. Instead, an oedipal illusion might persist and the child is caught up in phantasies about the nature of the parental union, which make it harder for the Oedipus complex to be resolved through the normal processes of rivalry and relinquishment (Britton, 1998b). By this means, the experience of the oedipal situation bears upon the child's capacity to distinguish between phantasy and reality, to differentiate between subjectivity and objectivity.

In his writings, Britton explores Klein's understanding of the primitive forms of the oedipus situation. In his seminal paper, "The missing link: parental sexuality in the Oedipus complex" (1989), he describes how the oedipal triangle creates a particular mental space in which the child can develop a different relationship with each parent. He examines how the resolution of the Oedipus complex is interwoven with Klein's concept of the depressive position. As suggested above, this position denotes a person's capacity to understand and relate to reality, rather than remain defensively in the realm of fantasy, in denial of lived experience. Britton suggests that, for a small child, the working through of the one (the depressive position) entails the working through of the other (the oedipal situation). If the child is able successfully to find her way through the Oedipus complex, she can reach an adequate acceptance of the "depressive position" without having defensively to resort to feelings such as contempt or triumph. Most importantly, the child will not have to rely on magical solutions in the face of difficulties.

Once the existence of the parents' sexual relationship is recognised, the child has to relinquish the idea of sole possession of the mother and this, in turn, leads the child to experience a tremendous sense of loss. This is not to say that the small child understands, at least initially, the specifics of sexual intercourse, but, rather, that the child comes to realise that there is an intimate relationship between the parental couple from which the child is excluded. The fact that many children grow up effectively in a "one-parent family" does not immunise the child from these experiences, since there will always be an "other" of some form in the mind of the mother or carer.

Britton explores the nature of the child's encounter with the parental relationship at a time when the individual has not yet been able to establish a secure and containing relationship with the mother or a maternal figure. Bion (1959) describes the consequences for some individuals when there is a failure of the maternal person's containment of the infant. He suggests that the effect of this type of failure could stimulate a destructive and envious component of the psyche that will interfere with the person's ability to learn, hindering the capacity to pursue positive and creative relationships with others. If the mother is unable to "take in" and contain the infant's distressing anxieties, the child might experience this as a destructive attack by mother on the good and loving bond between mother and child.

> The idea of a good maternal object can only be regained by splitting off her impermeability so that now a hostile force is felt to exist, which

attacks his good link with his mother. Mother's goodness is now precarious and depends on him restricting his knowledge of her. Enlargement of knowledge of her as a consequence of development and his curiosity are felt to menace this crucial relationship. (Britton, 1989, p. 89)

Britton argues that the child's continued curiosity will, in time, reveal to the child the existence of the oedipal situation. The psychic discovery of an emotionally intimate couple becomes part of normal development but is, nevertheless, a challenge to the child, because there will be a reluctance to admit the existence of another, significant person in mother's mind. If the two-person relationship between mother and infant, between the container and contained, is insufficient in some way and the mother is unable to respond to the infant's distress and/or loving feelings, this will have an impact on the child's capacity to resolve the oedipal situation. The challenge for the child is that the discovery of this "third" person might potentially undermine the child's belief in the goodness of his mother. Alternatively, if the child experiences a sustained, satisfactory maternal containment, then he is more likely to transition with greater ease from the exclusive mother–child relationship to a more complex situation where the third person, often the father, must be accommodated. At the same time, the child has now to accommodate the perceived relationship between the parents.

In the Kleinian understanding of the oedipal situation, as in Freud's original concept of the oedipal complex, one parent represents an object of desire, while the other parent represents a hated rival. As the child increasingly recognises the reality of the parents' sexual relationship, the understanding of who is the "good" parent or the "bad" rival parent changes. This is a crucial developmental juncture, since the child is confronted with the realisation that, for example, the hated father–rival is, in fact, an object of desire for the child's love-object, the mother.

The acknowledgement by the child of his parents' relationship ... with each other unites his psychic world, limiting it to one world ... shared with his two parents in which different object relationships can exist. The closure of the oedipal triangle by the recognition of the link joining the parents provides a limiting boundary for the internal world. (Britton, 1989, p. 86)

Britton refers to this as "triangular space", a space bounded by the three persons of the oedipal situation and all their potential relationships. This includes the possibility of being a participant in a relationship, for example, with the mother, observed by the father, as well as being an observer of a relationship between two people. The child's capacity to conceive of a creative and positive parental relationship will influence how the space outside the self is observed and thought about. It is this capacity of the person to be thought about and observed that provides a foundation for a belief in a world that is secure and stable. When there is a developmental failure and the child is unable fully to internalise the oedipal triangle in a manner that is felt to be containing and manageable, then this, in turn, could result in a failure to integrate and make use of lived experience.

Britton suggests that, if there is a failure in the very early relationship between mother and infant and if the child is unable to establish a secure bond with the mother before being faced with the oedipal reality of a third person, then this can lead to attempts at a primitive "wiping out" of the parental relationship. The person might be overwhelmed with a feeling that to acknowledge the reality of the oedipal situation would be psychically catastrophic. This makes the negotiation of the Oedipus complex impossible for the child. In adulthood, this can manifest as a lack of ability to occupy a "third position" and a denial of relationships between others. Britton introduces the idea of "oedipal illusions", where the purpose and function of the illusion is to protect the individual from psychic reality and the person's phantasies around the original oedipal situation. The psychic "wiping out", or denial, of the parental relationship creates an illusion that the relationship between the parents does not exist.

A different set of "illusions" can develop when the child is able to know about the parents' relationship, but is not fully able to take on board its significance. This type of defensive illusion is less severe in nature than the more primitive quality of a "wiping out" of the parents' relationship. Nevertheless, it manifests as a defensive organisation in the person's mind, in order to deny the psychic reality of the parents' relationship. This can lead to feelings of exclusion, rivalry, and hatred. Britton argues that, in normal development, such illusions are frequent, but transitory. Sometimes, however, these illusions can persist, preventing an adequate resolution of the Oedipus complex.

The illusions are often conscious and can be expressed as wish-fulfilling ideas and beliefs about the nature of relationships.

For example, a couple came for therapy because the husband could no longer tolerate his wife's long-standing "affair" with another man. In one session, the wife expressed her bewilderment about her husband's objection to the affair, since, in her own parents' relationship, her mother's ongoing extra-marital relationship had been accepted by her father, and the parents remained married despite this. It can, perhaps, be extrapolated from this vignette that the wife believed no one in this threesome should feel excluded, while the husband increasingly felt pushed into an observer role, looking at the relationship between his wife and her lover from the sidelines. Without going into details of the couple's early histories, it might be sufficient to say that, as children, they had both found themselves compromised in their oedipal struggle to find a "third" position. The "illusion" of maintaining a relationship where no one was felt to be "left out" might be seen as a defence against the psychic reality of the Oedipus situation. The defensive "oedipal illusion", in which the couple to some extent seemed to collude, contained a phantasy that rivalrous feelings could be sidestepped and obliterated.

Britton suggests that it is through the process of mourning for the lost, exclusive two-person relationship between child and mother that the child is able to begin the process of resolving the Oedipus complex. Through this process, "it can be realised that the Oedipal triangle does not spell the death of a relationship, but only the death of an idea of a relationship" (Britton, 1989, p. 100).

Oedipal themes in art and culture

Representations of oedipal manifestations can often be found in narratives of literature, film, and the visual arts. Of these, Hamlet is perhaps the most prominent. From the perspective of this chapter, we note, above all, Shakespeare's portrayal of Hamlet's consuming anguish and bitterness at his mother's hasty remarriage after his father's death, and of his guilt-ridden torment at the news of his father's murder. Within the drama, guilty feelings seem to arise from Hamlet's yearning for his mother and from his rivalry towards the stepfather, which combine to block Hamlet from genuinely engaging with Ophelia. Hamlet is shown as too caught up in his feelings towards the parental couple to avail himself of Ophelia's implicit invitation (Lanman, 2005). Hamlet's eventual murder seems intuitively to illustrate how a failure to resolve oedipal feelings can lead to annihilation. Freud proposes that Hamlet's hesitation in avenging the murder of his father derives from an unconscious sense of guilt, arising from his illicit passion for his mother. Freud notes that Hamlet brings down a punishment on himself, suffering the same fate as his father, in that he is being poisoned by the same rival for the mother's love. Freud linked the Oedipus complex with unconscious guilt and this idea was to become a cornerstone in his future thinking (1923b, 1924d, 1930a).

The Swedish film director, Ingmar Bergman, records in his autobiography a knowing account of his early upbringing, describing a small boy who did not experience the union of his parents as containing or benign (Bergman, 1988). It is fair to speculate, noting Bergman's childhood illnesses, that there may have been an early failure of containment in his relationship with his mother. His own subjective experience certainly seems to have been that he pined for his mother's affection, but was met by her coolness and calculated distance. Perhaps Bergman's hateful feelings towards his father, who executed premeditated beatings, heightened his oedipal envy and rage and intensified his feelings of guilt. In this way, he was left with the psychic inheritance of the apparent lack of oedipal resolution. This might have contributed to his complicated intimate relationships as an adult, something which he outlines with bitter frankness in his autobiography (Nyberg, 2005).

Bergman's childhood might illustrate the importance of the degree to which a person is successful in negotiating the so called "oedipal triangle". Perhaps it does not always have to be a triangle; maybe it can equally be a rectangle, or a pentagon, depending on the family constellation with siblings and extended family members. The significance is the person's capacity to manoeuvre and relocate along the spectrum of family relationships in such a way that a degree of freedom is maintained and, consequently, in the way, these different relationships are both perceived and experienced. The examples of Hamlet's dramatic narrative and of Bergman's account of his childhood illustrate in different ways how an individual can become trapped, as if in a spider's web, prevented symbolically from negotiating the complexity of the parental relationship. In this context, the individual is unable to find a more comfortable "third position" along the oedipal spectrum.

Britton observes that the child's recognition of the parental relationship can create a boundary for the internal world, making possible what he calls "triangular space".

> If the link between the parents perceived in love and hate can be tolerated in the child's mind, it provides him with a prototype for an object relationship of a third kind in which he is a witness and not a participant. A third position then comes into existence from which object relationships can be observed. Given this, we can also envisage being observed. This provides us with a capacity for seeing ourselves in interaction with others and for entertaining another point of view whilst retaining our own, for reflecting on ourselves whilst being ourselves. (Britton, 1989, p. 86)

Hamlet, in his enactment of unresolved oedipal feelings, is clearly not able to find the "third position" that Britton outlines. This third position might have allowed him to find greater freedom to be a "witness", able to tolerate his parents' union, rather than re-enact unresolved oedipal feelings.

If the Oedipus complex is understood as a symbolic representation of a person's psychic flexibility to move around these emotional pitfalls, tensions, and opportunities within family relationships, it also underlines the enduring presence of this universal challenge that must somehow be negotiated in the best possible way, with the aid or hindrance of our families of origin.

Oedipal tensions in intimate adult couple relationships

Almost all couples, in the course of their relationships, must confront and cope with major life events, challenges, and traumatic experiences. For individuals who have experienced failures in the primary infant–parent relationship, their early difficulties will leave them emotionally more vulnerable as adults and lead to problems in establishing a trusting and satisfactory intimate relationship with their partners, which includes the centrality of the sexual relationship. As Freud states, "The Oedipal complex . . . represents the peak of infantile sexuality, which through its after-effects, exercises a decisive influence on the sexuality of adults" (Freud, 1905d, p. 226).

Within the realm of the adult couple relationship, couple psychotherapists often observe how arduous it can be for certain couples to negotiate their positions, emotions, and tensions. Often, this relates to an experience of feeling either too close to his or her partner, or the opposite feeling of isolation, or even abandonment. The loss of the illusion of possessive exclusivity might be one of the most difficult developmental hurdles to be negotiated (Johns, 1996). Couple therapy, in contrast to individual psychoanalysis or psychotherapy, takes place within a setting of three people akin to an "oedipal setting", between the couple and the psychotherapist (Balfour, 2016). For some couples, the setting in itself could activate regressive behaviour and the couple psychotherapist might become aware of how one partner is trying emotionally to pull the therapist over to his side, against the other partner. This is sometimes manifested by one partner trying to persuade the therapist to side with him or her in regarding the other partner as the "ill patient" who is in need of help and treatment.

The "internal parental couple"

The notion of an "internal parental couple" is a means of conceptualising an unconscious "phantasy couple", which a person has internalised largely based on his or her experience of the parents' relationship. This is different from what might be thought of as an "external parental couple", which refers to the conscious reflections and understanding of the parents' relationship. The "internal parental couple" becomes a psychic and emotional entity that will influence the kind of unconscious expectations the couple have for their relationship. When partners have internalised an experience of a good enough parental couple with capacity for resolving differences, this contributes to a sense of psychic containment, which the partners then bring into their own adult relationships. In this scenario, the "internal parental couple" becomes an enriching and guiding feature for the couple to draw upon. Many couples who present for therapy, however, will bring early experiences of parents who, themselves, were overwhelmed by their own needs and difficulties, which might later influence and confine the couple's developmental capacity, as well as the creative potential for their own relationship.

The characteristics of the "internal couple" will greatly influence the nature of the relationship that the couple can create together. A couple will come together with a set of phantasies embodying their expectations of potential relationships, and "it is this compulsion to transfer that drives each half of the couple to choose someone who will fit or can be provoked into fitting in with their own unconscious need to repeat and relive past emotional experience" (Tarsh & Bollinghaus, 1999, pp. 126–127). A couple can enter into the relationship with conflicting attitudes towards the internal parental couple. There might be an inability to tolerate emotions stirred up by this "internal couple", or feelings such as envy, jealousy, or a wish to control. On the other hand, the internal parental couple might be split into one "good" parent and one "bad" parent, with a sense of irreconcilable differences, where one partner will always be right, while the other will be in the wrong. In this central oedipal struggle, with the intensity of ambivalent feelings towards the parents, the oedipal phantasies might include representations of parents who are both much loved, while simultaneously hated and attacked. The capacity for containing ambivalent feelings towards the other forms an important feature for a couple's ability to negotiate conflicting feelings.

Oedipal anxieties reawakened: the birth of a first baby

The birth of a first baby marks a revolutionary milestone in the life of the couple's relationship, accentuating the tumultuous experience of a two-person relationship becoming a threesome. Unresolved oedipal issues can mean that there is a denial of the parental couple and an assumption that the "real" relationship is between parent and child, with the interparental relationship relegated to secondary importance. Alternatively, there might be a belief that there is only a parental couple to the exclusion of the infant, where the infant can be experienced as an interloper, threatening the couple dyad. This dynamic can equally occur when the parent is a single parent, when the birth of the baby will reactivate early experiences and anxieties. The presence of the other parent, both in actuality and in the psychic space of the parent, will greatly influence the relationship between child and parent, and the child's experience of a threesome.

The baby's arrival could reactivate past conflicts and make demands on the couple as parents, temporarily stretching their capacity to contain the inherent tensions. The stress relating to the experience of separateness, following the arrival of the third person, can be experienced as a challenge for some couples (Clulow, 1982) because it can compound memories of previous separations. It is not uncommon for new parents who present in therapy to describe a situation where one partner experiences the other parent as over-involved with the child at the expense of the couple relationship, leaving the other parent feeling abandoned and rejected. The birth of a baby can profoundly disturb a couple's phantasies and illusions about themselves as the kind of couple they had perceived themselves to be, prior to becoming parents. The specific vulnerability of each couple varies depending on their own individual experiences, circumstances, and interpretations of the meaning of events.

Sometimes, a parent will identify with the new baby in ways that are dependent on their own early experiences. For example, Ted and Tania, who presented for couple therapy heavily invested in disputing their contrasting ways of responding to their one-year-old son. In the course of therapy, Ted spoke at length about the importance of mothers, and the concern that Tania was not sufficiently maternal towards their baby. The couple therapist discovered that Ted, despite the initially rosy picture of his family of origin, had experienced a mother with mental health problems and a father who was very absent. It appeared that the experience of emotional neglect had been dealt with, at least in part, by splitting off the longing for a providing and ideal mother, which was now projected to Tania. Simultaneously, Ted identified with the son, wishing for him to have a different experience than his own, to have the benefit of an emotionally present and involved mother, wishing for his partner to embody these imagined features. Tania's actual experience was of frequently feeling criticised for her mothering. However hard she tried, she would never be good enough in the eyes of her partner. This couple's history illustrates a situation where the birth of a baby disturbs the *status quo* of the couple relationship, where the partners' early experiences can lead to a splitting and polarisation of feelings. For this couple, the result was a rather primitive competition about who was the better parent, with

Ted becoming increasingly indulgent towards the baby, while trying to marginalise Tania. She experienced an equal challenge to assert her own maternal prerogatives once the baby was born. It transpired that she had her own unconscious conflicts, accentuated through the birth of their daughter. As a very young child, she had, in effect, experienced two mothers, because her own mother had soon returned to work, employing a full-time nanny. This experience of dual mothering seemed to have been reactivated in the way she struggled in her conflict of divided loyalty between her partner and her baby. As she put it, she was trying to please both, but felt she failed with both.

This vignette could illustrate how the birth of a baby can bring to the surface a parent's own yearnings to be parented and cared for.

> The adult couple relationship is one of the few other relationships that ... has the intensity and intimacy of a primary mother–baby relationship. A ... partner's unmet need in that early relationship can lead to an attempt to ... gratify them in the adult relationship. (Morgan, 2012, p. 75)

This experience can also expose unconscious incestuous longings, with the ensuing feeling of unconscious guilt, which may prevent the partners from establishing their own effective parental couple (Morgan, 2005). While past unresolved experiences can be re-evoked in problematic ways, with the arrival of a new baby, the arrival can offer the potential for past experiences to be "reworked" within the context of the new family constellation. This permits the possibility of new and creative features to be integrated into the couple relationship in ways that allow for psychological growth and development.

"Affairs"

Another presentation that is familiar to couple psychotherapists is a couple who present, sometimes after the birth of a new baby, having found that their sexual relationship has come to a halt. Erotic desire for the partner has dried up and, as a result, one partner might seek sexual satisfaction outside the couple.

An affair is ordinarily regarded as an event of infidelity, where one partner has had, or is having, an intimate relationship with a third party. This usually, but not always, encompasses a sexual relationship, and might occur around the time of pregnancy and childbirth, when the non-pregnant partner is the one having the affair. Other trigger points can include a serious protracted illness, redundancy from employment, the youngest child leaving home, resulting in an "empty nest", or major events such as retirement. A common factor is the experience of loss in different contexts (Nathans, 2012). This gives an indication of how an affair can represent a defensive act or manoeuvre, an attempt to avoid mourning, and facing difficult and changing circumstances in the relationship. Infidelity occurs across the developmental spectrum, and it can sometimes represent a movement towards health and an attempt to escape a loveless relationship. "Where they love they do not desire and where they desire they cannot love. They seek objects which do not need love, in order to keep their sensuality away from the objects they love" (Freud, 1912d, p. 183).

Freud is speaking here of his male patients who were impotent with their wives but were able to perform sexually with a mistress or prostitute. Freud's idea of libido can broadly be translated as an urge towards intimacy and sexuality. The idea of a splitting of the libido is well established, and the most florid example is, perhaps, the so-called "Don Juan complex", which refers to a person who splits relationships into the two realms: the sacred relationship, which represents the "purity" of a loving relationship, and the profane, which represents a more debased sexuality. There are many complex reasons for the loss of sexual desire in an intimate partnership, but the so-called madonna–whore split referred to above can often be traced in couples who present for therapy where one partner is having an external sexual relationship, or, occasionally, both are.

A psychoanalytic understanding of oedipal feelings is based on a child's phantasy of an internal parent that can be possessed, merged with, and somehow owned. In the course of psychic and social development, the child will usually be able to dispel this intense need for the parent. Instead, there will be a gradual recognition of the appropriateness of separation and the child's omnipotent wishes will diminish. The acceptance of the inevitable separateness between parent and child is used as a hallmark for an individual's capacity for psychological development. For some individuals who, for varied reasons, have been caught up in an over-identification with the parent, where perhaps the parent's need for merger has been over-dominant, the push towards separateness and individuation can be fiercely resisted. This means that the developmental pathway becomes blocked and this could lead, in turn, to unconscious anxieties, phantasies, and wishes attached to the original parental relationship, emerging instead within an adult intimate partnership. "For some couples, their early experiences of relating are not modified by development but become fixed in the unconscious as a belief about all subsequent relationships" (Morgan, 2010, p. 39).

Since the child might perceive the parents' intercourse as an act of infidelity, unresolved oedipal conflicts have the potential to engender defensive splitting, where the child experiences a sense of betrayal by the longed for, albeit "unfaithful", parent (Josephs, 2006). Depending on the strength of the underlying unconscious phantasies, this scenario, originating from the internal world, can be re-enacted *via* infidelity in the couple relationship. "Rivalrous triangulation" refers to a defensive reversal of the oedipal triangle, where, instead of competing for the oedipal object, that is, the child competing with one parent for the other parent's affection, the adult reverses the oedipal situation through the act of infidelity. The partner who has the affair is now in a powerful position, where he or she, rather than being the person who must compete and perhaps lose the longed for partner, becomes the object of desire and rivalry between the partner and the lover. In contrast, a "split-object triangulation" is based on a split between, on the one hand, a phantasy relationship with an ideal partner that is free from conflict and, on the other hand, a "bad" partner who symbolically represents a neglectful internal parental object (Person, 1988). This kind of split can manifest in different ways, as outlined in the following clinical vignette:

A same gender couple presented for therapy, where Erica was having an extra-marital relationship with an old school friend. It transpired that, while growing up, she had experienced her mother as aggressive and punitive. As part of the couple's projective system, these qualities were now firmly projected into her partner. Her father, in contrast, was described as loving and attentive and she was still extremely close to him.

She experienced her partner, Mona, as someone tyrannical, whom she had to flee from, while the lover was felt to represent a loving and idealised phantasy mother, the opposite of the experience of her actual mother. The affair seemed, in part, to be an expression of Erica's fear that she might be trapped and engulfed in an intolerable relationship with Mona, rather as she had felt entrapped by her domineering mother. Mona's aggressive, but, in effect, impotent, rants confirmed for Erica the need to escape from what was felt to be an intolerable situation.

The couple therapy uncovered aspects of the psychological "fit" between the couple, and how Mona's experience of a withdrawn and depressed mother had contributed to her own undiagnosed depression, which was interspersed with fits of rage. She was burdened by feelings of unworthiness in relation to her vivacious and attractive partner. Within the interrelational projective system, Erica seemed to carry some of Mona's disowned passion and liveliness, while Mona appeared to carry some of Erica's renounced sadness and hopelessness. In this way, the couple relationship became imprinted by the kind of "projective gridlock" identified by Morgan (1995). She describes

> a particular kind of couple relationship in which the couple have a problem feeling psychically separate and different from each other, and hence create between them a relationship in which they feel locked together in a defensive collusion within which there is only very limited growth. (p. 33)

This couple was helped by having the opportunity to uncover some of the unconscious expectations and anxieties that were clouding their psychic vision of their relationship. They began to understand Erica's infidelity as an unconscious rivalrous attack on her father for his perceived betrayal of her through his close relationship with the mother. She felt that her father ought to have joined up with her against the awful and "monstrous" mother. "How could he be married to her?" she asked. This seemed to liberate Mona from some of Erica's hostile projections and, within the context of the relationship, she could be perceived through a less distorted lens. This, in turn, seemed to free the couple from the need for the affair. When a couple can understand the "unconscious collusion" (Kernberg, 1995a), the symptom picture will often change, creating a more satisfactory relationship. A *ménage à trois* can act as a defence against powerful oedipal longings and wishes, and, although couple psychotherapy is often an uncomfortable and emotionally disturbing experience for many couples, it offers the potential to understand a manifest problem as a defensive function of the relationship.

Oedipus: different cultures and beliefs, and hetero-normativity

Some critics have taken issue with the prevailing assumption that the Oedipus myth, almost by nature, transcends different cultures. Hewison (2007) points to the Hindu divinity of Ganesh, a figure with four arms and the head of an elephant, a mythic character with an extremely close relationship with his mother and murderous battles with his father. Without diminishing the broader relevance of the Oedipus myth, Hewison highlights the importance of cultural subjectivities and variations. From this standpoint, Freud's understanding of the Oedipus complex might appear, in retrospect, Eurocentric.

A similar critique is advanced by Tseng and colleagues (2005), who argue that the classic Oedipus complex "is only one type of parent–child complex that occurs and needs to be resolved" (p. 11). They put forward the idea that there are other interpersonal emotional complexes rooted in parent–child issues, as illustrated by the Ajase complex, which involves the mother and son, rather than the father and son, and the parent–child conflicts described in the Ganesh complex, where the son is defeated by the father, rather than being subjugated to him.

Other critics have questioned the implicit assumption of Freud's theory of the Oedipus complex as essentially being hetero-normative, because it fails to offer an adequate understanding of analogous configurations within same-gender relationships (Hertzmann, 2011, 2015). "Oedipal rejection with scorn for the child's same-sex romantic desires, or with withdrawal of the parent who is desired, is an emphatic failure that can add to feelings of shame, condemnation, and isolation" (Lynch, 2015, p. 141). Clarke (2016) argues that, although the Oedipus myth captures something universal about the human condition, this does not mean we are all compelled to read it in the same way. He suggests that what happens at "the crossroad", when Oedipus kills his father, can be seen as encompassing a range of different developmental possibilities, including the possibility that Oedipus is gay. He suggests that the idea of someone having a "true" fixed sexual identity is fictional, and that an awareness of this will have consequences for the way in which the oedipal framework is applied across diverse or fluid sexual identities.

Our understanding of the conventional approach to the Oedipus complex is further challenged in *Oedipus and the Oedipus Complex: A Revision* (Zepf, et al., 2016). The authors, in effect, invert Freud's conception of the centrality of the child in the oedipal configuration and redirect attention to the significance of the parents' unconscious sexual feelings towards the child, that is, the parents' own formative oedipal longings. From this standpoint, Freud's original theory is seen as tending to neglect the critical role of the parental unconscious. The authors suggest that there are good reasons for assuming that the parental seduction remains unconscious. They propose that the child's oedipal experience should be seen as staged by the parents' unconscious oedipal strivings. From this standpoint, the parental strivings are seen as unconsciously projected into the child and then processed by the child through identification. The authors question the idea that children compete with mother or father for the love of the "rival" parent. Instead, they suggest that father and mother should be seen as competing with the child for the love of the other parent. This approach might go some way towards rebalancing the conventional understanding outlined above. It reinforces the intensity and complexity of the triangular psychic processes that take place within the emotional nexus of mother, father, and child.

Summary

This chapter has explored how oedipal feelings constitute a complex psychic reality. A small child will not only be full of his own oedipal longings, but might also be surrounded by others' erotised phantasies and frustrations that must be negotiated.

With the Oedipus complex, there is neither a happy nor an unhappy ending. However, we may hope that, in the course of a child's maturational process, he or she will be able to see off the "ghosts" of the internalised parental representations in such a way that a degree of mental space is created. The individual can then accept that he is not omnipotent and that he cannot possess his parents.

Britton's notion of a "third position" helps us better understand the importance of finding a standpoint from which the partners can make sense of their experiences. This allows for an observer position to be found, permitting each partner to move towards a position where they can also be observed. It is this kind of psychological flexibility that enables an intimate adult couple to tolerate observing each other, to know each other in a more rounded way and with less need for mental "blinkers".

The wish for a "happy ending" to sweeten the burden of the human condition is alluring, but perhaps an appreciation of the centrality of these recurring oedipal dilemmas can bring an acceptance that feelings arising from the experience of being excluded or included are forever with us, demanding to be recognised, negotiated, and confronted as part of our personal and intractable histories.

CHAPTER THREE

Projective identification processes in the couple relationship

Mary Morgan

The concept of projective identification is a psychoanalytic gift to those trying to understand the unconscious dynamics of a couple relationship. It is a clinically and theoretically rich concept that has been elaborated extensively since it was first articulated by Klein in 1946 (Klein, 1975e). We now understand projective identification as an intrapsychic and an interpersonal process, as a defence, and a mode of communication and way of relating. In couples and other relationships, projective identification can also be part of creating a narcissistic relationship in phantasy and in the way a couple function together, such as that seen in a "projective gridlock" (Morgan, 1995).

Projective identification is central to the couple analytic concept of the "couple projective system". This concept has been crucial in shedding light on why some couples who are apparently so unhappy together none the less cannot separate. The nature of the couple projective system, how communicative and flexible, or defensive, rigid, and intrusive, rests on the way that projective identification is being used by the projector and experienced by the recipient. The couple's projective system can be containing for the couple or result in something very narcissistic and anti-developmental. The projective system is also an overarching concept that includes an understanding of the couple's "unconscious choice of partner" and the "unconscious couple fit", two other important couple analytic concepts.

The concept of projective identification

Melanie Klein first described the process of projective identification in 1946 in her paper, "Notes on some schizoid mechanisms" (Klein, 1975e), although she did not use the actual term "projective identification" until a later version in 1952. She understood projective identification as a primitive phantasy of splitting off and projecting parts of the self and internal objects and identifying with them as if located in another person. For Klein, projective identification was a defence, an unconscious phantasy, and an intrapsychic process.

> Together with these harmful excrements, expelled in hatred, split off parts of the ego are also projected onto the mother or, as I would rather call it, into the mother. These excrements and bad parts of the self are meant not only to injure the object but also to control it and take possession of it. In so far as the mother comes to contain the bad parts of the self, she is not felt to be a separate individual but is felt to be the bad self. Much of the hatred against the parts of the self is now directed towards the mother. This leads to a particular kind of identification which establishes the prototype of an aggressive object relation. . . . It is, however, not only the bad parts of the self which are expelled and projected, but also good parts of the self. Excrements then have the significance of gifts; and parts of the ego, which together with excrements are expelled and projected into the other person, represent the good, i.e. the loving parts of the self. (1975e[1946], p. 8)

For Klein, the infant functions in this way to manage unbearable bodily and mental states. Bad parts of the self that were experienced as threatening to the self are projected, as are, sometimes, good parts of the self for safe keeping, if felt to be threatened by the bad inside. In Klein's picture of early development, a paranoid–schizoid universe, there were also aggressive and controlling impulses towards the object that threatened the subject. She was describing a complex primitive internal world in which the object is, at times, experienced as threatening, partly because the infant has projected bad and threatening aspects of the self into it.

Since Klein's first description of this process, the concept of projective identification has been developed by many others, not only as describing processes in early development, but in describing processes between patient and analyst and in other relationships.

Bion: container–contained

The person who has made the most significant development of the concept is Bion (1959, 1962, 1967c[1962]). Following Klein, he understood that, as well as being a defence, projective identification could be a primitive mode of communication. He described it as the most primitive preverbal way in which the infant not only gets rid of, in unconscious phantasy, unbearable feelings, both physical and emotional, into the mother, but in which the mother receives this as communication of the infant's psychic–physical state. If the mother can digest and process these inchoate states, which he terms "beta elements", the mother, through her reverie, performing a function that he calls "alpha function", helps the infant to take back these parts. Eventually "alpha function", the apparatus for thinking, is itself introjected, which helps equip the developing infant in processing his own emotional states.

This process of containment is what the ordinary mother provides for her infant, and what the ordinary infant seeks from the mother, though many things can go wrong in this exchange between mother and infant, the factors depending on mother, infant, or both. In offering containment, the mother allows herself to be affected by her infant's emotional state: for example, to feel the infant's primitive states of terror and falling apart. Some mothers will be overwhelmed by their infant's anxiety, which might make them feel they are falling apart and, consequently, they might try to force the anxiety back into the infant, unprocessed and amplified by their own anxiety. And some infants, it seems, might not be able to make use of a containing object: for example, if they are too affected by envy of the mother's capacities, which they do not yet possess themselves. Thus, it is easy to see how a vicious circle can be created, the overwhelmed mother quickly becoming an untrustworthy object for the infant. Many mothers and babies struggle in the early stages of being a parent and being a newborn, but mainly they learn from each other and the relationship develops.

In some cases there is very limited containment:

> Normal development follows if the relationship between infant and breast permits the infant to project a feeling, say, that it is dying, into the mother and to reintroject it, after its sojourn in the breast has made it tolerable to the infant psyche. If the projection is not accepted by the mother, the infant feels that its feeling that it is dying is stripped of such meaning that it has. It therefore reintrojects, not a fear of dying made tolerable, but a nameless dread. (Bion, 1967c[1962], p. 116)

If the mother is very disturbed or psychotic, not only are the infant's anxieties not contained, but the mother might project her own disturbance into the infant. This description of early development is relevant in thinking about couple relationships, not only because of the elucidation of the concept of projective identification, but also because the difficulties experienced in this early relationship will always manifest in some form in the adult couple relationship.

Some writers, following Bion, now consider the process of projective identification to always include the impact on the object who has been projected into and the potential for the projected feelings to be contained by that object: for example, Ogden states,

> In a schematic way, one can think of projective identification as a process involving the following sequence: first, there is the fantasy of projecting a part of oneself into another person and of that part taking over the person from within; then there is pressure exerted via the interpersonal interaction such that the "recipient" of the projection experiences pressure to think, feel and behave in a manner congruent with the projection; finally, the projected feelings, after being "psychologically processed" by the recipient, are re-internalized by the projector. (Ogden, 1979, p. 358)

For British Kleinian writers, this is not always part of the process, as the "projective phantasies may or may not be accompanied by evocative behaviour unconsciously intended to induce the recipient of the projection to feel and act in accordance with the projective phantasy" (Bott Spillius et al., 2011, p. 126). This view emphasises projective identification as an unconscious phantasy and an intrapsychic process, which might or might not include these other stages. In fact, I think it is useful, even in couple therapy that has at its centre an interpersonal dimension, to keep an understanding of projective identification as both intrapsychic and interpersonal. This is because in narcissistic relationships, each partner's intrapsychic projective identification affects their perception of the other, and they relate to the other distorted by this projection. However, the recipient might not accept the projection and so can feel trapped and misunderstood by the other's distorted perception.

Acquisitive and attributive projective identification

Another way in which projective identification has been elaborated is by considering that phantasies of the identification part of the process are sometimes felt to have an "acquisitive" as well as "attributive" properties, meaning that the phantasy involves not only getting rid of aspects of one's own psyche and identifying with these in the object but also entering the mind of the other in phantasy, to acquire desired aspects of the other's psyche. "In acquisitive identification, the phantasy is *I am you*; in attributive identification, it is *You are me*" (Britton, 2003, p. 167). In attributive identification, as in the usual sense of projective identification, some aspect of the subject is attributed to the object, and in acquisitive identification the projective phantasy involves entering the object to acquire some attribute that the object is thought to possess. This is similar to Bollas's idea of "extractive introjection", "a procedure in which one person invades another mind and appropriates certain elements of mental life" (1991, p. 163), or in a couple relationship, a partner recognises something in the other they themselves do not possess and take it over. Both ideas indicate the close relationship between projective and introjective processes.

It is also interesting to note that in couple relationships, a projected aspect that was originally attributive can become acquisitive, as the projected-into partner accepts the projection and takes over this aspect. That partner then carries what has been described as a "double dose" (Cleavely, 1993, p. 65) but not always unwillingly. A typical example of this is when a couple with young children temporarily attribute to the other aspects of themselves that are, in fact, useful to the other. The parent at home attributes her "outgoing competence", to the partner out working, while that partner attributes his "nurturing caring" capacities to the partner at home. When the children are older and the partner who has been at home wants to return to outside work, she might feel denuded of the capacities she needs. Her partner, who has relied on the "double dose" of these capacities, might be reluctant or unwilling to give them back. The opposite is also just as likely to occur—the partner who is out at work and after a while wants to play a more nurturing role with the young children might feel completely inept and be kept this way by his partner.

Intrusive identification and the claustrum

Although many writers, following Bion, have fruitfully elaborated the communicative aspects of projective identification, Meltzer returned to Klein's more defensive use of projective identification and elaborated this. He suggested making a distinction between Klein's original use of the term "projective identification" and Bion's development of it. For Bion's development of the concept, he suggested retaining the term projective identification as a process describing "the unconscious phantasy implementing the non-lexical aspects of language and behaviour, aimed at communication rather than action". For Klein's original use of projective identification, he suggested the term "intrusive identification" to describe the "unconscious omnipotent phantasy, mechanism of defence" (Meltzer et al., 1986, p. 69). In this formulation, Meltzer draws attention to the experience of the kind of object in unconscious phantasy that is being projected into, the former being a container, the latter a claustrum. In thinking about couple relationships, the unconscious phantasy the couple have of their relationship is important. Do they conceive of it as a container, "feeling that they exist within it—are contained by it" (Colman, 1993, pp. 89–90), or do they experience it as a claustrum, in which "the unconscious experience of being entombed inside one's partner leads to feeling suffocated, as there is no air inside the claustrum and little hope of reclaiming what is hermetically sealed" (Feldman, 2014, p. 145). I will return to this latter kind of phantasy in discussing the *nature* of the couple's projective system.

Projective identification in the couple: the couple's projective system, unconscious partner choice, and couple fit

The early pioneers of Tavistock Relationships set out from 1948 onwards to try to understand couple relationships using concepts drawn from the psychoanalysis of individuals. From quite early on, however, they realised these concepts needed modifying and extending and that new concepts that specifically addressed the unconscious relationship between a couple needed to be found. The "couple's projective system" is a key couple psychoanalytic concept, referred to in many clinical discussions or supervisions at Tavistock Relationships. It describes a way that couples relate through projective identification, creating a flexible, semi-permanent or more or less fixed unconscious system. At its centre is the concept of projective identification, particularly the way that projective identification can be seen to function interpersonally and reciprocally through mutual projective identifications and counter projective identifications.

> The marriage relationship provides a containment in which each feels the other to be part of themselves—a kind of joint personality. What at first attracts and is later complained of in the other is often a projection of the disowned and frightening aspects of the self. It might be imagined that the best thing to do with unwanted aspects of the self is to project them onto someone or something and get as far removed as possible. That would, however, be placing a part of oneself in danger of being lost forever, and of losing one's potential for becoming a more complete person. (Cleavely, 1993, p. 65)

Unconscious choice of partner and couple fit

Theoretically, the projective system can also be thought about as an overarching concept that includes other key couple concepts, particularly "unconscious choice of partner" and "couple fit", though these concepts themselves include, as well as projective identification, other elements such as transference and shared unconscious phantasy. Alongside the conscious choice of adult partner, sexual attraction, finding "the one", falling in love, or choosing someone with whom one feels a deep connection, or however one might describe this process consciously, there are many unconscious factors at play. These arrangements are like an unconscious version of a marriage contract.

In this way, a particular kind of intimacy is created in the couple relationship, in which they come to share a psychic life for good or ill.

Klein saw projective identification as a way in which the infant in its most primitive state first establishes object relations, even though early on this is a part-object relationship and the distinction between self and other is not clear. Following this, Rosenfeld thought that projective identification was the process involved in recognising objects and identifying with them, sometimes with the aim of making essential links with them (1983). In the early stages of a relationship, unconsciously "recognising" in another lost or denied aspects of the self can be a very powerful experience. We might be intrigued by these aspects, even though ill at ease with them, and wish to re-experience these parts of ourselves through contact with the other. The potential of being able to reintegrate these aspects into the ego, thereby enriching it, might feel risky but also create a sense of possibility. The other is experienced as psychically, if not one's "other half", an object with whom a relationship can help one feel more whole. Projective identification is often at play in unconscious partner choice for these kinds of developmental reasons but also for defensive reasons. Sometimes, we recognise parts of ourselves that we want to keep lodged in the other, so that we only have to experience that part of our self at one remove. In conflictual relationships, these unwanted aspects of the self are often still feared and, when brought to life by the partner, could be attacked in them.

Couple fit, in the earlier literature referred to as "marital fit", refers to the projective system as a whole, that is, the projections of both partners as they dovetail and then interact around core issues or shared unconscious phantasies within a couple. The partners in the relationship carry aspects for each other, that is, aspects of the self, projected into the other or, through acquisitive or extractive projective identification, aspects acquired from the other. Unconsciously, there might be a recognition in the other of the representation of some aspect of one's internal world that one wants to make closer contact with, an internal object with which one wants to work something through, or unwanted aspects that can be located in the other and controlled there. Dicks referred to "unconscious complementariness",

> a kind of division of function by which each partner supplied part of a set of qualities, the sum of which created a complete dyadic unit.

This joint personality, or integrate, enabled each half to rediscover lost aspects of their primary object relations, which they had split off or repressed, and which they were, in their involvement with the spouse, re-experiencing by projective identification. (1993[1967], p. 69)

Willi (1984) describes how the couple can collude together to avoid areas that make them anxious and become polarised, each carrying opposite aspects of a shared theme or issue. He describes this polarisation of behaviour patterns in relation to the couple's level of psychic development:

Partners may feel attracted by a mutually fascinating yet at the same time disturbing theme. . . . Often unconsciously, these central themes constitute the common basis of marital relations. Similar fears may cause the build-up of a reciprocally organised defensive system helping both partners to neutralise these fears, to compensate for offenses, and to avoid or master threatening situations. The consequence may be a collusion, an unconscious, neurotic interplay of two partners that is based on similar, unresolved, central conflicts and acted out in polarised roles. (Willi, 1984, p. 179)

The nature of the couple's projective system: developmental and defensive aspects

In thinking about the projective system in a couple, it is important to consider not just the content projected and introjected by each partner but the *nature* of the projective system itself, how evacuative, intrusive, controlling, flexible, or containing it is. Other writers, in different ways, draw attention to the nature of the projective system and the couple's unconscious relating. Novakovic (2016, p. 97) in describing the "couple's unconscious relations", emphasises "process" as well as "content". "What 'connects' the partners in a 'couple' are unconscious objects, internal figures, *contents* of the mind, and the *processes*, functions, or relations between the objects". Fisher in describing the oscillation in relationships from narcissistic relating to a psychological state of marriage, highlights the inevitable changing nature of relating in a couple, which he sees as "a fundamental human tension" (1999, p. 1). Ruszczynski argues, if we consider projective identification as part of what links a couple, then *all object relations are in part narcissistic*. The point at issue is the degree, flexibility and forcefulness of the projective identification. If the more primitive defences of splitting and projective processes dominate the nature of the interaction, such object relations will be more narcissistically structured. If there is less splitting and if the projective system is more fluid, so allowing for the projections to be withdrawn, then the nature of the relationship will be based that much more on the reality of the self and other. (1995, p. 24)

Flexible containment

When a couple projective system is working developmentally, we are really talking about containment in the relationship, but not necessarily or only or exactly in the sense that Bion described, in which one person is functioning as a container for the other who is contained. If the relationship is structured with one partner as mother, the other as infant, then the relationship will be functioning in quite a primitive way, be very limited, and under enormous strain. In more mature relating, aspects of the self are not so entirely disowned. Joseph describes that while in more primitive states projective identification has no concern for the object, this changes with psychic development.

As the child moves towards the depressive position . . . although projective identification is probably never entirely given up, it will no longer involve the complete splitting off and disowning of parts of the self, but will be less absolute, more temporary and more able to be drawn back into the individual's personality – and thus be the basis of empathy. (1989, pp. 169–170)

Something is disowned and, at the same time, "lived with" in the other who is in close proximity.

Developmental (and therefore therapeutic) potential lies in the fact that what is feared and rejected in the internal world, and is located in the person of the partner, is not lost but it is "lived with". It is therefore available experientially and may be assimilated. (Woodhouse, 1990, p. 104)

The projection, lived with in the other, and as it becomes less feared by the projector, might increase empathy in the relationship.

For most couples their projective system contains defensive and developmental elements: at times it functions more defensively and at other times more developmentally. Its defensive functioning can support the couple, as, for example, Cudmore and Judd found in working with couples who had lost a child. They found that while one partner temporarily carried the pain of the overwhelming loss, the other could function and contain. "All the couples we saw, who used their relationship to assist them in their mourning, demonstrated this flexibility, an ability to take turns in looking after and being looked after" (2001, p. 169).

This can work for the couple if what is projected is not too extreme or not whole parts of the personality, and, if there is flexibility, they can be given back by the object and taken back by the subject. However, if one of the partners is nearly always the angry one, or the rational one, or the depressed one, or the emotional one, unconsciously caught up in expressing these specific emotions and functions and depriving the other of expressing them, the projective system has become more fixed.

Psychic development

Deep in the heart of much of the early writing from Tavistock Relationships is the idea of the couple's relationship potentially being therapeutic, or, at least, one in which each partner can continue his or her psychic growth and development. We cannot always, if ever, function as whole, integrated people, and the couple relationship allows for some regression. Living in intimacy with a partner who contains unwanted aspects of ourselves is an unconscious arrangement that, over time, can lead to psychic development in each partner.

This is important, because, as a consequence of projecting, the ego is left depleted, which could result in a weak sense of self. For example, it might be that the capacity to feel and appropriately express angry feelings is disowned because such feelings are felt to be too destructive; consequently, one could live a restricted life, avoiding conflict and confrontations, or become depressed. Alternatively, loving feelings might be disowned, because they are felt to place one at too great a risk of hurt and disappointment: this might lead to living a falsely independent and lonely life. The advantage in projective identification in the context of an intimate relationship is that the disowned parts of the self are not too far away, and seeing these managed differently by the other could render these aspects less frightening. Either there is some kind of psychic balance in the relationship, whereby the other can be relied on to carry this aspect of the self, or it might be possible over time to reintroject this part of the self. As Scharff describes,

> the well-functioning, maturing projective identificatory system enables the person to take back impoverishing projections. It simultaneously enriches the self and maximises concern for the spouse as a separate person, as well as refurbishing the internal object or part of the self to which the spouse corresponds. (Scharff, 1992, p. 138)

In more detail, Ogden describes this process in the following way:

> The elicited feelings are the product of a different personality system with different strengths and weaknesses. This fact opens the door to the possibility that the projected feelings (more accurately, the congruent set of feelings elicited in the recipient) will be handled differently from the manner in which the projector has been able to handle them. ... These methods of dealing with feelings contrast with projective identification in that they are not basically efforts to avoid, get rid of, deny, or forget feelings and ideas; rather, they represent different types of attempts to live with, or contain, an aspect of oneself without disavowal. If the recipient of the projection can deal with the feelings projected "into" him in a way that differs from the projector's method, a new set of feelings is generated which can be viewed as a "processed" version of the original projected feelings. The new set of feelings might involve the sense that the projected feelings, thoughts, and representations can be lived with, without damaging other aspects of the self or of one's valued external or internal objects (cf. Little, 1966). (1979, p. 360–361)

Conscious container–unconsciously contained

In some couple relationships, it does appear that the arrangement is that one partner is a container for the other. However, this is not always as it appears, as "the obvious and conscious container is sometimes the unconsciously contained and, vice versa, the obviously and consciously contained is unconsciously and emotionally the container" (Lyons & Mattinson, 1993, p. 108). One partner in a couple described the other as "spineless", unable to take any kind of position in their discussions. He felt he was left to make all the important decisions. His therapist was aware of how fragile this supposedly more self-assured partner was and felt that were the "spineless" partner not prepared to take this projection, his partner would collapse. This is an example of a couple's unconscious projective system and the way in which the partner who appears on the outside to be the container, is, in fact, in other ways, the unconsciously contained. The way the projective system functions in a couple relationship can be defensive but in a way that supports the couple's relationship if it is not too constraining. The couple can unconsciously agree to carry a projection for the other, as this benefits both their relationship and, thereby, each of the partners.

The absence of a container

Some couples experience a failure in the use of projective identification. The projective identification might have occurred intrapsychically, identified in unconscious phantasy as in the other but, in all but the most narcissistic couples, the projector needs some evidence that the projection has been identified with by the object. Some relationships are suffused with anxiety. One partner in the relationship is overwhelmed with anxiety and deals with it by projecting it into the partner. However, that person's anxiety just makes the other too anxious and they push back the anxiety, increasing the original partner's anxiety. In this situation, instead of the projected anxiety being processed by the recipient and the couple eventually being able to think together, the anxiety escalates. Conflict between the couple can easily ensue, as there is a feeling of being attacked by the other's projection.

Defensive projective processes

In some relationships, the projective system is very defensive. The couple might join unconscious forces around a shared belief, expelling from the relationship anything that contradicts it. Together they might repeat an unresolved internal relationship that they share and cannot relinquish. Between them, there could be the attempt to disown an aspect of the self, projected into the other so completely that it is no longer identified with in any sense as belonging to the self. Instead, it is firmly lodged and controlled in the other. Couples like this often present in a very polarised way, each partner carrying a double dose of a particular set of feelings. In this situation, as Zinner describes it, the relationship becomes "a repository or dumping ground for externalised elements of intrapsychic conflict or expelled unacceptable inner objects. . . . the quality of the marital relationship is sacrificed to the need to minimize inner tension within the individual partner" (Zinner, 1988, p. 2).

In trying to understand a couple relationship, we need to think about the experience of both the projector and the recipient of the projection. In intrusive identification, the partner is related to as a narcissistic object, not as a separate object. The projection has a different motivation to that of communication; it is about wanting to lodge oneself inside the other and, in phantasy, to control the object from the inside. In terms of how the partners perceive each other, it is very different imagining what is going on inside the other from the position of being outside to that of feeling one knows what is going on inside the other from the position of being inside them.

From the point of view of the recipient of the projection, Fisher asks what it is like to be on the receiving end of intrusive projections, "a projection in which someone peremptorily defines both himself or herself *and me* without so much as a by-your-leave?" (1999, p. 239), like an uninvited guest, as evoked by the title of his book on couple therapy (1999). Here, it is not about taking in and containing something, but more like the experience of being taken over. As Meltzer says, "this factor of invitation, and consequently of receptivity, is crucial in object relationships" (1992, p. 70). Without this receptivity, the experience of the intrusive identification is "the experience of being manipulated, so as to be playing a part, no matter how difficult to recognise, in someone else's phantasy" (Bion, 1961, p. 149). Some couples do have a particular kind of narcissistic fit, each with a poor sense of boundaries. One of them functions through the use of intrusive (projective) identification and the other, who has a poor sense of self, is taken over by, and identifies with, the projections.

Projective gridlock

I described this dynamic in the idea of a couple "projective gridlock" (1995). Here, projective identification is used to deal with anxiety about separateness and difference. While at a cognitive level, the members of the couple recognise that they are two separate people, at an emotional level, the experience of the other as different, and, therefore, separate, is experienced as persecutory. In this situation,

> projective identification seems often to be used excessively and intrusively, with the aim or result that the other's separate psychic existence is denied. Instead, a comfortable sort of fusion or feeling of being trapped or imprisoned is created, which stultifies the relationship. (Morgan, 1995 p. 35)

The experience of being taken over and losing a sense of self was described poignantly by the wife in one couple:

> I have now come to a point—where I feel I want to be more independent—I have my own ideas and thoughts. Up to now I have sort of let my life go to one side and taken my husband's. I feel sometimes I haven't been living my own life but his . . . I would like to feel my own identity . . . (1995, p. 34)

Fisher describes this as the interlocking adhesive and intrusive dynamics that function in a particularly narcissistic way.

> The adhesive dynamics exacerbate masochistic tendencies and the intrusive dynamics exacerbate sadistic tendencies, mutually reinforcing each other in the couple relationship, as each partner feels increasingly locked into intensifying spirals of retaliation. The couple's *folie à deux* offered no way out. (1999, p. 243).

When projective identification is being used in this way, it has a distorting effect on intimacy. A partner using intrusive identification might feel that they know the other completely, better even than the partner knows him- or herself.

> Intrusive projections leave no space for the imagination. This helps us to understand . . . the fundamental difference between a genuine intimacy with the other and a "pseudo–intimacy", which is actually a narcissistic form of relating. The former is based on the reality that the other is known *only* from the outside. The latter is based on the phantasy of getting *inside* the other. (1999, p. 236)

Meltzer invites us to consider the difference between the picture of the inside of the internal mother, which results from the use of imagination, and the one that results from the phantasy of omnipotent intrusion. Seen from the "outside" (that is, through the use of imagination), the primary quality of this region of the internal mother is "richness", having the nuances of "generosity, receptiveness, aesthetic reciprocity; understanding and all possible knowledge; the locus of symbol formation, and thus of art, poetry, imagination" (Meltzer, 1992, p. 72). However, "experienced" from the inside influenced by the motives of intrusion, Meltzer suggests a very different picture: "generosity becomes *quid pro quo*, receptiveness becomes inveiglement, reciprocity becomes collusion, understanding becomes penetration of secrets, knowledge becomes information, symbol formation becomes metonymy, art becomes fashion" (Meltzer, 1992, pp. 72–73).

Thus, the couple projective system and the way in which projective identification is used by the subject and experienced by the object can manifest in very different ways. Sometimes, what is important to consider is the contents of the projective identification—why one partner disowns important aspects of him- or herself and why the partner identifies with the projection. At other times, what is crucial to understand is how projective identification is being used in the relationship, its intent, and the nature of the relationship created.

The relationship has a life of its own

The discussion of projective identification in a couple relationship can take on a predetermined slant. We often think about what a couple are bringing to the relationship from their past, what intrapsychic conflicts and anxieties they are seeking resolution of in the relationship. Although the aggregate that the couple forms is, of course, determined by what each partner brings to the relationship, the way the couple then relate together and function takes on a life of its own.

Even though unconsciously the relationship might be set up in a certain way, the partner choice meaningful, and the couple forming a psychic system for developmental and defensive purposes, this unconscious system will also develop in unpredictable ways. What one partner is trying to create unconsciously is not necessarily what the other one is doing, and the interrelationship of these two psyches creates something that is challenging for both. This creates the kinds of tensions and difficulties that bring couples for therapy.

What might have looked like a potentially developmental unconscious choice of partner might not turn out like that. Attempts to recreate an internal object relationship, to work something through in the relationship, or to use the relationship to defend the self against psychic pain might or might not be realised. It might not be possible to keep one's depression at bay projected into the other. Perhaps the depressed partner seeks help and recovers; perhaps the pressure of projections leads to increasingly forceful reprojection of one's own split off aspects, now added to by the partner's. Also, events in the external world, loss and change, will have an impact and might result in unexpected behaviours that could not be predicted, and what the couple do with this cannot be known. In a healthy relationship, this is what gives life to the relationship, as the couple find that together they are creative in ways neither could have predicted (Morgan, 2005), but the couple might also find that what happens between them is difficult, disturbing, and hard for them to process.

More creative functioning in a projective system

While excessive and intrusive projective identification in a couple relationship is clearly destructive of any creativity, there are ways that projective identification and the couple projective system can help the couple's functioning.

If projective identification is used flexibly and not excessively, each partner can feel contained by the other but, in a functioning relationship, it is not quite as the infant is with the mother, in which contents are entirely split off because they are unmanageable. It is more that it is not entirely split off, but attributed to the other, where it can be observed as lived with by the other. This can lead to psychic growth in the subject who becomes more interested in, and less frightened of, his or her projection.

In some relationships, projective identification is not so flexible, but, if not excessive, it can support a couple. There is an unconscious agreement to carry aspects for each other and even an unconscious recognition that this is the agreement. In this way, the couple create a relationship in which they function better together than either partner would alone.

In a more creative couple relationship, communication by projective identification, although inevitable, is less the normal currency, and the couple feel able to communicate more verbally. Of course, some of what they try to communicate might be the experience of something projected into one of them by the other, but being able to talk about a double dose of, say, "angry feelings", rather than act out the anger or try to push the anger or other feelings back into the partner, can enable this emotional experience to be thought about. The couple feel able, at least some of the time, to share difficult feelings, unprocessed feelings, differences, hate as well as love, with the belief that the relationship can manage it. With experience, there develops confidence in the relationship, and projective identifications, while being an aspect of the couple's relationship, can be processed and contained within the relationship.

CHAPTER FOUR

On container–contained dynamics in the couple relationship

David Hewison

In order to explore and describe the psychological dynamics between partners in a marriage or committed couple relationship, we need to understand the ways in which each person influences the other beyond those that are direct, behavioural, or conscious. Psychoanalytic thinking about the nature of the unconscious and its impact between people is based on a particular understanding of the growth of the mind in the mother–baby relationship, and psychoanalysis has developed a mature theory of how this is replicated in the special situation of the analyst–analysand dyad in psychoanalytic psychotherapy.

This chapter looks at the application of this body of thought to the adult couple relationship, and to the interactive experiences that happen during couple psychotherapy. It notes that the adult couple relationship cannot be seen solely as a replication of that between a mother and her infant, or, indeed, as a more mutual psychotherapeutic interaction between consenting adults. Couple relationships involve something more than this: the American psychoanalyst, James Grotstein, suggested we are all born with an intersubjective instinct (Grotstein, 2008, p. ix), and this has implications for how we conceptualise the nature of the unconscious communication between partners and for what might be seen in the therapeutic setting with couples.

The term "container–contained" is one that is particularly important in understanding couple dynamics, and is associated, in very different ways, with the work of Wilfred Bion and Carl Jung. Bion used the term to think about very early mental processes in the mother–baby relationship, and Jung addressed what happens in the committed adult couple relationship. Bion, in effect, looks backwards from the adult patient in analysis to the baby they once were, and shows how this dynamic is repeated in the analytic setting; Jung looks forward from the point of a couple committing to each other, to the person each partner will become because of the relationship between them, and shows how a mutually interacting, innate developmental process, which he termed "individuation", can go wrong and lead to relationship breakdown. The link between Bion and Jung is the idea of psychic development *through* relationship: surviving and giving meaning to emotional storms is essential in each of their conceptualisations, and failures in this process can lead to the need for couple therapy. This chapter addresses these different ideas about the container–contained relationship, and gives clinical vignettes to bring them to life.

Container–contained in infancy

Bion built on the work of Melanie Klein about the relationship between projective processes and the integrity of the personality (Klein, 1975e[1946]). Reading backwards in time from her work with young children, she posited that a particular psychic defence—projective identification—had a dual role in the communication of mental states between a very young baby and the mother. This dual role was to protect the baby from its own unbearable emotional states, and to build on an awareness that an "Other" existed in relationship to them. Klein felt that babies were born with a powerful but undifferentiated imagination (phantasy), which coloured their experience. Much of this experience was uncomfortable or even painful to the very small infant, and this meant that the ordinary processes of the development of the mind through projection on the external world and taking back in what was found there, leading to an accretion of experience, was highly subjective and fraught with danger.

As Klein felt this stage was before the use of language and the capacity to symbolise via words, internal bodily states (hunger, wind, bowel movements, or constipation, etc.) were experienced psychically as something potentially overwhelming. In order to cope with states such as hunger that has been left too long, becoming experienced as a sense of being eaten up from the inside, the baby has recourse to the very basic psychological mechanisms of defence that dominate at this stage of development: primarily denial, splitting, and projection. Denial takes the form of "this isn't happening to me"; splitting takes the form of "this is all only good, that is all only bad", and projection takes the form of "I'm not doing this, you are". When this happens, the baby stops experiencing something inside the boundaries of itself by denying and separating itself mentally from the experience and projects the internal feeling, coloured as it is with both phantasy and physical sensation, outside of itself, and ascribes it to something or someone else, such as the breast or the mother. Through splitting between "good" and "bad" experiences, and projecting the "bad" away, the baby achieves relief, at least for a moment. This protection of the baby's growing sense of self comes at a cost, however: not only is the internal sensation and its associated experience pushed away, but the part of the baby's growing mind that has the experience is ejected with it. The baby is, therefore, less able to link inner and outer experience through reality testing. This is a particular problem because the dangerous states that had to be evacuated are now felt to be external to the infant, and Klein suggests that parts of the baby's sense of his own mind are, too. The baby, in his extreme dependency, now becomes vulnerable to the actions of these external bad experiences.

Klein aptly named this state of development the "paranoid–schizoid" position ("paranoid" because of the level of anxiety, and "schizoid" because it involves splitting into good and bad). She redefined the projective processes involved as "projective identification" because of the particular mix of projecting and identifying with oneself that it comprised. The identifying is two-way: the baby takes in the external world through introjection, and the two processes of projection, via projective identification and of introjection, help to build the mind and the personality. Interestingly, in Klein's theory, good parts of the self are expelled as well as bad ones, and they help to build a good relationship with the mother as an object of projection.

It will be obvious that the actual qualities and behaviour of the external world—which, of course, really means the mother or other primary carer—is of extreme importance in helping the baby to survive this stage of psychological development. A mother who is attuned to her baby's shifting states will soothe rather than exacerbate the painful physical–emotional experiences that the baby is having, and the development of psychoanalysis in the UK around and after the Second World War produced different versions of how this needed to happen. Donald Winnicott developed the idea of "holding" to conceptualise this: the mother's sustained preoccupation with the baby, which allows her to shift and adapt to her child's capacity to use her in the service of development (Winnicott, 1960). He felt that the kinds of mechanisms put forward by Klein were of less importance because, he argued, there was not such a psychological separation between baby and mother at the beginning (going so far as to claim, somewhat rhetorically, that "there is no such thing as a baby, only a baby and mother"). He felt that Klein's view was too far in the direction of a one-person psychology (intrapsychic), because she appeared to give the environment much less of a role than internal phantasy; he preferred a two-person psychology (interpsychic), in which the baby's belief that there is no difference between himself and the environment is gradually modified by the mother's attuned adaptive responses. This distinction between intrapsychic and interpsychic processes—and what weight to give to each in articulating theories of human development and in clinical technique—remains a source of rich debate in the psychoanalytic field. It is found when thinking about the dynamics of the couple relationship, too.

Bion followed Klein in terms of theory but is close to Winnicott in practice, in that he characterised the processes of projective identification and introjection as being simultaneously intra- and interpsychic, as something that goes on *within* and *between* people. He expanded the usefulness of these concepts from the baby–mother interaction into the consulting room between analyst and analysand, into the experiences that happen in groups, and beyond that into organisations and interorganisational life. He focused on what happened to the parts of the self and their associated phantasy-shaped experiences when they were put into the mother/other in the way that Klein described, and what then happened when introjection (or reintrojection) followed. He went beyond Klein in emphasising the importance of the impact of the projection on the person receiving it (the other as a real person, not just as an aspect of the baby's unconscious imagination), and he added to her idea of what the process was used for by distinguishing between projective identification as *evacuation* (a getting rid of, or attack on, the other) and projective identification as *communication* (in which something is passed from one person to another, in order to be made sense of). This emphasis on the communication of unconscious material was a radical expansion of Klein's thinking, and has formed the basis for key developments in psychoanalytic theory and practice since.

He suggested that the use of the mechanism for evacuation should be considered "excessive" projective identification, as it was characterised by envy and frustration. He considered that the use of the mechanism for communication should be thought of as "normal" projective identification, as the process is used to enable the mother to know something about the baby's internal emotional experience and, implicitly, therefore, to have the other do something with it. He developed the concept of "container–contained" to describe what happens as a result of this normal projective identification process (Bion, 1967a).

Bion's theory of container–contained

Taking Klein's idea that the baby will experience painful and terrifying internal emotional states, and will try to deal with them through splitting and projection, expelling not only the state but also a part of his mind (his capacity to experience or know about these states), Bion suggested that the emotional response of the mother was key. He indicated, like Winnicott, that an attuned mother can receive the projection and tolerate it, without denying that it is happening or without becoming overwhelmed by it. When the hungry baby cries and cries, and becomes more and more distressed, the mother who is tuned in to the baby's experience through her capacity for reverie—a deep interest in her infant—can know that the baby is experiencing not just hunger but a sense of terror and a feeling of being about to fall apart, to become fragmented. The baby's experience is, in effect, one of dying. The mother attends to the baby physically, verbally, and emotionally. She might talk to the baby, saying something like, "Oh, darling! You're so hungry! Don't worry, I'm here. Here we are. Ssssh.

Gently now," as she holds the child and prepares to feed. The words themselves are, of course, not understood, but the sense that the mother is not put into the same state of mind as the baby but can know about it and tolerate responding to it is conveyed in the mix of sounds and physical actions. In addition, and importantly, the mother's emotional state and focus on the wellbeing of the baby—her love—is also communicated and the experience of the resulting feed and the calm mind that the mother has is taken in by the baby, who becomes less fragmented and frightened. As a result of this interactive experience, the baby increasingly is able to tolerate his own bodily–emotional states for longer, and his mind begins to grow. The mother is the container and the baby is the contained. This container–contained experience can be put slightly differently, as the capacity to be open to another's emotional distress meeting the need to have that distress known about and understood, in both its conscious and unconscious forms.

"Container–contained", then, is a description of the transformative conjunction of difference; when the container is unable, or refuses, to accept the impact of the experience (if mother is depressed or unduly panicked), then the normal projective identification process is replaced by excessive projective identifications, and communication stops, fragmentation increases, leading ultimately to breakdown, whether this be of an individual's sense of themselves, a psychotherapeutic treatment, a couple relationship, or interactions between groups or parts of society. Where dependence is used for destructive purposes, Bion suggested it was *parasitic*, and where the dependency was more mutually developmental, he used the term *symbiotic* (Bion, 1970, p. 95). Unfortunately, Bion did not go into detail about these in his writing, and appeared to define them differently, depending on whether he was talking about the development of thinking (the mother–baby relationship) or the relationship between members of a group (Bléandonu, 1994, p. 229). In both instances, however, he emphasises the relationship between an emotional experience and the capacity to know about, and be changed by, it. In relation to groups, he suggested that growth is the product of the contained working on the container, and *vice versa*, without one destroying the other, and it is this idea that is of such relevance to the adult couple, whose relationship is so much more symmetrical than that between a mother and a new baby, though both kinds of dyad make use of the processes of projective identification in the struggle to move from paranoid–schizoid to depressive position ways of relating. Don and Carol were a couple whose struggle was too great for them to manage.

Don and Carol: a destructive container–contained couple relationship

Don and Carol were a white, heterosexual couple in their early sixties. They came for therapy because, as Carol put it, "We are unable to communicate without descending into bitter arguments and recriminations." Don agreed, suggesting that it was impossible between them, and that they either sorted it out or they divorced, as Carol would not let things rest. They appeared to have some interest in their internal worlds, but it soon became clear that this was only a front for a continuing grievance between them over who was to blame for their current state. They had invested money into a risky business venture that had failed, leaving them without savings and no prospect of being able to retire for many years to come. Each time one of them began to tell the story, the other would interrupt to clarify a detail or dispute the imputation of what was being said. There was a pervasive atmosphere in the therapy of deception: although they claimed to have no money, they arrived in an expensive car and were always dropping into the conversation the latest expensive holiday or event they had planned. They were often late paying their bill.

Each had had a very difficult upbringing, with parents who were unavailable and preoccupied (Don) or overinvolved and intrusive (Carol). The sessions were characterised by insistent demands that the other submit to their point of view and that the therapist become an ally in the fight against the other. Any observation or interpretation that was made by the therapist was met with either a stony silence (with an implicit "what on earth do you possibly imagine we could do with what you've just said!?") or with glee and vengeful delight (with an explicit "See! The therapist knows just how bad you are!"). There was no space in which they could see themselves as a couple relating to a difficult circumstance together (having what has been described as a "couple state of mind" (Morgan, 2014a)). Instead, they used the therapy sessions to accuse and rebut, to confuse and obscure, all at a heightened pitch of emotional intensity. It was impossible, at times, to follow the fast-switching argument between them, and the therapist felt battered and bewildered, often unable to think clearly. After a while, it became clear that this was not simply a matter of anxiety driving desperate attempts to get through to each other, to be heard, but a deliberate campaign of chaos so that the only thing that was in anyone's mind was the latest sense of outrage and excited grievance. Calm reflection or the slow going over of details of their interaction or exploration of what something meant to them or reminded them of in their backgrounds was anathema to them. It could be tolerated for a moment, before it became used again in the service of complaints and misunderstanding.

There was a particular difficulty in that, in many respects, they understood each other quite acutely: their accusations against each other were not arbitrary, even if they were overblown and wild. They were used, however, not to further understanding and sharing, but to pre-empt and defend against, to turn knowledge into victory. At the same time, the couple were panicking, because the arguments were escalating and each was feeling increasingly out of control. At one point, they began legal action against each other, and were only persuaded by the lawyers to desist, as the professionals became more aware of the irrational and volatile forces driving the dispute. The couple abandoned the therapy shortly after the therapist interpreted that they were more interested in using the therapy as a weapon to continue wreaking revenge than in looking at why they were doing this, and that they appeared to wish to use the therapist as a regulating function, whose sole purpose was to ensure they could keep the fight between them going for ever, at exactly the right pitch of excitement and indignation. Too little excited fighting and they risked falling into guilt and shame about what they were doing; too much and they risked either harming each other or the relationship actually breaking down.

The difficulty that Carol and Don had was that they were operating at an early level of splitting and projection, and seeing each other as a kind of enemy that they could not escape from. Their emotions overwhelmed their sense of themselves as each having a mind that could bear to think about things, and this spread into the therapy, too. Rather than be helped to see what they were doing to each other, they split even further, turning the therapy wholly bad, and they left. Their sense of being contained by another was not one that promoted a safe dependency leading to development, but, rather, a kind of prison in which only destructive things could occur. Repetition of the old was safer than risking something new.

Most couples, however, expect something much more mutual between them as adults, and are building on the developments of mind and the capacities for emotional self-containment that they have made, not just as very young children but also through the developmental expansions of adolescence and beyond. As individuals grow up, they can make couple relationships in which there is the opportunity for further transformative conjunctions of difference—the capacities for which depend on what each brings to the relationship and why, as well as their abilities to bear further emotional challenges and demands. This adult-focused container–contained conjunction is essential in different ways to this capacity, as Jung described. To understand the links with Bion's work, we first have to survey Jung's ideas on what is *psychological* about the adult couple relationship.

Jung's writing on container–contained in the adult couple relationship

In 1925, Jung wrote a paper, "Marriage as a psychological relationship", in which he described a process of the influence of marital relationships on the individuation process, and of the particular difficulties involved in moving from a state of identity (fusion) to one of consciousness (psychological separateness) (Jung, 1954[1925]). In this work, he uses the image of a mutual interaction between partners in a relationship, where one is "contained" by the other, who is then the "container" for them, in a different way to Bion. He suggests that a "psychological relationship" is one in which consciousness is involved, most particularly the ability to discriminate between oneself and another. Jung points out that even adult relationships are largely ones of unconsciousness, particularly ones that are entered into while the participants are still young. He suggests that the gradual emergence of consciousness out of the depths of the unconscious reaches a crucial point: that of the establishment of continuity in the sense of ourselves. "With the rise of a continuous consciousness, and not before, psychological relationship becomes possible" (para. 326). This consciousness is only partial, however; large areas of unconsciousness exist that bind a person's sense of self into a primitive identity with others, an identity that precludes relating to an Other. What this means is that "the greater the area of unconsciousness, the less is marriage a matter of free choice, as is shown subjectively in the fatal compulsion one feels so acutely when one is in love" (para. 327).

Jung outlines what the unconscious motivations for marriage are, dividing them into personal and general in nature. The personal motivations stem from the conscious and unconscious implications of the relationship each individual has to his or her parents, and particularly to the parent of the opposite sex. Jung points out that although conscious love for a father or a mother will favour a marital choice of someone similar, the nature of the unconscious relationships—which are unlikely to be a matter of simple love—will introduce complications into this picture. The main complication, in Jung's view, is the area of psychological life that the parents have refused to live for themselves: their children are then forced to carry it for them. At times, where the parents' emotional state is simply one-sided, the children are required to embody the other side: excessively "moral-minded" parents will have "unmoral" children, and *vice versa*. The dynamic qualities of this influence become heightened and worsened when one (or both) of the parents has kept him- or herself "artificially unconscious" and has refused to face up to knowledge of him/herself. He suggests, similarly, that a relationship that is purely "instinctual", in the long run also leads to difficulties: the obstacles of the parental failure continue to make their presence known, and the instinctual choice of partner will not be something that is necessarily in the best interests of the individual, who really needs to make a marriage with someone who can match or endure their increasing differentiation as they develop psychologically. Instinct, in this sense, is opposed to individual happiness, and is more a function of the need to maintain the species. Any relationship that stems from this more biological need will be both unconscious and impersonal. As Jung puts it,

> If we can speak here of a "relationship" at all, it is, at best, only a pale reflection of what we mean, a very distant state of affairs with a decidedly impersonal character, wholly regulated by traditional customs and prejudices, the prototype of every conventional marriage. (para. 329)

An instinctual marriage choice is made on the basis of a non-differentiation between the partners, based on a supposition, arising from the state of unconscious identity (Jung's version of projective identification), that the partners share the same psychological structure. This unity is strengthened through a satisfactory sexual life in the couple that binds the pair closer together. He suggests that, in a way, the individual is put aside in favour of the preservation of the species; as a result, when children are born, the couple who have been latched together in this way then shift into another instinctual and collective role: that of mother and father.

Jung is clear that these features of the couple are not to be considered attributes of a real relationship between two individuals; theirs is not a *psychological* relationship (para. 331). He suggests that all marriages stem, initially at least, from instinctual roots, from collective factors that are influenced by the impact of the partners' upbringing and the impact of the state of the parents' psychological development (cf. the work of Henry Dicks, 1993[1967]). This shift from an instinctive relationship to a psychological one is something that can only come about when the partners, brought together by collective instincts, slowly and painfully separate themselves out from their state of unconscious identity, and become aware of the individual elements of their relationship. This means becoming more conscious, a painful and shocking change that Jung links clearly to the individuation process.

Jung describes this initially in general terms, noting that a sense of passion can turn into one of duty, and later become "an intolerable burden". Looking forward, building and establishing a family, developing creatively, is gradually replaced by an involuntary looking backward and wondering how one reached this point. Jung suggests that this gives rise to insight into one's individual peculiarities, but "only by the severest shocks". Meaning begins to be more important than doing, and the personal begins to be more important than the collective. Jung suggests that there often develops at this point an internal disjunction between conscious wishes and drives and those of the unconscious. This disjunction produces a sense of unease in the individual, which, because the causes are unconscious, is seen only in projection, and so is blamed on the marital partner. This gives rise to an atmosphere of criticism that leads, in turn, to a particular dynamic in the relationship. This dynamic—itself a function, we would now say, of projective identification between the couple—is based on the fact that no two people are the same, and so the process of psychological development progresses unevenly in a couple; the chances of them both being able to understand what is happening to them at the same time *and* seeing it as an internal process within the relationship are slight. We can see the challenges that this gives rise to, and the way it links to Bion's idea of the developmental container–contained relationship, in which partners engage with each other to their mutual benefit, in the case of Sade and Errol.

Sade and Errol: a developmental container–contained couple relationship

Sade and Errol were a couple who could make good use of their therapy. They had come because their relationship had become stale and distant. Neither wanted to leave the relationship, but they were no longer getting pleasure from it. They slept in separate beds, and sex had stopped between them after the birth of their second child, eight years ago. Sade was Black African from a middle-class professional family in Nigeria, and Errol was Black British, with a working class St Lucian heritage. They were both lawyers, and had met at a dance, introduced by mutual friends. They characterised their interventions as being formal and stiff or else subtly niggly, sometimes provoking each other into arguments that became more and more disagreeable, and which would occasionally lead to one or other of them storming out of the house. There had been an argument immediately before starting therapy that worried both of them, because they felt as though they were going to become physically violent to each other. It became clear that there were themes to these arguments. There were two main things: how to raise their children (particularly in terms of expectations and discipline) and what each expected from the relationship. Sade's upbringing had been strict and a lot had been demanded of her academically, to the extent that she felt that she had been pushed too far and punished too often for what she felt were minor infractions of her parents' rules, and she was determined not to repeat the same thing with her children. What this meant in practice was that she was inconsistent in what she thought the children should or could do, and would sometimes veer from being very controlling and demanding to being completely *laissez-faire*. This meant that the children did not know how seriously to take her instructions, and they would look to Errol for some kind of clue, leaving her furious. Errol's parents had been very warm and loving, but were often away from the family, because they each had two jobs, meaning that he had to take responsibility for bringing up his two sisters. This left him with a great sense of responsibility for others, but also, at times, a resentment that he had to put their needs before his. He was also very playful, and, sometimes, this could veer into a kind of irresponsibility that Sade described as "childishness", particularly when she felt he was on the side of the children, in opposition to a request of hers.

What each expected from the relationship had its roots in their families of origin and in different cultural expectations, as Jung indicated. What this meant, though, was that Sade, when angry, would subtly denigrate Errol, suggesting that he was not a real man, and Errol, retaliating, would accuse Sade of being stuck up and thinking herself better than him. It seemed that neither's extended family had really accepted the relationship, suggesting that each would have done better to have "stayed nearer to home" in their choice of partner. The therapy focused on how much each could really trust the other, and there was a kind of turn taking, with each of them exploring the reasons behind why they sometimes doubted each other. These times were very painful for the person speaking and required a great deal of compassion from his or her partner, as each of them tried to give voice to things that they did not consciously want to know about. They realised that each of them felt disappointed that the other was not how they imagined a perfect partner to be, and that this had been fine until children arrived and their different responses to parenting became more obvious. The distance between them was really a way of managing their upset—which they were not really conscious of—and the lack of sex was linked to their anxieties about another child forcing them back into this very painful dynamic. The therapist always felt engaged with them and interested, in contrast with the experience of Carol and Don. Over the course of the therapy, the couple relationship improved, and the couple felt warmer and closer to each other.

We can see how Sade and Errol had to deal with the impact on them of their families of origin, and the need to focus on the family, to the detriment of the couple relationship. Fortunately, they had enough internal early development to make use of therapy and each other to get the relationship back on track. In his paper, Jung suggested that partners differ in the degrees of fragmentation or dissociation that they bring with them into the relationship, and one of them is likely to have a rather more complicated personality (we can call them partner M). These complex personalities act in a way as to become in effect the *subject* of their less complicated partners (partner L), who is taken up by them and by trying to understand them. Partner L can lose their own sense of being a subject in their own right when with them, and can become "contained" in the other in a passive way, rather than in the emotionally transforming way identified by Bion. Tensions arise because the more complicated personality (partner M) is forced to try to be simple enough to feel related to properly by partner L, and partner L begins to understand that they, too, have areas of fragmentation and association that need to be understood in order to relate. Although this is ultimately a spur to the development of both people, initially it is something of a nightmare, not least because the more complicated personality feels misunderstood and effectively pushed out of the relationship, and partner L notices this wandering of attention, begins to feel uncontained, and so pushes and pushes, trying to regain their place in partner M's mind, and projective identification becomes more excessive, evacuative, and controlling. This has the continued effect of making the containing, more complicated, partner M feel claustrophobic and so more likely to seek relief elsewhere. This makes the contained partner L even more insecure, and so the risk of splitting up rises. It is at times like this that the true value of the relationship between them is tested: does it have enough sense of a link between them that keeps them together and keeps them thinking about each other, no matter how painful it seems? Are they really able to keep in mind the relationship between them? If the despair at the state of the relationship between the partners and the inner state of crisis in each of them can be borne, then *both* partners have the opportunity to develop psychologically.

What this means, of course, is a state of absolute turmoil and pain; the relationship itself has lost a great deal of its gloss and apparent value, and both partners might feel themselves to be in a rather desolate and arid place. Each will be highly disappointed in the other. Partners who were previously the containers will feel themselves highly constrained by the demands of their partners, who, in turn, will feel let down and betrayed by them. The more complicated partners will begin to feel the pain of their dissociated state more keenly, and they might feel that they are experiencing a kind of breakdown, and that this is being forced on them by the obduracy of their partners. They have to bear feeling that the relationship is impossible. Apparently less complex partners, on the other hand, will begin to find in themselves something richer and more interesting; this could, itself, lead to them withdrawing a great deal of their energy from the relationship. They will have to bear feeling that the relationship is, in some way, becoming irrelevant to them. The key to the shift from an instinctually based relationship to a psychological one is the lessening of excessive projective identification, and the corresponding development of a richer inner world that is then used to relate with. Jung suggests that we choose our partners based predominantly on an instinctual feeling about them, and that, over time, we have to withdraw these archetypal projections and face the reality of who we are truly relating to. In addition to this, we also have to face a growing realisation of who we truly are as individuals, something that we can only find in the mirror of our relationship.

Container–contained in the individual and in the couple relationship

The couple psychotherapist and Jungian analyst, Warren Colman, in his development of Jung's paper, "Marriage as a psychological container" (Colman, 1993), explores this tension between the marital/couple relationship and the individual, linking Bion's perspective with Jung's. He points out that the individual partners must have had sufficient individual containment in their development to be able to risk relating to another person, and that the committed adult relationship between the partners can itself serve as container, with particular implications for clinical technique. For Colman, following the model developed at Tavistock Relationships and its forebears, it is the *relationship* that is the "patient" treated in couple therapy and not the two partners *as individuals*. The reason for this is that, as both Bion and Jung have suggested, the development of the personality requires a relationship that is capable of being sufficiently solid and resistant to regression, so as to require growth, but sufficiently flexible not to shatter when the growth happens. Couple relationships are in a state of flux between feeling too constraining to one or both individuals (because no one relationship can provide everything for everyone) and feeling too insubstantial, so that the couple feel that breaking up is a matter of small consequence (there is not much of worth to be lost, anyway). This tension between togetherness and autonomy is one of the engines that drive change in the couple. Another—and perhaps the most important one for conceptualising how it is that the relationship becomes a "containing skin" (Cleavely, 1991, p. 66) for the inner worlds of each partner—is the fact that couples get together not just because of the unconscious recognition that the other knows something about their very early experience and so has the potential to repeat or to repair prior container–contained states that have their roots in infancy, but also that they bring into the relationship elements of the personality that are still *in potentia*. Individuation is not simply the shift from a defensive to a developmental relationship to one's past and to one's inner world, vitally important though this is, but it also involves a move towards establishing the relationship as a shared unconscious function that allows for the projection and introjection of elements of the experience of *difference*.

This difference has been conceptualised in psychoanalytic and Jungian thinking as the difference between internal male and female elements, taking the image of heterosexual intercourse as its model (Jung's *Mysterium coniunctionis*, or mystical marriage (Jung, 1963), Freud's and Klein's internal parental couple in intercourse (Freud, 1909b, Klein, 1975a[1927]); Bion's ♂♀ (Bion, 1970), and Meltzer's nuptial chamber (cited in Colman, 1993, p. 79), but this gendering is really better thought of as a *façon de parler*, a way of making something easier to describe, rather than something meant literally. In couples, it is true that both gender and sexuality (and the relationship to same- and cross-gender parents and their sexualities) are important elements of the relationship, but what is also meant by difference is the relationship between one's own conscious and unconscious, and between these and the conscious and unconscious of one's partner, between part and whole, and between past and future within the field of the relationship. This is the terrain of the container–contained couple relationship, in which a third thing, the relationship, is used and related to by both partners, and itself changes and develops, to the benefit of all three, where projective identification is used for the process of communication, understanding, and growth by each partner (Zavattini et al., 2015).

Conclusion

Bion's suggestion that the container–contained relationship may be destructive or developmental, and Jung's and Colman's ideas that the container–contained dynamic is an essential part of an adult couple relationship indicate that failures within these dynamics will affect a wide range of areas of relating, both between the couple and within each partner. Together, they can give us a model for understanding the ebbing and flowing of development in relationships. All couples have times when partners find it difficult or impossible to contain the other's feelings, or to put their own to one side in the face of something that feels unacceptable or outrageous, but most couples do not forever stay in a state where lying and fighting are preferable to more empathic and supportive feelings between them. A degree of containment *is* needed to have a relationship with another person, and the emotional demands with which couples face each other mean that sometimes one partner has to contain the other (in a symbiotic way, as with Sade and Errol), and, at other times, there is a breakdown of the capacity to bear the demands of relating (in a parasitic way, as with Don and Carol). If this can be managed, held, as it were, within the "containing skin" of the relationship itself, the relationship grows and develops, and the capacity for containment grows within and between the individuals in the couple, too. In couple therapy, the therapist is sometimes asked to be a container for the relationship between the couple, holding it in mind and addressing interpretations to it and about it, when the couple are unable to value it for themselves. The aim of the therapist is to help the couple move from paranoid–schizoid states, in which destructive container–contained relating predominates, to one in which the couple can rely more on developmental container–contained dynamics, in which mutual and healthy relating predominates, to the benefit of the relationship and the individuals within it.

Acknowledgement

The clinical material in this chapter is heavily disguised and composite, while retaining a clear portrayal of the container–contained dynamics at play in the couples.

PART II

COUPLE STORIES AND CLINICAL COMMENTARIES

In this part of the book, we present four "couple stories". These stories are based on the clinical material generously provided by colleagues and supervisees of Marguerite Reid. Each couple story is discussed by several contributors, and these discussions are presented in the form of clinical commentaries.

The clinical material in the "couple stories" is not only very brief, it is also very limited in various respects. Partners' individual histories and the history of the couple relationship are not included, or, if there are references, they are minimal. In the reality of the consulting room, and over time, there would be far greater understanding as to whether there were any links between the partners' individual histories, their experience of their own parents' relationship, family dynamics, and the influence of the wider cultural and social context. Likewise, in the course of the work, it would become more apparent what the couple "brings", that is, the experiences they jointly create in their relationship, the way the partners relate to each other, and how they relate individually and as a couple to the therapist.

Considering the limitations to conceptualisation of the couple dynamics based on only one clinical session, clinical commentaries are, as stated in the title, just commentaries or therapists' reflections on the partners' interaction with each other and with the therapist. The contributors, in their reflections on the clinical material, apply concepts presented in the first part of the book, and there are four clinical commentaries for each couple story.

Authors' note

We would like to express our deep gratitude to students and colleagues—who, with regard to confidentiality, wished to remain anonymous (though we would like to point out that the material is heavily disguised)—for their generous contribution and help in providing couple stories based on a consultation or couple therapy session. In some instances, the couple therapist shares his/her own experience or feelings about the couple—that is, their countertransference. In other cases, this was not shared, but we think this is also helpful in a different way, as it provides a space for contributors to have different ideas about the conscious and unconscious effects the couple might have had on the therapist, and what that might indicate and reflect about the couple.

CHAPTER FIVE

Marco and Rosa

The couple, Marco and Rosa, have been attending couple psychoanalytic psychotherapy for four months. They attend their sessions punctually and regularly, on a weekly basis. They are seen by two therapists: therapist A is male and therapist B is female.

Both members of the couple come from Italy. Marco, thirty-five years of age, is from Naples, and Rosa, nearly thirty years of age, comes from northern Italy. The couple have been together for ten years. They met when Marco was on a wine course in the Piedmont area and Rosa was doing some temporary work in the company that ran the course. Marco found her attractive, very much liked her style, and later admitted that her fluency in English was another factor in this attraction, as he had dreams of opening a restaurant in the UK. Rosa found Marco attractive, liked his drive and enthusiasm, and saw marrying him as giving her an opportunity to leave Italy. They moved to the UK almost eight years ago, and they set up their restaurant three years ago. Marco sees this restaurant as his, but Rosa helped with décor and choice of location, something Marco can occasionally acknowledge. The restaurant is successful, but involves considerable hard work.

Marco's mother became pregnant when she was in her late teens. She was given support by her mother, but when Marco was four she abandoned him, leaving him in the care of her mother. During subsequent years, she would occasionally appear, usually being driven in fast cars by different men. Marco was brought up by his grandmother, who worked hard in a nearby restaurant, as well as taking care of some elderly ladies in their neighbourhood. When Marco was about ten years of age, his grandmother quite unexpectedly inherited money from one of the elderly ladies whom she cared for, and this not only enabled her to buy a flat, but also meant that their way of life improved considerably. She did not tell her daughter of her inheritance. Marco's grandmother taught Marco to cook, something he loves. She encouraged him to go to the UK to set up a restaurant. She died not long after the couple moved to the UK and Marco remains distressed that he was not there at the time of her death. He has found it difficult to mourn her loss. He is fond of Rosa's mother, who visits them regularly.

Rosa's mother, Francesca, came from quite a wealthy family in Northern Italy. When Francesca married against the wishes of her parents, they disinherited her. The grievance continued and the parents gave Francesca little support when her husband was killed in a road accident, leaving her with two small children. At the time of her father's death, Rosa was five years of age and her brother Paolo was seven. Rosa seems to know little about her father's death, as her mother has not wished to talk about it. Rosa's mother subsequently earned a living as a translator and tourist guide and this meant that she was often away from home during the summer months. As a result, the two children, Rosa and Paolo, were invited to stay with their mother's two brothers during the long summer holidays. Rosa found this difficult, as their way of life was different to hers. She felt sorry for her mother and painfully envious of her cousins, who had different opportunities to her and Paolo. Her mother, however, helped to ensure that Rosa was fluent in English. Rosa dreams of going into the fashion industry.

Waiting room

The receptionist calls to say that Marco and Rosa have arrived promptly for their appointment and ask if she should send them through, and the therapists agree. As usual, they open the door for the couple, so that they can walk into the room when they arrive.

Consulting room

Rosa sweeps into the room as though she is making a point and Marco follows, looking tired and irritable. As they come in, therapist A suddenly remembers Marco describing his mother as having swept into his life on odd occasions, usually being driven by different men in fast cars, while therapist B is aware of Rosa's characteristic child-like quality in the way she looks, although, as usual, she is extremely well groomed and prettily dressed. The couple sit in their usual chairs, and Rosa begins to speak immediately.

Rosa: It's been an impossible week. I was really angry at the end of last week's appointment. I thought you were both on Marco's side. You didn't listen to what I was saying about how frustrated I feel and how unfair Marco is.

Marco: Raises his eyes and looks directly at the male therapist. This look seems to say "We men know about this sort of thing".

Therapist A: Thinks he is being pulled into colluding with this thought and, looking at therapist B, sees she also has silently registered this.

Rosa: [looks at the therapists] Yes, when I told you that Marco had said that we couldn't go away for the weekend for my birthday, as he couldn't close the restaurant or leave the staff in charge, you sympathised with him. You didn't think what it was like for me. It's always the restaurant. It always comes first, and when he's not stuck in the kitchen, he's making plans for the next "special event" or change of menu. I am so fed up, it's no life. I'm nearly thirty, not sixty. There has to be more to life than this. Why can't he think that my birthday is as much "a special event" as one of his "themed evenings"? [Rosa looks angry and is also close to tears.]

Marco: [looks at Rosa] I've told you we can celebrate your birthday later. It's just before Christmas. I can't let customers down. They expect me to be there.

Rosa: [sweeps a glance around the room in an exasperated way] Who wants to celebrate their birthday in February when it's in December? It would be lovely to go away, the hotel would be decorated for Christmas and the atmosphere would be great. The staff would all be happy, they are always happy just before Christmas. In February everyone is miserable and it's cold and wet.

Marco: [looks at Rosa] I've told you, go away for the weekend. Take your mother, and your friend, Maria. Go to a spa hotel, you would all love it.

Rosa: [purses her lips and looks ahead] Yes, I'd probably enjoy it more. There's nothing worse than trying to get you to do something when all you want to do is stay in the kitchen. But then you would sulk, just as you did last time I went away with Maria. You know you get jealous and think we just want to attract different men when we're away. All you want to do is work. All you're interested in is the restaurant.

Marco: [glares at Rosa] You enjoy spending the money. My grandmother was right. "Don't marry someone from the north. It's all about style! We people in Naples know what hard work is.

Rosa: [looks at Marco for the first time] You didn't think like that, though. You thought it would be great marrying someone who was pretty and stylish. You kept talking about front of house and welcoming the customers. Of course she told you it was a mistake; she didn't want to lose you!

Marco: [explodes in Italian] *Basta così. No, non devi parlare della nonna in questo modo.*

Marco: [looks as though he will leave the room but then leans back in his chair. He glares at Rosa] You do not look welcoming now. Your face is always miserable. There's nothing welcoming about you now.

Rosa: Hhh, that's not what you said last week. You accused me of flirting with the men in that large party. You sulked all weekend about it.

Marco: No. I was tired. I have to work hard. You don't like hard work.

Therapist A: [looks at the couple] I wonder about what's happening now. We've often thought about the sense of disappointment that you both feel, as though neither of you live up to the other's expectations.

Therapist B: [after a short silence] Yes, and I think you, Rosa, felt quite disappointed with us last week. You wanted us to agree that Marco was in the wrong, that he wasn't being fair. But you both feel that you have right on your side. It's so difficult for either of you to think about the other's point of view.

There is a moment when both members of the couple seem to reflect on what has been said and then—

Marco: [looks at the therapists, and speaks rather sadly] I love cooking. I love being in the kitchen. It's my passion. I've always felt like that. When the kitchen is right, I feel right. I've always wanted a restaurant. Rosa knew that. Now she's not interested. Now she just reads fashion magazines and goes to the beauty salon.

Rosa: [in a furious tone, glaring at Marco] That's not true, you know I've always wanted to go into fashion. I should have gone to art school but my mother couldn't afford the fees. You know that customer said my fashion designs were good and I should try to market them. All you do is expect me to help in the restaurant. You don't think that what I want to do is important. My brother always says, "It's Marco, Marco, Marco all the time. What he wants, happens." What I want just gets put on the back burner!

Marco: Your brother knows I think his dealings are shady. I don't like his friends. He never helps your mother. Who helps her financially?

Rosa: My brother's wonderful. He's a wonderful husband and father. He adores his children. You've always criticised him. You know he told you that your grandmother's flat near the Cathedral should be earning us more rent than it is. You won't listen to him. He could help you let it for more money.

Marco: I don't trust him. I've heard things about him I don't like. You forget I still have friends in Naples.

Therapist A: When the two of you talk in this manner, you just miss one another and the meaning of what you are both saying. It is as though you don't think that what the other says *could* have some meaning, *could* be important. Instead, it just leads to another argument. Marco, you say you love cooking and being in the kitchen, it's your passion, but you, Rosa, can't bear to think what that means to him. Perhaps it is because it stirs for you feelings of loss about what you haven't done, what you haven't been able to achieve yet . . .

Marco: [interrupts Therapist A] She talks as though she's deprived. It's as though I don't give her anything. It's Paolo this and Paolo that. She thinks her brother's perfect.

Therapist B: Marco, you talk about your grandmother in a very similar manner, how good she was to you when you were a child, how

	she worked very hard to give you a home, how she taught you to cook, how wonderful it was when you cooked together, but you and Rosa are the couple now.
Therapist A:	Yes, I was going to say that I think that when Marco talks about how much he enjoys being in the kitchen, it leaves Rosa feeling excluded, shut out, not part of Marco's world.
Rosa:	[looks ahead stubbornly] I don't want to be part of his world. I want him to show some interest in mine.
Marco:	[explodes again, this time in English] Fashion magazines and the beauty salon? OK, some of your drawings are good. But they won't feed us. They won't provide for us. Suppose we have children. You won't want us starving in the gutter then.
Rosa:	That's right, remind me how difficult life became when my father died. That's just like you. You and your grandmother didn't exactly start life with masses of money.
Marco:	I'm not reminding you. I'm just saying we must work for the future. We must work hard in the restaurant. It's doing well.
Therapist B:	When A talked about you, Rosa, feeling excluded from Marco's world, it made me think that in a way you both had that experience in childhood. Marco, you felt excluded from your mother's world. She seemed to enjoy life without you, and I wonder if it was very painful for you to feel your mother preferred the company of others to you. Rosa, you've also talked about your mother having to leave you with her family, and about the fact that, although they were wealthy, they did little to help when your father died. You've spoken of the way that you felt excluded from their family and their grand life style when you stayed with them. You've used the phrase "poor relation" and how upset that made you feel.

There is silence for a few minutes and the atmosphere in the room has softened.

Therapist A:	[looks towards B and they note the time] We have to stop now, but there are painful and shared feelings about being excluded.

Co-therapy, containment, and the couple
A clinical commentary for Marco and Rosa

Christopher Clulow

Humans are meaning-making beings. We constantly strive to process new experiences in ways that have meaning and that confirm the meanings we have already established for ourselves. We like stories, and we are prone to believing that they have a linear trajectory, starting at the beginning and moving through various vicissitudes to a conclusion that gives coherence to the whole. Coherence makes us safe in our assumptions. It confirms the world as we know it and helps us feel secure, even if that world has been hateful or harmful. It is the contradictions and unpredictability that life presents us with that are disturbing, generating emotions that fuel the hard psychological work of resisting and adapting to the new and unfamiliar.

Psychoanalytic psychotherapy is a meaning-making process. While meaning and truth do not always coincide, we therapists hope to be able to make sense of the often non-sense that finds expression in our consulting rooms. Coming to our senses, we hope to be able to help those struggling to come to theirs. Simply by sharing the same space as those who consult us, we become part of their experience, and they, part of ours. Our conscious intent is to create a sense of safety, and to adopt a receptive stance that attends to, and takes seriously, the apparent non-sense that can affect all intimate relationships. This intent interacts with the intentions, both conscious and unconscious, of those who consult us, generating an experience that is shaped by everyone in the room.

Marco and Rosa enter a therapeutic space into which the door is opened by a hetero-gendered couple. As well as invitation, there is a balance in this arrangement, an implicit message of likeness—a couple for a couple. This might provide a sense of welcome and security, but it might also constitute threat and challenge. What lies beyond the consulting room door needs to be rendered safe, and there is an implicit message of unfamiliarity in being greeted by a couple: neither Marco nor Rosa has grown up in a family environment where there was a parental couple. How will they view and manage this unfamiliar environment? How will their therapists make sense of, and use, the strange situation created by the four?

Let us begin by exploring the senses of the therapists in recounting Marco and Rosa's problems. The couple story begins with history: his story, her story, and their story. What Marco and Rosa tell us of their history might not be historically accurate, and it will have been edited by their therapists, but their accounts will represent and convey meaning about how the past is having an impact on the present.

Marco and Rosa's histories have some external and internal similarities. Each lost a parent at a tender age: Marco's mother left him in the exclusive care of her mother when he was four (ostensibly to party with other men); Rosa was left in the exclusive care of her mother when she was five (after her father died in a road accident). True, Marco's mother appears in his life story, as do various uncles and cousins in Rosa's, but the primary relationships were, respectively, with a grandmother and a mother. Marco's grandmother made up for part of Marco's loss and became his primary attachment figure, a tie he developed and continued with her through his interest in cooking and his professional career as a restaurateur. Rosa's mother was her primary attachment figure, with whom she identified through becoming fluent in speaking English and aspiring to the glamour from which her mother had been disinherited. When Marco's grandmother died, we might surmise it was akin to the death of a mother, a bereavement that remained unmourned for him. Rosa, similarly, had not mourned the death of a father, whom she barely knew; in the absence of information from her mother, he might have become the idealised fantasy object she hoped Marco might become for her. Neither partner had the experience of being fathered or of having a parental couple working on their behalf. Marco's grandmother cut her daughter, his mother, out of the financial windfall from a bequest. Rosa's mother was cut off by her parents when she married against their wishes. The structure of their relational worlds, and those of the people who cared for them, consisted of exclusive dyads, not inclusive triangles. Against this background, a twenty-five-year-old man from the south of Italy and a twenty-year-old woman from the north met, fell in love, and left their respective families to make a new life in the UK, setting up a family restaurant business that could be their "baby" together. Except that *their* baby turned out to be regarded as *his* baby, leaving her feeling shut out and him feeling abandoned and overburdened.

For therapeutic purposes, this affective information (that is, the *value* placed on experience) is the key dimension of their histories. Negative affect brings couples to therapy. When couples can no longer contain the negative value attached to their experience, they might seek outside help either to restore and strengthen affective balance in their relationship or to enable them to relinquish the hope of doing so. Negative arousal (affect dysregulation) is associated with misattunement in relationships, or the rupture of a previously attuned state associated with a positive affective sense of life and vitality. Affect regulation (balance) is often restored by an experience of misattunement being repaired. How is this played out with Marco and Rosa?

Very broadly, Rosa and Marco are angry about feeling abandoned and excluded by each other. The first affective "hotspot" is triggered by Rosa's recollection of feeling frustrated and excluded by their therapists seeming not to have heard what she was saying in an earlier session, siding with Marco instead. No distinction is made between the therapists, and, in her mind, they might as well have been one person. Marco appears to encourage this pairing against his wife, perhaps against women generally, by making contact with the male therapist through raising his eyes. Rosa continues and recharges the affective theme in the context of their marriage, when she describes her anger at feeling discounted by Marco, representing his concern to ensure their restaurant customers celebrate Christmas as prioritising their needs over her need to celebrate her birthday with him. All of this, as the therapists pick up on, is likely to have resonated unconsciously with Rosa's experience of feeling she came second to her mother's work and customers and was the "poor relation" in her family.

Rosa is not alone in her susceptibility to negative affective dysregulation, and she heads unwaveringly towards the two relationships most capable of upsetting Marco. First, she plays with his unconscious invitation for her to become the playgirl mother who abandons him to his responsible restaurant grandmother by suggesting Rosa celebrate her birthday apart from him. She turns the knife by homing in on his jealous imaginings that she will attract the attentions of other men. Then, when he retreats to valuing the "hard work" ethos of his grandmother and her advice to avoid the type of woman he represents Rosa as being (that is, like his mother and the Rosa he was initially attracted to), she enrages him by observing that his grandmother's motive might have been to hold on to him. The possibility that Rosa might have helped him achieve some needed distance from a grandmother upon whom he had depended for so long for his sense of value and security is discounted, as he rebukes her (in their mother tongue, one he might imagine excludes their therapists from understanding).

The splitting within and between them continues, as Marco defends and idealises the work ethos associated with his grandmother and sets this against the (maternal) seductions that he locates and attacks in Rosa. Rosa, in turn, responds in kind, idealising the brother she depicts as the perfect family man and financial adviser whom she sets against the Marco who holds her back and prevents her from realising her dreams and potential. Their interaction fuels their disappointment with, and attack on, each other and cries out for containment.

How do the therapists respond to this challenge? First, they allow themselves to experience something of what it might be like to be the partners. The male therapist senses from the way Rosa enters the room that she might be the seductive maternal object in Marco's internal world, sweeping into and out of his life in a tantalising way. The female therapist senses something quite different: the prettily dressed child seeking attention and acceptance from the grown-ups. Together, they resist both Rosa's and Marco's attempts to enlist their exclusive support through an unspoken exchange between them that provides the assurance that each has registered the collusive pressures they are being put under. Their relationship as a therapist pair survives this attempt to divide them. The conflict is then articulated primarily between the couple.

The first interpretation attempts to contain their dysregulated state by inviting the couple to think about what is going on between them and offering the suggestion that the attack they have launched on each other is being driven by the anxiety that they are disappointing to each other. The therapists work together with this thought, therapist B supporting her colleague by linking this to Rosa's disappointment with her therapists for seeming to support Marco rather than her. While this allows for a pause, the invitation to think about each other's position is not taken up and each partner goes on to advocate their own position, resuming their fight in the process. Maybe this initial invitation to see the other's point of view, and how they might be contributing to the things they complain of, came too early. The challenge to the therapists was then to find a way of conveying that they had heard and valued the feelings of both partners, and that their attention was not mutually exclusive.

The next interpretation again pulls the partners back to consider the other's position, this time focusing on why this might be hard for them to do. The male therapist affirms the importance of the kitchen for Marco, and invites Rosa to think about why she might find this hard to hear, a potentially dangerous move, since it invites the perception that he understands and values Marco's passion but sees Rosa as the problem because of her frustrated aspirations. Marco takes this as a cue to pursue his attack on Rosa until the female therapist balances things up by pointing out how he can behave in very much the same way (towards his grandmother) as he complains of Rosa doing (in defending and extolling the virtues of her brother). At this point, the therapist pair could be on the verge of replicating the stand-off in the marriage. The therapy couple is restored when the male therapist reinforces his partner's observation and tries to help Marco see that his passion for cooking might leave Rosa feeling excluded.

The fact that there were two therapists will have helped restore the ruptured connections in the session. The female therapist built on her colleague's intervention about how Marco's behaviour could make Rosa feel excluded and made this into a joint interpretation. The feeling of being excluded was then defined as a shared affective experience, to which each partner was seeking a solution in their marriage, perhaps along with their feelings that they had disappointed their mothers, or were not important enough for them to have ensured that their needs had been understood and given priority.

By resolving the countertransference invitation to replicate the marital argument, the therapist pair changed the relational environment in which Rosa and Marco were being held, offering an opportunity to experience a more inclusive way of being with others than their histories had led them to believe might be possible. Therapeutic structure (two therapists) and process (resolving the countertransference between the therapist pair) combined to offer this couple containment for their dysregulated affective experience.

Finding a story
A clinical commentary for Marco and Rosa

Joanna Rosenthall

Marco and Rosa's relationship is dominated by a fight. If the fight were removed, would we see two very undeveloped, vulnerable people, who are ill-equipped—perhaps too needy themselves—to be able to form a relationship in which both partners can be taken into account?

Normally, when faced with a couple, I try to absorb them and their communications, offer my thoughts/interpretations, listen carefully to their reactions, my own reactions while in the presence of the couple and afterwards. All of this contributes towards understanding. In the absence of that live process, and only hearing one session, any thoughts I can offer are tentative and hypothetical.

Did they fall in love? This was not mentioned. We hear about their relationship as a transaction more than as an engagement; he wanted help to get to the UK and set up a restaurant, and she wanted help to leave Italy and become a fashion designer. I suspect that each of them was aware that they had, at least in part, been chosen to help their partner achieve something, which might leave them doubting whether they had been chosen for love, something that is likely to cause an underlying and potentially crushing doubt in the relationship.

I was struck by the symmetry in their histories: he lost his mother, aged four, and she lost her father, aged five. In addition, neither of them was raised by a couple, and, therefore, had little or no lived experience of a couple or the potential "team-like" quality from which a child can benefit so enormously.

In this session, the couple are desperate to be heard and frustrated by the way this experience eludes them, but also, I suspect, deeply lonely as a result. Neither can receive the other; an "intercourse" is not possible. Early on, Rosa says, "You were both on Marco's side," as if they are on different teams. She adds, "You didn't listen to what I was saying . . .", as if she is convinced the therapists, too, ignore her and there can be no possibility of their both being heard and taken into account. The quality of the interaction, therefore, becomes like a fight for survival, and they are then locked in a battle on this basis, each wanting to defeat the other in order to survive themselves.

As the session continues, the fight heats up; he invokes his beloved grandmother, she attacks the grandmother, and he then insults her. The interaction has a ping-pong quality, there is no communication taking place—the fight has taken on a life of its own.

Without doubt, most of us at times engage in this kind of barren fight, but when it becomes repetitive, even habitual, it raises questions about whether the partners have been in receipt of a containing presence in their early experience (Bion, 1963). Individuals who have not received enough of that containing experience can be left unaware of what their feelings are and confused about what belongs inside and what can be attributed to the outside or to others. In this dilemma, individuals might seek external solutions to solve internal problems, as Marco and Rosa seem prone to do.

For Marco, maybe the beloved grandmother can live on forever via cooking and his restaurant (external things). For Rosa, it is possible that her interest in fashion and design is a way of attempting to set things right, by making things look beautiful on the outside. For both, the UK is an idealised place where there are resources, unlike Italy, which seems to have involved pain, abandonment, and being second rate. Marco's grandmother and Rosa's mother both conveyed that the UK was desirable, as if the mothers they had had, the mother country they had come from, and even the mother tongue, were not good enough: a message that they needed to find what was missing elsewhere (moving to a different place).

The infant's first passionate relationship is the one with his mother. When this relationship goes well, she is nurturing and loving but also gets to know her infant through close attention to the minutest details about him. Bion's theory of the "container–contained" describes the vital function she performs for her infant's emotional development when she is able to be receptive to the feelings and sensations that her infant cannot manage. She holds and thinks about them in her mind and ultimately conveys the thinking/containing function that the child can absorb.

Marco and Rosa show little sign of bearing their internal experience inside, or knowing that others also have internal experiences that inform their behaviour. They share a resentful preoccupation with the other's passionate engagement with an activity. It is as if they are saying, not only do you not attend to me, but it is unbearable that you are engaged with someone/something else.

The kitchen is Marco's passionate love. Perhaps cooking with his grandmother became the activity that stood for love, contact, and containment. He now has an intense, perhaps idealised, attachment to it, and giving it up would feel life threatening. He is attached like a baby at the breast. Rosa is left on the outside, forced into the position of watching "a couple" in a passionate engagement who are excluding her. She feels enraged, denigrated, and alone, in despair about finding contact. Marco's experience of her interest in "fashion magazines and visiting beauty parlours" seems to have taken on a similar significance.

This experience of being left out is unbearable. They feel neglected, excluded, and usurped. The attacks followed by retaliations gather momentum, and seem to be a way to evacuate the overwhelming experience of pain and rage into the other.

Both partners seem convinced that only one person can be heard, not both. We see this again when we hear about the "birthday" fight. He needs to have the importance of the restaurant understood and she needs to have the importance of her birthday understood.

Each seems to be suffering from an emotional void, a desperate longing for something. At the same time, there is confusion about whether this need can be satisfied by external things (cooking, art school) or through a relationship. The latter is something Rosa might have more of a sense of. She wants to go away for a weekend to celebrate her birthday. I presume that, in part, she longs to be treated as the special one who is attended to, but it is also true that she does not want this from her mother or a friend, she wants to be with Marco. Does she have an inkling that the couple relationship could provide nourishment to them both?

Marco and Rosa both have histories that indicate they might not have received enough from early figures, and appear to be looking for the missing love and containment from a partner. Imagine the disappointment and anger when they discover that their partner is not only unable to respond to that need, but also has a similar need of their own. The ensuing fight escalating between them in this session can be understood as a shared defence, something the couple unconsciously construct together, with the purpose of helping them remain unaware of how vulnerable they are, of what pain they are in, and how unknowing they are about how to manage themselves.

McDougall (1986) describes individuals who cannot manage to digest their experience and resort to externalising inner conflicts by relying on substances like drugs or food, or else on other people. She describes a "transitional theatre", in which the individual plays a part and chooses others to enact parts that cannot be borne psychically. The wish behind these complicated dramas is to "try and make sense of what the small child of the past, who is still writing the scripts, found too confusing to understand" (p. 65). She argues that these individuals, instead of forming symptoms, are dominated by "action symptoms", which perform a similar function, binding together psychic experiences that cannot be borne or known about. In a couple, both partners derive relief from externalising unresolved mental pain, for example, via repeated rows. However, this defensive strategy tends to mean that the relationship can only take place in a restricted zone, which might look deeply unhappy, even hate-filled, but, nevertheless, it protects the couple from a more terrifying experience: for example, of disintegration or vulnerability.

The therapists

We are not told what it feels like to be with this couple, but the therapists come across as shadowy, their interventions muted, and struggling to meet head on the interaction they are faced with. I was struck by their wish to be sensitive and receptive, but I was left unclear about how they understood Marco and Rosa. We see in this account how difficult this work can be. The couple are intent on proceeding with a defensive row, while the therapists possibly feel shut out, not quite able to engage or intervene at the deepest level that the couple need.

I have often felt overwhelmed by a rowing couple, who so easily knock you out of your therapeutic stance. Let us think what would make sense to the couple.

The therapists do talk about "feeling excluded", and this seems to resonate with each partner's experience; however, it leaves unattended perhaps deeper, more primitive communications: the way each partner feels not loved, ignored, abandoned, not heard, and lonely. There is a desperate quality, "the void", a yearning or need, like a hungry baby crying, unheard in the cot.

Of course, it is very difficult to provide a real, meaningful, and emotionally in touch response to a couple who are intent on a fight, and especially when that fight has a life and death quality. It can feel as if you are faced with an impenetrable wall, and interventions are dangerous, in case they are heard as taking sides and adding fuel to the fight.

In this case, I found it hard to sense what the therapists were thinking, or to get a feel for what they might have made of their own intercourse in between the sessions. I wondered if perhaps they had not yet managed to form a working couple alliance and, therefore, were "firefighting", but not yet using each other by supporting or complementing, which possibly left them mirroring the loneliness and lack of intercourse in Marco and Rosa's couple relationship.

As therapists, it is part of our task to discover and put into words a meaningful story with a beginning, a middle, and an end, including, conscious and unconscious elements of each partner's histories as well as the story of their couple relationship. This has the power to be integrative and developmental and affects the way the partners function together.

Many couples come for help in a chaotic state, helplessly unknowing about their own and each other's internal states. They are without a meaningful narrative, which involves not just memories of experiences, but some capacity for thinking about them and linking them up into what amounts to a personal story. For example, understanding that being abandoned by one's mother (Marco) or feeling treated as second rate (Rosa) leaves an important trace in the individual's inner world. One's own "personal story" is a crucial part of the development of personal identity. When someone is cut off from his or her past and does not understand the significance of it, they not only seem unreachable and "thin", but they also speak of things in a current way as if they have no resonance in the past or with other people. Wollheim (1984) describes them as having "broken the thread of life", and he has shown that the thread of life is at the core of personal identity and the person's sense of inner unity. Rosa and Marco show a need to discover their individual and shared stories. Through the therapy, they need to build up an awareness of events, of memories, of what they each have made of past relationships and absences. Only then will they start to develop a sense of what they share and how they are different, and they will have more of a chance to start developing, deepening, and considering their shared journeys, both past and future.

Projective identification: rivalry, competition, and exclusion
A clinical commentary for Marco and Rosa

Stanley Ruszczynski

Background information

On reading the brief background to the clinical vignette, I was struck by two factors, both fundamental in establishing the setting for engaging in a psychoanalytic couple psychotherapy treatment.

The first relates to the question about what brings a couple together. As has been described in the first part of the book, the unconscious choice of partner is driven by mutual unconscious motivation and needs, for both defensive and developmental purposes. What attracted Marco and Rosa to each other? There is never a simple or single answer to this question, but I was struck by what read like a rather "functional" dimension to the mutual partner choice. Describing his attraction to Rosa, Marco "admitted that her fluency in English was ... [a] ... factor in his attraction, as he had dreams of opening a restaurant in the UK". Describing her attraction to Marco, Rosa "saw marrying him as giving her an opportunity to leave Italy". Does this rather functional description of each other suggest a significant "parental" aspect to their choice of each other?

The second factor relates to the other major area of interest to all clinicians using a developmental or psychoanalytic model of the mind and relationships, but is of special interest to couple psychotherapists. This refers to an understanding that relationship patterns and experiences set down in early family life contribute to the nature of the adult relationship, mutually created by the two adults who form the sexual adult relationship. When reading the histories of this couple, there emerge remarkable parallels in their experiences of their families of origin.

In their early experiences of childhood, it is noteworthy that Marco, aged four, was abandoned by his mother and brought up by his grandmother who "worked hard in a restaurant". There is no reference to a father. Rosa's mother was disinherited by her own parents and then lost her husband, Rosa's father, when Rosa was five years of age. Her mother, who must have been depressed and possibly emotionally absent as a result of these losses, was away from home for work reasons, and Rosa was brought up, in part, by her uncles, a difficult experience, because "their way of life was different to hers".

So, for both Marco and Rosa, there was no experience of a functioning parental couple, but the experience of absent fathers and preoccupied and absent mothers. It is difficult to see where, for either of them, there was a parental figure who, to paraphrase Winnicott, was emotionally "preoccupied" (Winnicott, 1984) with them so as to provide a safe and consistent presence for their emotional and interpersonal development.

This absence of a primary containing parental structure would probably lead to a fragile sense of self, to a self-protective narcissistic personality and not only to an absence of an internal model of benign relationships, but probably also a persecutory model of relating to another. Beneath this fragile psychological structure, there is likely to be a very frightening sense of betrayal and anger. Further, this lack of a containing parental relationship, and fragile parent–child relationships, would have militated against the developmental potential, achievable through the resolution of the struggles and dynamics of the oedipal constellation (Britton, 1989, Ruszczynski, 2005).

Perhaps, in an attempt to secure some sense of self, Marco developed an identification with his grandmother's "hard work" in the restaurant, in his desire to set up his own restaurant. The text says, "Marco's grandmother taught Marco to cook, something he loves". He is reported as having found her death, not long after the couple moved to the UK, "difficult to mourn" and we know that unresolved mourning might, in part, be dealt with by identification with the absent person. More speculatively, was Rosa's wish to go into the fashion industry unconsciously driven by a desire to produce a beautiful self that might attract her mother's attention?

Given these shared emotionally deprived and difficult beginnings, the couple's unconscious attraction to each other might have been, in part, determined by a mutual sense of recognising something familiar in the other and of being recognised by the other. This recognition of something similar to themselves in the other, an identification with each other, could have felt for them both comforting and safe. Although this is likely to be part of most couples' initial attraction to each other, does this point to why there might be a somewhat over determined "functional" or parental aspect to this couple's choice of each other?

The treatment session

As the presented session opens, there is evidence that both Rosa and Marco are immediately struggling with the dynamics of a threesome. Rosa accuses the therapists of siding with Marco; Marco invites collusion with the male therapist, leaving out the females. There is then an argument regarding the restaurant. Rosa feels left out, because Marco appears to "prefer" the restaurant to her and Marco affirms her anxiety by confirming that his priority is to not let down his customers.

At this point in the session, and possibly at this point in the treatment overall, Rosa is the one who feels rejected/pushed out/left out (by the therapists and by Marco/the restaurant/customers) and Marco clings to, and claims ownership of, a primary attachment (the attempt to seduce the therapist and his prioritisation of the restaurant/customers over Rosa). Marco's attachment seems to be at the expense of Rosa's sense of abandonment. He projects his fears of abandonment into Rosa, and she projects her longed for attachment into Marco and his involvement in the restaurant.

Rosa desperately wants to feel special (the special event of her birthday), but Marco dismisses this, suggesting that she celebrate her birthday two months after the event. He compounds this rejection of her being "special" by suggesting that she celebrate with others and not with him, again seeming to prioritise the restaurant and its customers over her.

Rosa then appears to retaliate by reminding Marco that he sulked and accused her of being attracted to other men when she last went away without him. She then makes a barbed reference to Marco's special relationship with his grandmother, to which he reacts very angrily, nearly walking out of the consulting room.

At this point, we might be getting a glimpse that the feelings of being left out (Rosa) and the feelings of having one's partnership "attacked" (Marco) might be close to being paranoid, with both aggression and vulnerability experienced by both Rosa and Marco. We are witnessing a relationship experienced as competitive rather than collaborative.

The oedipal theme continues with a further competitive series of mutual attacks, accusations, and criticisms: Rosa is accused of looking miserable; Marco is criticised for accusing Rosa of flirting with other men; Rosa accuses Marco of sulking when she returned; Marco criticises Rosa for not liking hard work.

The therapists pick up on this sense of competition and disappointment and the sense each has of being alone and isolated from the other. This appears to touch both members of the couple, but then, very quickly, as if to reject the possibility of making use of what the therapists offered, Marco refers again to his primary attachment to the restaurant and cooking, and then attacks Rosa by suggesting that she does little other than "[reading] fashion magazines and going to the beauty salon". Rosa is infuriated by these comments and describes her sense of being isolated and not supported by either her mother or Marco in her desire to go to art school or develop her interests in fashion. This lack of interest and support, she says, results in her apparently having no role other than supporting Marco and his primary concern with his restaurant.

The therapists' attempt to show the couple the shared nature of their psychic conflict appears to fail, with both partners returning to their isolated, anxious, and angry positions, mutually accusative and paranoid. The sense of depression and sadness that might come with recognition of their shared problem is unconsciously felt to be too difficult. Marco clings to his "relationship" with the restaurant, and Rosa is left not only rejected, but abandoned in relation to her own interests, and serving only those of Marco.

As the session continues, Rosa tries to link herself up with her brother, Paolo, and uses that relationship from which to attack Marco's narcissism ("It's Marco, Marco, Marco all the time. What he wants, happens", Rosa reports her brother saying). She also suggests that her brother might have something to offer Marco, financial advice in relation to the rental of his grandmother's flat in Italy. Marco rejects this offer, attacking Rosa's potentially useful connection with her brother and aping her reference to what her brother had said about him, by saying, "It's Paolo this and Paolo that. [Rosa] thinks her brother is perfect." He further minimises Rosa's relationship to the brother and his potential usefulness by referring to his "friends in Naples".

When therapist A tries to address this constant sense of competitiveness and shared inability to hear each other, Marco talks over him and refers again to Rosa's special relationship with her brother, whom he sarcastically describes as perfect, but whom, he says, he does not trust.

Both therapists comment on Marco's special relationship with his grandmother, and how this is perhaps reflected in his interest in the restaurant, and how this shuts out Rosa. Rather than hearing this as something she might have found supportive, Rosa hears it as suggesting that she join Marco, about which she protests and asks him to show some interest in her world. Marco attacks this by making reference to his being concerned about financial security, to which she does not contribute. Rosa experiences this as attacking and accuses Marco of making some critical reference to her family of origin and its difficult beginnings.

Again, it feels as if the therapists do very briefly touch one or other or both members of the couple, but very quickly their comments are talked over or misunderstood. Perhaps this puts the therapists in the position of feeling that they do have something to offer, but that it is quickly rejected and often misinterpreted as hostile, mirroring the way each of the couple feels.

With the session coming towards an end, therapist B, the female therapist, makes a comment addressing the couple's shared experience: of feeling excluded from their mothers, and envy of what they were excluded from, and implying, but choosing not to spell out, that, at present, there is a painful repetition of this sense of exclusion and envy in the way the couple are functioning with each other at present. Perhaps, unconsciously, it felt too painful to spell it out for this couple at the present time. The session ends with an atmosphere that has "softened".

In summary

My understanding of this couple, at this point in the treatment, is that their shared lack of a secure early family environment, results in their lack of the developmental possibilities achieved in the working through of the Oedipus complex, and, therefore, the struggle to develop the capacity to be what Mary Morgan has described as "a creative couple" (Morgan, 2005). Their primary ways of relating are more narcissistic, often rivalrous, competitive, and driven by more persecutory, rather than more benign, states of mind.

Processes of projection dominate this couple's interaction. Rosa projects her envied but longed for intimate relating into Marco and his restaurant and feels persecuted and excluded by it. Marco projects his fear of being excluded and isolated into Rosa and behaves in a manner that keeps her separated from him. Both struggle to make full use of the functioning therapist couple relationship, of which unconsciously they could be very envious, only briefly allowing themselves to hear their comments, but then ignoring them. In their emotional experience of this couple, I suspect that the therapists have to manage their sense of having something to offer but it being rejected or even tarnished and misunderstood. Under this assault, the therapist couple are challenged to sustain their "couple state of mind" (Morgan, 2014a), as a setting within which Rosa and Marco can go on trying to address their relationship difficulties.

This reported session is early in the treatment and it is a sign of hope that the problematic dynamics between this couple are displayed as well as they are.

Narcissism and loss of a shared ideal, oedipal exclusion, and sibling transference affecting a couple state of mind
A clinical commentary for Marco and Rosa

Jill Savege Scharff

We are given some introductory history and process notes on a single session from the fourth month of couple therapy in which co-therapists A (male) and B (female) have already developed a working alliance and a therapeutic relationship with the couple. My task is to provide a commentary on this highly condensed material, not to analyse the couple *in absentia*, but just to show how I address the material from an object relations analytic perspective, showing how I associate to the material, select a focus, comment on the nature of the relationship between the partners and their therapists, and on the therapists' work towards therapeutic action.

The therapists introduce us to Marco and Rosa, an Italian Anglophile married, heterosexual couple, who have been living for the past eight years in the UK. There they are fulfilling Marco's dream of owning and running a successful restaurant. Marco invests heavily in developing the restaurant, working long hours in the kitchen and planning special events as well. Rosa would prefer to pursue her dream of becoming a fashion designer but, although she has talent, she cannot afford the training that could lead to a career with a steady income. Investing all their money in the restaurant to support their life and build for their future has the unfortunate consequence of diminishing the importance of Rosa's individual development, which leaves her in a child-like status, dependent on Marco, spending money on clothes, and rebelling against the demands of the business. Marco's preoccupation with the restaurant business is at odds with Rosa's need to feel special to him. His feeling of success is in sharp contrast to her disappointment in not finding a place for herself in the fashion and beauty industry. To Rosa, Marco thinks life is all about him, and she resents being in second place, whereas he thinks he is doing the work of both of them to build their life. To Marco, Rosa seems to be all about Rosa, and he is angry that Rosa fails to support him in the business.

Marco and Rosa cannot identify with and support each other's professional passions. It is as if there is room for only one passion, the one that makes the money to support the couple and any future family, the one that is Marco's, the one that requires talent and drive but no formal training. When they first met, Rosa liked Marco's drive and Marco liked her fashion sense. These qualities attracted them and brought the couple into being, but they are now a source of discord, pulling the couple apart, mainly because they are evidence of their other attachments outside the couple. Marco sees Rosa's love of style as proof of her attraction to other men and her preference for the ways of her brother, who enjoys a wealthy, stylish life (the basis of which Marco is deeply suspicious about). Rosa sees Marco's drive as proof of his narcissistic me-first personality and his attachment to the grandmother who raised him and imbued in him the love of cooking. I wonder if the restaurant was founded on money willed to Marco by his late grandmother, who had received an unexpected inheritance. If Marco had money and Rosa did not, this disparity could remind Rosa of the distance that she and her mother experienced, comparing their family resources to those of her mother's siblings in the family that disinherited her mother.

In preferring to wed herself to the fashion rather than the restaurant industry, is Rosa now disinheriting herself from the comfortable life she could now be investing in with Marco? In single-mindedly pursuing his goals for the couple, and sending Rosa without him to celebrate her special event with friends, has Mario connected to his beloved grandmother and left Rosa feeling abandoned, while he sees her as the abandoning one, a woman like his mother, who will go off with other men? Is Rosa envious of Marco's dedication and success, as she was of the cousins with whom she stayed when her mother (like Marco) was too unable to care for her needs, because of having to make money?

Therapist A notes the spouses' disappointment in each other. Both therapists having already questioned their own collusion with Marco's point of view, Therapist B follows immediately with a comment on Rosa's disappointment in the therapists for failing to agree how unfair and selfish Marco is. When Therapist B ties this to the couple's main problem of each wanting to be right instead of seeing each other's point of view, the two therapists have worked well together to create a thinking, feeling space in which Marco can then express his sadness and Rosa can express her outrage. The couple then gets into an argument about Rosa's brother, as ideally good or ideally bad, helpful or untrustworthy. Here, I think the couple is unconsciously associating to the therapists' intervention and experiencing them, or one of them, as a helpful or suspect brother.

Therapist A reflects on the couple's miscommunication as an effect of their not connecting over their painful feelings of loss. This intervention seems right on, but it is interrupted by Marco's returning to complaining about Rosa's brother. I think that this disconnect happened because the transference to the therapists as successful siblings has not been addressed in this session. When therapist B responds, she points out that Marco adores his grandmother as much as Rosa adores her brother, and that this prevents the couple from being primary. Everyone ignores this. Again, this is right on, but it has a retaliatory ring to it, rather than feeling usefully explanatory about their competing, intense attachments to others. Therapist A addresses Rosa's exclusion from Marco's world. This leads to an explosion of affect. Rosa challenges Marco's narcissism directly, and Marco reveals the trauma behind his single-mindedness—fear of utter poverty, a fear that Rosa shares and from which Marco protects her through his investment in the business. Therapist B, following Marco's line of thought, speaks to Marco's exclusion from his mother's life and Rosa's exclusion from both her mother's wealthy background and the fine life style of her cousins. In the ensuing silence, the therapists experience a "softening" of the atmosphere. Acknowledging the shared pain of exclusion and poverty, the therapists together end the session.

Therapists A and B work closely together as a couple. They build on what each other has said. We learn that they are a male–female couple but that is otherwise not evident in their differentiated interactions with the couple or its individual members, except where they mention a collusive glance from Marco to the male therapist. We do not hear them associated to in ways that would remind us of the internal couple. They make a space into which Marco and Rosa enter, freely expressing their anger, hurt, fear, and outrage. The therapists select the themes of miscommunication, lack of empathy, and exclusion to work on in this session. They refer to the transference of disappointment in them for appearing to take sides (which fits the theme of exclusion), but they do not gather the transference to them in the here-and-now of this session. Had they done so, the couple might have examined their conflict in its displacement to the couple-therapists' relationship, and then might have moved towards developing a shared reflective stance. Admittedly, Marco and Rosa do seem far from that in this session, and so it might be too much to hope for at this stage in the treatment. The male therapist experiences Rosa as a woman who, like Marco's mother, attracts men, while the female therapist sees Rosa as a pretty little girl. The therapists must be finding it hard to relate to Rosa as a woman with her own needs for creative expression and independence, and to help Marco attend to and support his wife, which, if he could support her and her dreams, would enable her to more fully support him in the business and in their life and future together.

I noted cultural differences, but these did not attract the therapists' attention in this session. We are told that Rosa is from the north of Italy, Marco from Naples. Within the couple, we find cultural stereotypes—the north being seen as stylish (Milan being the fashion capital) and Naples being controlled by Mafia gangs. The session is conducted in English, but the couple's mother tongue and culture is Italian. When Marco has a moment of deep feeling, when he prohibits Rosa from speaking ill of his grandmother, he speaks in Italian. The fact that he uses his mother tongue (or should I say his grandmother tongue?) to express his fierce loyalty to his grandmother underscores his enormous attachment, gratitude to, and identification with, her. Rosa's attachments, on the other hand, are to her own generation, to her brother and cousins, which speaks of an attenuated attachment and disidentification with her hardworking, single mother. This difference in specificity of attachment seems to me to be reflected in the history in which we are told that Mario comes from Naples (a city) and Rosa comes from the north (an area, not even a region).

As for the therapist couple, in being named Therapist A and Therapist B, not Mr A and Ms B, they make themselves seem impersonal, gender neutral. The male therapist takes the moniker Mr A. Alphabetically, he comes first, as does Marco, in terms of his name and his centrality in the couple. I do realise that their task in writing up the case is to give brief notes of one session. They cannot bring us the rich detail of four months of work, the family relationships current and past on each spouse, the shifting projective identifications as the couple recognise what they see of themselves in the other, and the development of the transference to each therapist individually and to them as a couple. However, to provide a commentary that really does convey analytic work in couple therapy, I wish I had more of that to go on. Other than the description of their perceptions of Rosa as the couple entered the session, and a sense of relief as the atmosphere softened at the end of the session, we learn little about their countertransference. Do they really feel pulled to Marco's side? Or is that a figment of Rosa's imagination? Are they able to maintain a state of involved impartiality? How do they feel about their work together? What do they say to each other when they meet to process and review this session? Christmas is coming—will they be on vacation, and, if so, for how long, and does the couple know a break is coming? Is that anticipation affecting the couple as they postpone Rosa's birthday? I am guessing that at least one of the therapists speaks Italian, which would explain why Marco's outburst in Italian demanding respect for his grandmother is not felt necessary to be translated.

I see the patient couple as a group of two individuals who were drawn together by a shared ideal and who no longer have a shared couple state of mind. Marco subsumes the couple in himself, and Rosa feels shut out and ignored. They come together only to argue, which is frustrating for them, and yet gives me some hope, because they are fighting to get back what they once had. It might be useful to apply Ezriel's (1952) "because clause" to the couple relationship. I would say that the required relationship is that of two separate individuals defending against the fear of intimacy, in which love may be felt and lost; the avoided relationship is the longed-for, elusive mother–child relationship exemplified in Marco as the central figure and provider, and Rosa as the ungrateful, spoiled child, and the catastrophic relationship is one in which they are joined in experiencing abandonment and poverty. This catastrophic level is spoken by Marco, reacted to by Rosa, and is formulated briefly in Therapist B's closing statement. It seems to me that abandonment with poverty is the basic anxiety. Over the next months, the therapists will be helping the couple analyse their defences and contain the anxiety so that it no longer tears them apart.

CHAPTER SIX

Peter and Helen

The couple Peter and Helen have been attending couple psychoanalytic psychotherapy for eleven months. They attend on a weekly basis. The couple are usually punctual, although Helen often appears to fly in at the last minute: they have an early evening appointment. The fees are paid relatively promptly by Peter, who, in the past, usually gave the impression that he would prefer not to be spending this money. Recently, however, this attitude seems to have lessened.

Both members of the couple are nearly sixty years of age. Peter is Scottish, and Helen is English. Peter is proud of his Scottish roots. They have been married for thirty years, and Helen thought that it was this anniversary that made her decide they needed to do something about their marriage. Helen's description was that "as a couple we have rather lost sight of each other, and we could have another thirty years together—unlikely, perhaps, but possible!" Both members of the couple thought something was missing, although Peter seemed less concerned than Helen. He thought they had different interests and that bringing up three children had been their priority. Initially, the therapist was discussing in supervision his observations about how this couple was "stuck" in relating, or, rather, in not relating, with each other: they did not argue, they just seemed rather tired of each other, often wanting to talk about their children rather than themselves.

The couple have three children. Fiona, who is now working in finance, Hamish, who is in his second year of university, and Catherine, who will be taking A levels this year, and then plans a gap year before university. Helen admits that the thought of Catherine leaving home makes her feel sad, but she knows that this has to be the next stage in her daughter's life. She speaks of the "empty nest syndrome" in quite a poignant way. Their therapist has pointed out that he thinks the knowledge that Catherine would shortly be leaving home also contributed to the couple seeking help with their marriage at this time.

Both members of the couple work. Helen has worked part-time, since she returned to work following the birth of their three children. She derives satisfaction from her work. Peter is happy about the path his career has taken, but is now beginning to look forward to retirement. He occasionally has to travel abroad for work, and this is something he no longer enjoys. He would, however, agree that it was something he enjoyed when he was younger. Peter is in charge of the couple's shared finances. Helen seems to keep the money she earns separate from Peter's, and the impression she gives is that he is rather mean about money, or, at least, not very generous towards her or the children. Peter's argument is that with three children and the remainder of a mortgage that has to be paid, it is necessary to be prudent about money.

Helen has also derived pleasure being a homemaker and bringing up their three children. In fact, both members of the couple have enjoyed being parents, and feel that they have made a good team. They both agree that family life has gone fairly smoothly with the "odd blip". Their therapist thinks that there is nothing smug about this feeling; it is, rather, that the couple have seen bringing up their children successfully as the central part of their marriage.

Peter likes golf, although he is not particularly keen on social events at his club. Helen says she thinks he is happiest when he is either on the golf course, pottering in the garden, or mending things in his workshop. Helen has some good friends, she loves singing in two choirs, and reading; she attends a book group, visits stately homes and, in particular, she is interested in the gardens. She is the first to admit, however, that "hands on gardening" is not something she particularly likes. Peter has told their therapist that he is tone deaf. He has also made odd comments about thinking that Helen has a crush on the music director of one of her choirs. Peter has never seemed particularly bothered about this, but their therapist has noticed that he has heard this comment less often during more recent sessions.

Of significance to the work is the fact that Helen's mother, who had been adopted as a child, died nearly twenty years ago. Helen's father subsequently remarried, and both Helen and her younger sister thought this marriage took place too quickly following the death of their mother. Helen can, however, acknowledge that, as a couple, her father and stepmother seem to enjoy life: they travel a great deal. Peter's father died of a heart attack in his late fifties, and this left Peter, the only son in a family of three, feeling responsible for his mother, who now lives nearby, and who has various health problems. Helen describes her mother-in-law as possessive, and says that she has never got over the fact that her son married someone English.

The therapist thinks that the couple have made quite a lot of progress during the time they have been in therapy. They seem somewhat depressed, but now also seem closer, and appear to be more in touch with their feelings. He is also aware that for this couple, talking about intimacy and sex has been difficult, if not impossible. The subject is always sidestepped, as though it is of little consequence.

Waiting room

The therapist goes to the waiting room at the time of the couple's appointment. It is obvious from the way that Helen is talking to Peter that she has only just arrived. The therapist observes that Helen looks somewhat distraught and upset, and that, quite unusually, Peter has his hand on her shoulder, as though giving her some comfort. The therapist asks if they would like to come up, and they go upstairs to the consulting room.

Consulting room

Once in the room, the couple sit in their usual chairs, and Helen immediately begins to speak. She looks at the therapist, but then includes Peter in what she is saying.

Helen: I've just driven back from visiting Fiona, and there had obviously been a terrible accident on one the country roads. A car had come off the road, and hit a tree. Looking at the car it's difficult to imagine the driver has survived. The police were there taking measurements, but the ambulance had gone. There was quite a build-up of traffic, even though it was a country lane. [She looks at Peter.] The accident was quite close to Walnut Tree House.

Peter: Oh, I think I know where you mean. It's quite a dangerous spot in the afternoon, the late afternoon sun can be quite low there.

Helen: I just feel terribly upset. [She begins to cry quietly.] It's silly, really, because as far as I know, I don't know the chap involved, but there was something about the state of the car, and the fact that I'd had such a lovely lunch with Fiona, and it's been such a beautiful day.

Peter: No, these things are always upsetting. I hate seeing road accidents. It just puts you in touch with how things can just happen out of the blue.

Therapist: I was thinking that we were talking about the death of your mother, Helen, and also the death of your father, Peter, during the last session. You both gave the impression that you still feel shocked by the suddenness of both their deaths.

Peter: Yes, it's funny you should say that, but I've been thinking about my father, this afternoon.

Helen Looks at Peter with interest, and the therapist thinks that there is something about this look that seems to indicate that she is more engaged than she usually is.

Helen: What were you thinking?

Peter: Well, you know that clock that always seems to be at the wrong time when we visit my mother?

Helen: Do you mean the carriage clock that had come from your father's father?

Peter: Yes, that's the one. I decided to take it apart this afternoon. I'd finished the project that I had been working on for Friday, and I thought, let's see if I can make this work a bit better. I told Mum weeks ago I'd look at it. It's been standing in the workshop for a couple of weeks. I immediately saw what the problem was, there was a bit that was simply sticking, so that was slowing down the mechanism. I just thought it was a pity Dad hadn't had a health check-up when he kept suffering from what he thought was indigestion! I know Mum blames herself that she didn't insist.

Helen: Well, your Dad wasn't that biddable was he? He had to make up his own mind about things before he would do anything. But I know what you mean. It just seems such a waste!

Therapist: I was thinking that, as a couple, you have both outlived your parent of the same sex. Helen, your mother died when she was quite young, very quickly. Peter, your father died in an equally tragic way when he was away from home. You've spoken of how shocked your mother was when the police arrived on the door step.

Helen: Yes, I sometimes feel guilty that I get irritated with Peter's mother, when she makes it so clear that it's Peter she wants to see and not me. When I think about it, I do realise that when you've lost your partner in that way, you obviously want to hang on to what is left. [She turns to Peter and says] But, that said, she was always cross that you married someone English, so it's been a bit of a losing battle!

Both members of the couple laugh as though realising that the reference to "a losing battle" was one of the *leitmotifs* throughout their marriage.

Peter: [stops laughing] Yes, but it would have been nice if she had been a bit more on your side when your mother died, especially once Catherine was born. I probably should have said something to her, but Dad was always so protective of her, it felt as though I would have to take them both on.

Helen: Well, she always blamed me that you moved to London to work, whereas, of course, it was much more about a good opportunity that came up for you. It makes it hard, though, now that she lives so close, and expects you to be there whenever she wants you.

Therapist: Do you have any idea why your father was so protective, Peter?

Peter: No, not really, although I vaguely remember my aunt saying something when I was quite young, about their father and some scandal about money. My parents gave her a look that stopped her in her tracks, and I don't remember it ever being mentioned again. I've asked my sisters about it, and they don't seem to have any recollection. That might have something to do with it.

Therapist: Secrets in the family.

The couple reflect on this for a moment.

Therapist: We have talked before, Helen, about the way you felt when your mother died. You've said that, with your father marrying again so soon afterwards, it made you feel as though you had lost both parents. Perhaps that is another factor in the way you feel about Peter's mother. Her husband dies, and my impression is that you feel she ignores the fact that he is married to you, and wants Peter only for herself. You rather felt that your father's new wife acted as though he didn't have a family, people who needed him to be there, and to share their feelings of grief."

Helen: Yes, that's right.

Peter: [addresses the therapist] I wouldn't have been able to have heard what you've just said about my mother when we first came here, but now I know what you say makes sense.

Therapist: [addressing Peter] I think you want to let us both know that you feel you had an important insight [and, turning to Helen], Helen, I was thinking that when you first came into the room, and were talking about the accident, that you made it sound as though you were certain there was only one person in the car, a man. It didn't sound as though you thought there was a couple or even a family. Did you know that for a fact, or was it just something you imagined?

Helen: [thinks about this question and then says] No, I simply thought it was a young man who had wrapped himself around a tree.

Therapist: Any idea why you might have thought that?

Helen: [looks at Peter and says] Do you remember me talking to Catherine about the book we were reading in my book club? I had chosen it. I'd heard the author speaking about it at a literary festival—Graham Swift. It just gripped me. It's called *Mothering Sunday*. It's about a young girl in service; she is an orphan, so she doesn't have a mother to visit on Mothering Sunday. She has been having a long affair with a young man from one of the nearby large houses. It was just after the First World War, and I think his brother had been killed. He was engaged but didn't seem to have his heart in the marriage, although his fiancée was rich. It was all rather surprising, because the orphaned girl, Jane, spent the morning in bed with him in his house. He was meant to be studying; his parents were having lunch with the parents of his fiancée and, of course, the servants were visiting their mothers. The house was empty except for them. Afterwards, he left Jane alone in his house, and drove off to have lunch with his fiancé. He drove the car into a tree. He was late, perhaps he was driving too fast, but the author leaves you questioning whether it was a suicide or not. Strange, really, but that book came to mind when I saw the accident.

Therapist: What do you think it was about the book that you found so gripping?

Helen: Well, someone in the audience asked the author if he had any thoughts about the girl's parentage, because it seemed to her that the main character, the orphan, Jane, seemed unfettered by her parentage, in a way that might be unusual for an orphan. The person who asked the question was interested, as she thought another girl might have dwelt on who her mother was, and that this might have got in the way of her being so much her own person—behaving exactly as she wished. Not hemmed in by social mores and conventions. I kept thinking about the word, "unfettered", and, of course, it just made me think about my mother, and how she was not unfettered. She would have loved to have known who her mother was, and I always thought it was there—a millstone round her neck. You know, life might have been different, if she had known who her mother was. It still makes me feel sad that she died without finding out. More recently, I've often thought that I should have helped her to try to find out. As a child, you don't understand. It's only when you become a mother yourself that you realise how important your genetic roots are. Of course, I know about my father's family, but not my mother's. It makes me feel as though there is something missing, and also there is something I didn't do for her.

Helen begins to cry again.

Peter: [looks concerned and says] You've never mentioned that you feel like that. But I can understand what you're saying. I'm always proud of my Scottish roots, and knowing where my family has come from. That makes it even worse that my mother didn't welcome you into my family.

Therapist: You seem to be thinking about parents in a different way today. Not just you as parents of your children, but the parenting you both received. But there is another point in this story that you've spoken about. Passion and the unfettered enjoyment of sex. You've clearly brought that into the room today, Helen, and it does seem to me that when you think about your marriage, that neither of you is keen to think that your sex life could be important now that you are older. It's time now, but perhaps you can begin to think about that too.

The couple say goodbye as they leave the room, and that they will see the therapist next week.

Over the hill to Oedipus
A clinical commentary for Peter and Helen

Andrew Balfour

Within a psychoanalytic frame, the dynamics of the couple's relationship are understood in the context of their expression in the transferences that unfold in the therapeutic sessions, the interactions in the consulting room representing, at least in part, the defensive patterning of the relationship, as enacted between the partners in the couple and with the therapist, the current coinages of historic problems, in which the couple are not simply victims of their past, but also agents in the reproduction and perpetuation of their difficulties in the present. It is the fact of this enactment of the "past in the present" that is the site for the therapeutic agency of psychoanalytic work. From the supervisory point of view, one is interested in details of the process that give a sense of how the couple shape their interaction with one another and with the therapist, encompassing the movements towards and away from emotional contact in the session. Listening in this way, one is less preoccupied with the content of the material alone, but also with the therapist's experience of the emotional encounter with the couple. In offering a commentary at one remove from the work itself, one is discussing thoughts and associations arising from the material, extrapolating from the case to observations that could be of more general relevance to working psychotherapeutically with couples.

At the outset, we might wonder why they are presenting for help at this point in their lives. We are told of "the empty nest" and of the prospect of retirement, and how the couple have prioritised their parenting role in relation to the children, their own relationship taking second place to this. In this detail, what might be signalled is the couple's difficulty with managing the shifting inclusions and exclusions that are necessarily a part of family life, where the parental couple are also a separate couple, with their own relationship to one another, as well as with the children. Indeed, the picture we are given is of a couple for whom such (oedipal) conflict has been particularly difficult. We are told about the impending loss of the "parallel lives" they have lived, of the "good team"—the parental couple whose children will soon all have flown the nest. As well as the losses contained in the development and growing up of the next generation, we might wonder, are they losing the emotional structures that have held them psychically and helped to obscure what is missing in their relationship? Are they now faced with the development in themselves that has been defensively avoided in the couple relationship as they have lived it until this point in their lives?

Although there seems to be a message from the couple, that "everything is OK, apart from the odd blip", it is striking that the therapist needs to say that this is "not a smug" attitude. Perhaps this is an example of what Freud called "negation"—the couple's retreat into complacency registered by the therapist, even as we are told it is *not* the case—is negated. Yet, the couple have come for help, and though the invitation they make might be for us to believe that this is not particularly significant, one cannot help but feel that, in fact, this is a couple who would not easily seek help. The comment that "they might have another thirty years together" brings in the dimension of time, and the anxiety, unconsciously, may be, as the therapist suggests, that each of them lost their parent of the same sex who died at around the age they are now: they did not have another thirty years. However, as well as these losses, the couple might also be conveying the fear of bringing to life the relationship between them, of intimacy and sexuality, and perhaps it is this "not brought to life" relationship that is expressed in the recognition in their presenting complaint that there is "something missing".

Each partner seems to be happier in a more self-sufficient state, in their own separate worlds. He is happiest on his own in his workshop; he likes golf, but not the social life of the clubhouse. Although she is interested in gardening and music, there is a somewhat distanced quality—she is "not a hands-on gardener". In her involvement in music and the choir, there is a hint of life that she is engaged in, and a glimpse of his felt exclusion from something, from the "music in her", perhaps expressed in the fantasy that she has a "crush" on the musical director. We are told that they are not intimate and cannot broach the subject of intimacy between them. This is expressed in their agreement that there is "something missing" between them, and they appear to convey this in a lack of passion or urgency, a sense of things not mattering one way or another. In telling us of the problem in this way, are the couple also showing us how it is established and maintained between them; how they keep themselves at a safe distance from one another and from any real engagement with their difficulties, defensively avoiding contact with potentially disturbing anxieties or states of mind? Perhaps what we are seeing here is evidence of a retreat into a state of mind that has a quality of complacency, the "smugness" that the therapist has alerted us to.

One way of thinking about the situation, is that the couple might have withdrawn into a state of retreat from psychic realities, such as oedipal struggles and recognition of the losses and displacements brought by the passage of time, seeking instead to maintain a defensive equilibrium. If it is the retreat from such psychic conflict that is at the heart of things for this couple, then perhaps the *leitmotif* is not so much a "losing battle", as the therapist suggests, but, rather, a battle that is not faced and which, therefore, cannot be worked through. Perhaps it is the evidence that realities, such as the passage of time, are now impinging which means that this retreat cannot function for them in the same way any more. The "losing battle" might be the difficulty in maintaining their familiar defensive structures in the face of ageing and the realities of time passing, these developmental changes displacing them from the role of parents who have had the children largely as the exclusive centre of their focus, perhaps meeting their own infantile needs through caring for children, but avoiding being a sexual couple and the oedipal anxieties this entails. Are they now, in their impending displacement, to be relegated to the other side of the oedipal divide, before they have ever really inhabited their primary position of being the sexual couple at the heart of it?

Ageing can be a powerful site for oedipal anxieties, with one generation's displacement by the next. In the novel referred to in the session, the consequence of sexual coupling is death: the conflation of intercourse with death is evident in the ambiguity of the phrase, "the young man wrapped himself around a tree". Is there a fear that bringing in sexuality at this point in their lives would be too dangerous, tantamount to a "suicide" of their relationship? Were both partners unconsciously terrified of the sexuality and aggression involved in "killing off" the parental generation, in order to take their own place as the potent sexual couple? Perhaps we are being told about a very split world, where things are "very nice", but then sexuality, aggression, and destructiveness crashes in, conveyed in the juxtaposition of the "lovely visit" with the accident. The therapist draws attention to the fact that there is no couple imagined as victims of the accident, that it seems their coupling has been killed off, even as a possibility. Perhaps the aggression that has been kept out of the picture, and the awareness of the "killing off" of their couple relationship, the losses involved in this and in the passage of time, are now "crashing in", triggered by the "dangerous spot" they are in, in the "late afternoon" of their lives, with the inescapable realities of time passing, of children growing and leaving them. As we cross into the later phase of our lives, we move over the brow of the hill, to face the prospect of our mortality ahead (see Segal, 1984), and this can bring both the threat and the opportunity of the re-emergence of earlier developmental difficulties.

We do not know anything much about their early histories: there is the theme of loss of the same sex parents and, linked to this, in each perhaps there is evidence of reparative wishes: of the clock that is always "out of time"; her mother who did not know her own mother. There is the sense of loss and of the repair that it was not possible to effect, and that, in actuality, is too late now. In working with couples in later life, one encounters the situation of losses that cannot be repaired, but, of course, what cannot be changed in reality does not obviate the need for internal reparation, for the need to ". . . put some order inside with respect to objects that were important" (Quinodoz, 2009). Perhaps what is signalled is that the psychic task of effecting some internal repair is linked to "repairing the clock"—the importance of recognising the realities of time passing, and the losses entailed in keeping themselves out of contact with one another, repair in the marriage entailing facing the time that has been lost, now that they are both nearing sixty.

In thinking about the case, I found myself wondering about the nature of the relating as it unfolds in the session, and in how these dynamic themes might be lived out between the partners and with the therapist. It is difficult to generalise from just one session, but it is striking that the contact within the couple and with the therapist is very polite and civilised, there is nothing "unfettered", not even "the odd blip", so to speak. The "parallel lives" of the couple seem to be evident, with interactions tending to happen between one or other partner and the therapist, with relatively cursory and conflict-free exchanges between the couple. What is interesting is the therapist's awareness of sexuality being a dangerous and fragile area for the couple, and yet the way in which it is brought in. We might wonder why interpretations are often focused outside the room, and then the couple's sexuality is shunted in, right at the close of the session. It is striking that sexuality is tagged on to an interpretation at the end in this way, without a place of its own within the session or in the relationship. Might this be linked to frustration or to a sense of it being unsafe for sexuality to be integrated into the session, as within the marriage? Or might it be a dutiful inclusion of something that was felt needed not to be left out? These thoughts can only be raised as questions, given the limits of the material available—we are seeing only a snapshot of the therapy. To understand more, we would need to know about the therapist's countertransference.

For the therapist, stepping back, to reflect upon the behaviour one finds oneself enacting in the session is an important way in to understanding—through one's lived experience with the couple—the emotional truths of their unconscious preoccupations and anxieties. Such understanding is hard wrought from the emotional encounter, and is part of a provisional, shifting process of understanding. The psychotherapeutic offering for the couple is of the experience of a therapist who is seeking to help make thinkable what was previously enacted between them in repetitive ways, allowing for the possibility of new ways of thinking and feeling their experience—for this couple, a way out of their defensive retreat from one another, perhaps.

Facing death: mourning and reparation in a late middle-aged couple
A clinical commentary for Peter and Helen

Warren Colman

The introduction to this couple's story shows that they are at a significant point of transition in their lives and in their relationship. As they approach sixty, they are in the process of leaving middle age behind; in a few more years, they will begin to grow old. Their time as parents to a growing family is coming to an end, retirement beckons (at least for Peter), and they have both lost their same-sex parents, though Helen's father and Peter's mother are still alive. They have a sense that "something is missing", and have come to therapy in the hope of finding a way of revitalising their relationship for what could be "another thirty years together".

To my mind, the theme of the session is primarily about the need to face the reality of death, and whether it is possible to recover from loss through mourning and reparation. This theme is introduced in a sudden and shocking way by Helen's account of having seen a terrible accident on her journey to the session that she thinks must have killed the driver of the car. She contrasts this with the "beautiful day" and "the lovely lunch" with her daughter, so it becomes for her a stark reminder of how death and destruction can strike out of the blue. As the session develops, it becomes clear that the accident evoked an acute sense that everything can be lost in a heartbeat, that the beautiful moments with our loved ones are fragile and precious, and should not be wasted. *Carpe diem!*

The therapist links the sudden death on the roads with the sudden deaths of their parents, an intervention that brings out an unexpected synchronicity: it turns out that Peter has been thinking about the death of his father that very afternoon. He tells a deeply symbolic story about his efforts to mend a clock that "always seems to be at the wrong time", a clock that belonged to his grandfather, thus referencing historical time and the passage of the generations. In his efforts to repair the clock, he is seeking to set the time aright, and, in so doing, to make symbolic reparation for the death of his father, due to an illness that apparently could easily have been put right, if only it had been attended to early enough. Like the couple's marriage, perhaps? Peter even says that the clock's mechanism was "sticking", a metaphorical link with the therapist's observation that the couple were "stuck" in not relating to each other, and in need of repair, like the intergenerational clock that, for them, too, is inexorably ticking towards death. Helen resonates with the symbolic meaning of his story, saying, "I know what you mean—it seems such a waste," implicitly referencing the terrible waste of the man killed in the car crash, as well as the couple's hopes and fears for their own future that brought them to therapy. Can they yet live again, before they die?

While the therapist stays with the theme of the early loss of their same-sex parents, the couple pursue their own implicit dialogue about making the best of life in the face of death, the need to "hang on to what is left" (Helen), and Peter's reparative regret that he has not been as protective of his wife as his father was of his mother. "I probably should have said something," he remarks ruefully, linking up again with the stuck clock that could easily have been repaired, and the missed opportunity to save his father's life by an early health check.

The therapist does not pick up on any of this, but seems to stay with the history ("why was your father so protective?"). Now, it might be that the therapist has a hypothesis in mind here, and hopes to elicit more evidence for it, but I did wonder whether this was an illustration of what happens when a therapist gets caught up with "memory and desire", pursuing thoughts and aims from previous sessions, rather than focusing on what is going on between the couple in the "here and now" (cf. Bion, 1967b). The couple seem so full of poignant emotion in the "here and now" of the session—loss, regret, guilt, hope, longing, and the aching transience of life—that it seems to detract from that to go on pursuing historical information about the past. Maybe the therapist sensed that too, as she or he then returns to the so-far unexplored story about the car accident, wondering why Helen had assumed it was a single man in the car rather than, say, a couple or a family. It is not clear why the therapist took this up but, whether consciously or not, it seems to have arisen from an intuitive hunch that there was more to this story (and its impact on Helen) than had yet been revealed. This would be an example of what Bion calls a "selected fact", something that arises spontaneously in the therapist's mind out of their unconscious immersion in the emotional field; it contrasts with the previous questioning about the couple's parents, which seems to have become more like what Britton and Steiner (1994) called "an overvalued idea".

However it arose, the therapist's question enables Helen to reveal a crucial association to the Graham Swift novel, where the illicit love between a young couple ends in death. She says, "He was engaged, but didn't seem to have his heart in the marriage," precisely the problem that this couple brought to their therapy. Now it is Helen's turn to feel a remorseful sorrow for her orphan mother, who could never be "unfettered". As she herself grows older, like her husband, she now wishes she had helped her mother more and tried harder to set things right before it was too late. So it seems that the couple are beginning to recognise the intergenerational burden they carry from "the unlived lives of their parents", and how they may free themselves (become "unfettered") by making reparation—to each other as much as their dead parents. From a psychoanalytic perspective, I was reminded of Henri Rey's proposition that people come to therapy to repair their "damaged inner objects" (Rey, 1988), meaning, their sense that their loved ones and their relation to them, especially parents, are, or were, in need of repair. More poetically, I was reminded of some of Bob Dylan's late work, writing as an older man in his sixties. In his reworking of the blues classic, "Rollin' and Tumblin'" (2006), the penultimate verse refers to the shadows of early doom and long dead souls. The final verse expresses the wish for mutual forgiveness and reconciliation, and concludes "let's put our heads together, let's put old matters to an end".

However, there is clearly another theme in the *Mothering Sunday* story that the therapist picks up in terms of "passion and unfettered enjoyment of sex". Here, too, I was reminded of a poetic allusion that famously links the unfettered enjoyment of sex with the transience of living—Andrew Marvell's "To His Coy Mistress" (1681).

> But at my back I always hear
> Time's wingèd chariot hurrying near;
> And yonder all before us lie
> Deserts of vast eternity.
>
> . . .
>
> Now therefore, while the youthful hue
> Sits on thy skin like morning dew,
> And while thy willing soul transpires
> At every pore with instant fires,
> Now let us sport us while we may

Nevertheless, I was left wondering whether the issue was necessarily the couple's actual sexual relationship or was more to do with the emotional quality of their passionate engagement with each other. In terms of the latter, it is clear from this very moving session how much is actually being achieved, how their love and concern for each other is deepening as they rework their own past and future possibilities in the face of loss, mourning, and death. It is true that many couples enjoy a sexual relationship well into old age, but there are also many who do not. Whereas the absence of sex is almost always diagnostic of a problematic relationship in a younger couple, this is not necessarily the case in an older couple at a time "when the fires of our love have stopped burning". Then, as Peter Green sang, the question is "will you love me tomorrow, like you say you love me now?" (Green, 1968). And for this, it seems that what really counts, according to couple researchers John and Julie Gottman, is not sex, but kindness and generosity (Smith, 2014)—the very qualities that this couple are discovering and learning to share together in their couple therapy.

Therapy: anxieties, defences, and the couple
A clinical commentary for Peter and Helen

Susan Irving

From this history, I noticed that "the couple" is usually punctual, but Helen represents a part of the couple that appears to "fly in at the last minute". What anxieties is each expressing for the couple? Is Helen expressing ambivalence or a disorganised manic defence, while Peter, the steady "rock", is overtly representing reliability, responsible for paying the fees regularly, a more obsessive defence? His reluctance to spend the money is lessening, suggesting he increasingly values the work: a sign of gratitude, the depressive position.

The couple are both "nearly sixty"; what does this milestone mean to them: aging and proximity to death, or time to reassess the meaning of their lives? I am curiously noting the "calculator" in my mind, working out their ages when they married and had their children; this could be *my* defence against knowing nothing. In this state of mind, I am wary of making false assumptions, drawing premature conclusions.

We hear *nothing* about the pre-children part of their relationship, and what attracted them to each other.

Helen is aware "they could have another thirty years together; unlikely but possible". It seems that it is this thought that is disturbing; they will be left alone together. Is the prospect of another thirty years depressing, unbearable, or does it represent a *denial* of the proximity of death, as they both lost their "same sex" parent at an early age? One might wish for death, the other fear it; both might be denied.

"Something is missing" captures my interest. I wonder "what is missing" and, "what does each of them understand this phrase to mean?"

We learn that argument is "missing". Why is this lively "passion" absent, a dynamic noted by Grier (2005c) as coinciding with "no sex" couples? Fear of conflict is a common primitive anxiety, with no room for two different positions.

The children represent the creative core of this marriage. Helen seems to fear their absence being added to the sum of whatever is "missing", making an undeniable void.

As always, I question, was the "something" once there and has gone, or was it never there in the beginning?

Helen keeps the money she earns for herself, yet feels Peter is "mean with money" (or his emotions?) This could be projection on Helen's part, as Peter rather sounds anxious about money; we learn later that money is central to a "family secret", and suggests that mismanagement has been a cause of scandal and, therefore, deep (unconscious) shame, so his tight control could be a defence.

They identify themselves as "a good team". However, a team of oxen comes immediately to my mind, yoked together, diligent, but each looking straight ahead and not at each other.

There has been "the odd blip". This acts like a blip in my mind; I become instantly alert and curious. Experience suggests this *could* be minimising what other less defended couples would have recognised as critical points, prompting them to take action to repair much earlier.

Peter likes golf, gardening, and "mending things" in his workshop. No original creativity, then? He seems a bit of a loner, frequently a euphemism for some autistic spectrum defensive traits. Golf is a single-handed sport, played ostensibly against another but mainly against oneself. *A partner is preferable but not essential in this game.* Could this be a metaphor for marriage in Peter's mind, with no overt conflict?

Helen sounds more sociable, singing in harmony with others, joining a book group.

I am struck by the *potential* complementarity of their interests: Helen likes gardens, and Peter likes gardening, possible foundations for creative coupling. However, Helen sings in a choir, but Peter is "tone deaf". Does he find the "sounds" she makes discordant, or does he become "deaf"? Music can stir up deep preverbal pain that some cannot bear to hear. Peter intuits that Helen has a "crush" on the music director. The word "crush" trivialises: has he curiosity about the music director's phallic power, as there seems to be little passion in the marriage; does primitive envy or oedipal jealousy prevent Peter imagining a more symbolic excitement this person could ignite in his wife?

The premature loss of parents by death is recognised as significant by all. Helen lost her mother when she was having her own children, twenty years ago, around the time of Hamish's birth. When the experiences of birth and death coincide in time, neither can be properly metabolised. Neither grieving properly nor bonding is fully managed.

Helen feels her mother-in-law never got over her son marrying "someone English", maybe another piece of projection: has Helen never forgiven herself for marrying a Scot, thereby contributing to her own sense of "not belonging"?

The therapist feels that the couple are becoming more in touch with their feelings; this would suggest less of their own feelings are being projected, moving from paranoid–schizoid to depressive functioning.

Sex and intimacy are, however, still treated as of "little consequence", rather than as the major thing that may be missing between them, along with curiosity.

The session

Helen is clearly quite traumatised. Something has dramatically broken through her defences. She has not directly witnessed, or been involved in, or caused, an accident, but is it "as if" she unconsciously believed she has? Peter quickly cognitively "understands" how the collision could have occurred. He also emotionally identifies with her sense of a trauma. One hallmark of trauma is that something dreadful comes "out of a clear blue sky". This malignantly deceptive "clear blue sky" being as relevant to the "total situation" (Joseph, 1985) as the traumatic event itself.

Peter picks up the therapist's link to the sudden death of parents, and a real emotional link is created between them, manifested in Helen's curiosity. Peter approaches his father's death via the unconscious metaphor of the carriage clock, which symbolises "something" that came from Peter's paternal line. Probably this "something" is a faulty gene causing his heart to stop or "stick". The "ticker" (heart) inside Peter's father had needed examining for some time. When Peter "mends things" in his workshop, is this a compulsive need to "make reparation" for the damage he unconsciously fears he has done via the phantasied attacks made primitively on his internal father? Hopefully, parents survive these attacks, but when a real parent dies, the child can believe they have killed them. Peter is unable to refuse his mother anything; he might believe this would be an attack on her, leading to a similar outcome.

Helen, in losing her mother, felt she had "lost both parents", and could not appreciate her father's capacity to continue to invest in life. This feeling in Helen is probably due to her own anger with him. The "woman who has lost both parents" reminds me of Helen's mother, identified as "like Jane" in the Swift novel, that is, an orphan. Helen believes her mother never worked through the loss of her birth mother, and, presumably, her biological father. Helen never felt fully "adopted" by her mother-in-law, unconsciously feeling like an unwanted orphan. Helen can express ambivalence towards her mother-in-law and empathise with her loss, but still feel angry at being made to feel that she did not really belong.

The "losing battle" could mean many things, as the battle to come to terms with loss is ongoing. The early need to separate *vs.* the fear of abandonment, plus the need for closeness *vs.* the fear of engulfment, or (s)mothering, evolve into depressive position mourning. Border territory is frequently referred to when emotional "borderline" issues are around, the border between Scotland and England in this work, for example. Borderline problems manifest within any couple dynamic; "how does one retain one's separate identity and yet fully commit to being a creative couple?" (Morgan, 2005).

Lack of intimacy and sexual difficulties point to problems in this area. Peter manifests oedipal difficulties, trying to avoid forming a couple with his mother. Possibly, when Helen became a mother, Peter could not extricate himself from identifying her as "his" mother, triggering an incest taboo that curtailed their sexual relationship.

The main indicator that someone has regressed from a more depressive position to an early defensive paranoid–schizoid position is that fantasies develop that are treated as reality. Sudden trauma can trigger such regression. An example of this is when Helen believes that a young, single man was the only occupant of the crashed car, despite having no evidence for this; she develops a fantasy narrative that the man has committed suicide. Fiction, from the novel she has just read, and reality are in collision, and then the "driver" is missing from the controls in her internal world. Helen recovered to a place of self-reflection, held by the therapist's gently containing curiosity and comments that the hero in the novel does not have his heart in his marriage.

Helen's overt curiosity and envy is focused on her belief that the orphaned girl, Jane, is "unfettered", described as "not hemmed in by social mores and conventions". Is this envy towards Jane about her freedom from concern regarding class barriers (borders) or sexual inhibition? Helen is consciously thinking about her real biological mother, but much of what she says could apply to herself. Helen intuitively knows that her mother, in not knowing her origins, had "something missing" in *her* internal world. Consequently, Helen could never have had full access to knowing her *own* mother. As she explores these feelings, she gradually recognises that there is consequently "something missing" for her, too; knowledge of her family tree and her genetic roots.

Discussion

Working psychoanalytically, the therapist uses their own responses to the material as a very important tool, part of what we call "countertransference". My initial response to this vignette was of slight disappointment and uninterest. Working on this commentary, I found myself becoming increasingly involved, interested, and curious about this couple. This is a common occurrence in live practice, but might also be particular to this case. Emotional development is a process of opening oneself up to another, who opens themselves in return to being known. At birth, mother and baby are strangers; the early process of knowing and being known is mainly non-verbal. Unbearable feelings are projected through splitting and projection, and one loses contact with those feelings that become located in another, particularly the therapist or other half of a couple. This couple manifests much ambivalence about their primitive feelings being known.

Peter is probably more acutely anxious about his death, being currently the age at which his father died. Peter has lost his interest in travelling for work, as if he fears a repeat of dying suddenly, when alone overseas. In the absence of effective mourning, melancholic identification with the dead person sets in. Helen, consciously fantasises about a sudden death, the death by suicide of a "young man". These are likely to be unconscious phantasies of what might occur if she allows herself the freedom to think about an affair or the possible thirty extra years of life with another more exciting partner (replicating her father's second marriage), as this would involve symbolically killing off Peter.

Unconscious fantasies tend to bear the hallmark of dramatic life and death scenarios, like fairy tales and replicating infantile wishes.

I have read this novel by Graham Swift. Where a therapist knows something in reality about a subject being discussed in a session, one needs to take extra care about one's associations. The story is, by the author's admission, a very sexual novel. Sexuality seems so obviously the "something missing" for this couple. The novel was described as "a heat soaked carnal encounter" and "suffused with passion and sorrow". Emotional freedom, self-recognition, and the possibility of a complete rebirth is captured in this short novel. It is impossible for me to not know these things; frequently one can intuit what the "missing something" is by sketching, in one's imagination, the metaphoric "shape" of what is absent.

Couples come in twos and threes: an oedipal perspective
A clinical commentary for Peter and Helen

Molly Ludlam

This powerful account of an important meeting heralding development in a couple's therapy brings alive not only the couple, Peter and Helen, but their relationships with the many threesomes in their lives. In this commentary, I highlight the oedipal and three-way relationship aspects of the couple's story, to show why triadic relationships are so significant for them, and, indeed, for all couples. It has been observed that wherever there is a couple, there will always be a third. Phillips (1996, p. 94), writing that, "Coupledom is a sustained resistance to the intrusion of third parties ... Two's company, but three's a couple", perceives that the couple needs an outsider to establish its identity. Ruszczynski (2005), however, sees an alternative configuration of a dyad–triad relationship, as a "marital triangle" composed of the couple and their relationship; the psychoanalytic couple psychotherapist's task, thus, lies in enabling the couple to use a shared perception of this third entity as a therapeutic resource. It is important, then, to keep in mind that, in Peter and Helen's story, there are three principal characters—Peter, Helen, and their therapist.

When considering the significance of threesomes in couple psychotherapy, we might do so from each of three perspectives:

1. How do the couple and their therapist use their three-way relationship?
2. What makes threesome relationships particularly significant for this couple?
3. What stage have the partners reached on their Oedipal developmental journeys?

How do the couple and their therapist use their three-way relationship?

When considering the therapist's role in any couple's psychotherapy, I suggest that what happens between the couple–therapist threesome could be judged to be as important as, if not more important than, what happens between the couple.

Couples often seek therapeutic help when a crisis in their lives coincides with a challenging, developmental period, affecting them both individually and as a couple. This appears to be so for Peter and Helen. At the outset of their therapy, Helen says that, as a couple, they have "lost sight of each other", wondering aloud about the prospect of continuing to live in this way—apart but together—for another thirty years. At times of crisis, awareness of loneliness of this kind might resonate with other painful experiences of being on the outside, excluded from an understanding that others appear to share. (Here, we might recall Helen's perception of Peter's closeness with his mother.) Thus, couples, finding themselves at such a loss, might unconsciously seek out a relationship with someone who, in terms of transference, can be for *both* of them a good "parent" whom they can share.

All of this underlines the importance of their therapist's ability to provide a containing, trusting, and open relationship, in which it is safe to be curious. As with all good and "good enough" parents, the therapist's capacity to foster a healthy, supportive curiosity about her or his own and another's emotional world is vital in promoting growth. Britton's (1989) delineation of the development of a healthy curiosity in dispelling the illusion that "a third always murders the dyadic relationship" (p. 100) has been invaluable in the development of couple psychotherapy. Morgan and Stokoe (2014) describe curiosity's "essential role in the development of a creative couple stage of identity" (p. 42). The ability to be curious about our emotional experience is modelled by the therapist's lively curiosity about the significant relationships in the world of the couple she or he is getting to know, these being those to which the couple directly refer and, of course, those that they seem to overlook or disregard. (Peter and Helen, we note, focus on their children, to the exclusion of themselves.) The therapist's focus is, however, not only on the couple's external relationships, but on those inhabiting each partner's internal world. There, they operate as templates of relationships, to which each can, if only unconsciously, refer. As these templates are developed in infancy or early childhood, they are most likely to form patterns of twos and threes, mirroring the child's close relationships. We might usefully wonder, then, what internal pictures each partner has formed, and how each might see her- or himself and their place in relation to these inner couples or threesomes. For example, in someone who, in childhood, negotiated the oedipal hurdles, the internal couple characteristically represents parents, while a threesome would represent her- or himself as a witness in relationship to the parental couple. Alternatively, if there was an oedipal victory, with the child triumphantly claiming mother or father as "partner", the internal couple represents a parent and child, while a threesome is invariably one in which the other parent is the excluded third.

The open-minded therapist will be prepared to learn that each partner's significant internal relationships differ. But, because the pair has formed a couple relationship, their respective internal relations might have much in common, even overlapping considerably, to the extent that they could be thought of as part of the couple's shared belief system or fit.

Nevertheless, at the beginning of couple therapy, while it is always possible, it is probable that neither partner will be conscious of their inner world, *or* object relationships, and so will not previously have thought together about the possible impact of inner relationships on their shared emotional life as a couple. Commensurate with the idea of the "marital triangle", the psychoanalytic couple therapist facilitates a joint exploration and discovery of the meaning of the couple's internal relationships, identifying them as they emerge in the therapy between the couple and in the therapeutic threesome. Because one person is always at risk of being the outsider, threesome relationships are intrinsically challenging. Yet, paradoxically, because this is so, and because couple psychotherapy itself presents a living configuration of this three-way relational difficulty, it offers two unparalleled opportunities: simultaneously, couples can re-experience and discover the particular significance of unresolved past triangular relationships, while experimenting with, and discovering, new strategies with which to manage them.

What makes threesome relationships particularly significant for this couple?

Alongside the many questions that the therapist entertains—often privately—as possible routes to a shared understanding of their difficulty is the key question: Why has *this* couple sought help *now*?

The therapist recognises that Peter and Helen face two impending, major life changes: lives once so preoccupied with family and work must soon find new meaning in retirement in an "empty nest". When their therapy begins, we learn how much is at stake for them. In saying, "As a couple we have rather lost sight of each other and we could have another thirty years together—unlikely perhaps, but possible!" Helen portrays something of the complexity of their anxieties about an uncertain future. Before they will have been able to enjoy (and make sense of) their couple relationship, beyond that of being parents, potentially, they are on the threshold of a new relationship. Either one of them dies, as has happened in their parents' lives, or one of them becomes physically dependent on the other, so changing their already non-sexual couple relationship into that of carer and invalid, more akin to one of parent and child. Indeed, in losing sight of each other, and in their sessions seeming to be tired of one another and preferring to focus on their children, they were telling their therapist that each of them was missing, or had even disengaged from, something supportive inside themselves that might fill the gap. This suggests to me that the internal "creative couple" that Morgan describes (Morgan, 2005) was not available as a resource to them. That they also "always sidestepped" talking about intimacy and sex, "as though it is of little consequence", further expresses their disengagement from an inner couple. In fact, both Peter and Helen appear to see themselves as outsiders in relationship to their significant other and to a significant other couple; for Peter, Helen's relationship is with the choir, if not with its music director; for Helen, Peter's relationship is with golf, the garden, or his workshop, if not with his mother.

Nevertheless, it is notable that we are introduced to the couple at a crucial moment in their therapeutic work; at the end of the session it feels as if they have reached an important turning point. Despite repeated expressions of their shared ambivalence about committing to the work, she through her last-minute arrivals, he through concerns about its financial cost, and both through seemingly "'stuck' in relating, or, rather, in not relating, with each other", they have actually attended regularly for eleven months. It would seem that during this time something vital has been germinating—the growth of a capacity to symbolise, and, thus, to recognise, the links between everyday events and the emotional worlds that they can now share with one another and their therapist. Now ready to make use of a therapist with whom it is safe to be vulnerable, they can embark on a journey of exploration.

While all this has prepared them, this session's development, however, was probably triggered by the trauma of the road accident. Its intimation of mortality reminds them both that death can arrive "out of the blue" to separate a couple. Like Peter, that day, unsticking the mechanism of his father's clock, they implicitly agree it is now better to allow their relationship to be worked on in the therapy workshop and to unstick it before death intervenes and it is too late. In her or his interpretations that reveal links between the many metaphors they use and their emotional lives, their therapist can help to free their emotional vocabulary, and so unstick and "unfetter" their relationship.

What stage have the partners reached on their oedipal developmental journeys?

Taking up Britton's extension (Britton, 1989) of Freud and Klein's elaboration of the myth of Oedipus, we can envisage the child moving from a phantasised position of being the parent's partner to one of adopting a "third position" that allows the child to become a witness of, rather than only a participant in, her or his parents' relationship. Britton suggests that, "through mourning for this lost exclusive relationship", the person can realise that curiosity about, and discovery of, the oedipal triangle does not mean the death of the couple relationship, "only the death of an idea of a relationship" (1989, p. 100).

Hypothesising about what shared unconscious belief or idea of a couple relationship Peter and Helen might have had until now, we could wonder whether it concerned the need not to enquire too closely into a parental couple's relationship, lest something vulnerable be destroyed. Little detail is given about Helen's parents' relationship, except that it was too quickly replaced by remarriage after her mother's death. Helen's mother had carried "like a millstone" the inability to be curious about her parents' relationship. In this session, Helen expresses grief for her mother for that loss, and for her own loss of parents and potential parents. Importantly, Peter can hear her and acknowledge the therapist's intervention.

Peter has carried different, but related, burdens. He did not challenge his parents for disparaging his non-Scots wife, nor for guarding the family's "secret". Perhaps to have confronted them would have meant uncovering his place in their oedipal triangle before he was ready to do so. On his father's sudden death, Peter took over his father's protective role with his mother, so prematurely forgoing his place as a son. That might have required him to be somewhat self-sufficient; perhaps he projectively identified this self-denying experience into his wife and children by withholding generosity. Thus, in sharing the experience of prematurely losing a parent, Peter and Helen found themselves unable to risk making sense of their respective places in their family triangles, for fear of what else might be sacrificed.

Happily, the potential development of "triangular space" now presages recurring family and couple rewards. Through focusing on their couple relationship, Peter and Helen can also now unfetter their children, allowing them to progress more freely into adult life.

CHAPTER SEVEN

Daniel and Caroline

Waiting room

This is Daniel and Caroline's first appointment. When I go to the waiting room, my first impression is that the couple do not look as though they are together. They are sitting close, but look quite detached from each other. I only know that they are the couple booked in to see me since they are the only two people in the waiting room. I introduce myself, and shake hands with them both. Caroline says she is Caroline, and smiles anxiously, and Daniel looks me directly in the eye, in what seems to me more like a "summing up" than a "challenging" way. Daniel says, "Hi, I'm Dan," and I query if he would like me to call him Dan or Daniel. He says, "Dan." Caroline is casually dressed, and Daniel is dressed in a perfectly ironed white shirt and well-cut suit.

Consulting room

Once in the room, I indicate the chairs the couple should use and introduce myself again. I mention that the couple had requested an urgent appointment.

Caroline: Yes, it was good of you to fit us in so promptly. The clinic was easy to find. I was a bit worried it wouldn't be.

Daniel: Yes, this is a good time for me, and it's quite easy to get here from the City.

Therapist: We have one hour and fifteen minutes for our first appointment, and towards the end of that time, we can think about whether you would like further help, and, if so, how best we might arrange this. I am wondering what has brought you here?

There is silence.

Therapist: While waiting, notices that although both spoke briefly, the atmosphere became even more tense. The couple glance at one another in what feels like quite a hostile way.

Caroline: Begins to cry.

Daniel: Looks at her angrily.

Caroline: Continues to cry, and starts pulling, one after another, tissues from the box.

Therapist: [reflects that this activity has an aggressive feel to it and waits for a few more moments] Would it be possible for one of you to tell me what has been happening?

Caroline: [continues to sob, but then looks directly at the therapist] Dan's been having an affair. I found a text on his iPhone. I wasn't checking up on him, but it bleeped when he was out of the room, and I just picked it up. It's obvious he's been having an affair with someone at work.

Daniel: Looks exasperated but doesn't say anything.

Therapist: When did you find this text?

Caroline: At the weekend. That's why I wanted an urgent appointment.

Daniel: I've told her repeatedly that I am not having an affair. There's just a girl at work and we've been having some fun, just some fun . . .

Caroline: [looking at Daniel angrily, interrupts] Huh, fun! It sounded more than that. She couldn't wait to see you on Monday. Were you having a dull weekend without her?

Daniel: [in an exasperated tone] I've told you, I am not having an affair. I've told you, I don't play away from home. It was just some fun, these things happen, it was just some fun.

Caroline: [still crying] I don't believe you! You've obviously deleted her texts and yours. You've even saved her name under a pseudonym. I bet her name isn't Computer Dealer. How could you, I feel such a fool, how could you?

Daniel:	[irritated, looks directly at Caroline] I am not having an affair! But well, what do you expect?
Therapist:	Looks from one member of the couple to the other. Daniel looks angry. Caroline continues to sob. Daniel's phone bleeps.
Daniel:	[looks at his phone] I'm sorry, I meant to put it on silent. I forgot.
Therapist:	Dan, you said, "What do you expect?" I am wondering what you meant by that?

The couple look at one another briefly. There is another silence. Caroline glances at Daniel, who looks at the floor.

Caroline:	I thought you'd bring that up.
Daniel:	Well!
Caroline:	You know how I feel.
Daniel:	I have feelings, too.
Caroline:	You've never understood. Ever since Tom was born, you've been jealous of him. I know you say to everyone, "He's my son", as though you are really proud of him, but really you're just jealous.
Daniel:	That's what you always say when I try to discuss this.
Caroline:	Look, I know jealousy when I see it. You hate it when Tom wants my attention. I see the look on your face. You are only happy with him when you've got him on your own. You hate it when all three of us are together.
Daniel:	That's because when I'm alone with him it's different. It's the only time that he feels like my son.
Therapist:	[looking at both] There's something here that I don't understand, but I gather it's to do with one of your children?
Daniel:	[addressing the therapist and looking distressed] Our only child, Tom, he's nearly four years of age.
Therapist:	[looks at the couple] Can you tell me what the problem is?
Caroline:	[looks at the therapist as though avoiding eye contact with Daniel] Dan's furious that Tom still sleeps in our bed. He doesn't understand that he's frightened of the dark, and doesn't like being on his own at night. Dan gets angry that I don't put him in his own bed, but Tom gets upset when he is alone, and, anyway, there are lots of cultures where the child sleeps with the parents.
Daniel:	[angrily, looking towards Caroline] That's not the point.
Therapist:	What do you see as the point, Dan?
Daniel:	He's nearly four years of age. He should be in his own bed. He interferes with our sleep, because he tosses and turns. We

	hardly ever have sex, because he's there, and Caroline won't think about another child, because she says we haven't sorted out having this one yet. I'm fed up with the whole thing.
Daniel:	[looks dejected and, after a short silence, addressing the therapist, exclaims angrily] There's this beautiful nursery, I spent a fortune on it, it's every woman's dream, and Tom's hardly been through the door, and it doesn't look as though there will be any other babies in there either.
Therapist	Notes that Caroline looks even more distressed, and there is yet another silence.
Therapist:	[looks at the couple] Would you like more children?
	The couple look at the therapist, and speak together. *Dan:* "Yes." *Caroline:* "Eventually."
Therapist:	[after few moments] Do you think you could give me some sense of your relationship. How and when you met, how long you've been together as a couple?
Daniel:	Yes, I guess that might help. [Dan looks towards Caroline, as though he wants her to begin.]
Caroline:	We met through work, about five and a half years ago. [She looks at Daniel and says, in a rather ironic tone] We knew pretty quickly we wanted to be together.
Daniel:	[although looking as though this irony was not lost on him] Yes, I knew Caroline was different. I didn't feel I wanted to put the brakes on in the same way that I had in previous relationships. I asked her to marry me not long after we met. We've been married nearly five years.
Therapist:	So Tom was conceived quite quickly.
Caroline:	Yes, it wasn't quite the plan, but these things happen, and we were both pleased.
Daniel:	I come from quite a big family, so I was quite happy that we got started, but then things have just gone downhill.
Therapist:	Do you mean with the pregnancy or following Tom's birth?
Therapist:	[As I say this, I am flooded with a feeling of panic, and am shocked by the intensity of feelings. I cannot think. I want to get rid of the feeling, yet struggle to process it in some way, and Caroline immediately starts to talk to both me and Daniel.]
Caroline:	Look, Tom is still small, he still wants to be in our bed. Lots of parents have their children in their bed until they are a lot older than Tom. I know. I've talked to a lot of mothers. Most of them say their children spend more time in their bed than they do in

	their own. It's just the way it is. We have to wait until he's more confident.
Daniel:	That's different. Henry says his kids come into their bed during the night, and they either take them back or, if they are too exhausted to get up, they sometimes just turn a blind eye, and hope they'll all get some sleep.
Caroline:	[interrupts angrily] What does Henry know? Jane says he's always working, and the children are often asleep by the time he gets back.
Daniel:	[responds in an equally angry tone] Tom is up most of the evening, so we never get any time on our own. Then when he does go to bed, you put him in our bed. He starts in our bed every night. He's there all through the night, and he's there in the morning. I never sleep with you on our own now. He's four, he's not four months.
Caroline:	[looks at the therapist] Am I right when I say there are cultures where the child sleeps with the parents until they are quite big and everyone seems happy?
Therapist:	[first addresses Caroline, but includes Daniel in her response] Yes, there are, but, usually there is an agreement between the couple that this is what they want to do. The problem here is that one of you wants a co-sleeping arrangement, but the other is clear that they do not. I wonder if perhaps Dan wants to reclaim you, and that he is saying he always feels he has to share you.
Therapist:	Sees that the couple engages in a different way. Daniel speaks in a gentler tone of voice, as does Caroline.
Daniel:	Exactly. Night time's bad enough, but look at the trouble we've had getting him to settle at nursery. It's been a nightmare. He never wants to leave you.
Caroline:	Dan, that's not true.
Daniel:	You know it is!
Therapist:	Caroline, do you think that separating from Tom is quite hard?

There is a long pause.

Caroline:	I suppose so. He's quite happy with my mother.
Therapist:	Perhaps that's because you trust her.
Caroline:	Yes, I know he's safe with her.
Therapist:	[addresses the couple] I would just like to backtrack. When I asked Dan if things had gone downhill during the pregnancy or after the birth, we didn't stay with that question, and I am wondering about that.

There is a poignant silence.

Daniel: [puts his head in his hands and says] Well, she nearly died. Giving birth, I mean.

Therapist: [looks at both] Do you want to talk about that?

Caroline: [looks at Daniel] Well, we never have, but, yes, if you think it could help. I've always thought it happened, and we've just had to get on with it.

Daniel: [begins to weep quietly, but says] Caroline haemorrhaged very badly after the birth. They couldn't stop the bleeding; she had to be taken to theatre. At one point, they thought they would have to do a hysterectomy, but, in the end, they didn't. I sat outside the theatre holding Tom, thinking, here I am with this beautiful new baby, and my wife is going to die. It was awful.

Caroline: [moved, looks at Daniel with affection, then, addressing both Daniel and the therapist] I didn't want a blood transfusion, but I probably should have had one. I felt ill for months. Tom cried all the time. I couldn't get breastfeeding started, he didn't seem to be able to latch on to the breast.

Therapist: It seems you both feel Tom's birth went terribly wrong. You were all traumatised, and it sounds as though you haven't recovered since. The delivery, separation from your baby, was so extremely difficult, traumatic, and it seems that separating from him since has become a problem.

The couple sit in silence; I am aware of the sadness in the room, and that we are close to the end of the session.

Therapist: We have thought about very painful issues today, and I am wondering if it would be helpful if we arranged a further session.

They agree they would like to come next week.

Containment and the couple
A clinical commentary for Daniel and Caroline

Eve Ashley

The pared down description of this first session enables the processes of containment and holding to be brought into distinct focus, and it is the concentrating on essentials that gives this session such a strong form. I had the image in my mind of a mother looking at her child who had hurt his knee, holding the child with her gaze on his face, a stripping away of inessentials, and concentrating on the important part—the containing of the pain by the link of understanding.

In the session, there was the initial contact between the couple and the therapist, the hesitation before the problem began to unfold, a strong countertransference response, then, a further unfolding of material, leading to the couple and the therapist both beginning to understand what the problem might be about. On further thinking about this sequence in terms of the containing process, there are different kinds of processes coming in and out of focus throughout, depending on the material, and the states of mind of the couple and the therapist. "The containing process represents an active integration of observation, clarification and emotional resonance" (Sorenson, 1997, p. 121).

The containment work of the therapy began before the first appointment, when fantasies and expectations about what the therapy might mean to this particular couple at this time were generated and held. The pre-meeting thoughts of the therapist were also activated, and, as she walked into the waiting room, she was making observations, adding them up, to be discarded or saved as the session goes on. This process of observation, in itself, is an unconscious act of containment, made conscious when describing the situation verbally or in the form of notes. The unconscious act of containment was recognised by each partner in the couple, and observed by the therapist when Caroline smiled anxiously at her, and Daniel "sums up" the therapist. Caroline felt she could be unguarded; Dan felt he had to be more distant, and it might be that he already felt he was the guilty one. There is a sense of two different maternal transferences to the therapist from them both.

They had requested an urgent appointment, and this request was met by the clinic, so they were offered an initial container to their distress quickly. In some ways, they seemed a little disarmed by this. Caroline said that the clinic was easy to find, and Dan that it was easy to get to from his work. They might have been showing that they found it hard to know if their distress was really urgent, or if they should have been able to manage it for longer on their own.

Caroline began crying after the therapist asked them what had brought them to therapy, and said she had discovered texts on Dan's phone that she thought were evidence of his having an affair. Dan denied it, and repeated that the texts were from a girl at work and they were just having fun. The bitterness with which Caroline responded to this highlighted the fact that there was not much fun in their relationship at the moment, and led Dan to ask her what she expected anyway. At this moment, his phone bleeped, as if to remind everyone that digital distraction from unhappiness was so close all the time.

The therapist queried Dan's expectation, which led to an exchange between the couple where they acknowledged the lack of fun (sex) between them, and then Caroline accused him of being jealous of her relationship with their son, Tom, ever since his birth. She observed that Dan was only happy on his own with Tom, and Dan admitted that that was the only time it felt as though Tom was his son. As the therapist continued to gently clarify what was happening, Caroline revealed to her that Tom still slept in their bed, as he was frightened of the dark and being alone, and that Dan did not understand that. In his turn, Dan said that Tom disturbed their sleep and their sex life, and that Caroline would not think of having another child as "we haven't sorted out having this one yet".

He described the beautiful nursery that was never used, and repeated the fact that he felt there would not be any more babies, either. Then the therapist asked them both if they wanted any more children, exploring their feelings about having another child. Once they had told her that they did, she then went on to ask them more about their relationship. They had been strongly attracted to each other when they first met five and a half years ago, and then Tom had been conceived soon after they were married.

When she asked about the pregnancy and the birth, the therapist was flooded with feelings of panic coming from the couple, and this experience was so intense she could not immediately think about what was being communicated. Using a term from the work of Bion, it was as though she had been assailed by beta elements from the couple. When considering the development of emotional life, Bion (1962) used the term beta elements to describe "not so much memories as undigested facts". He thought that beta elements occur when "the sense impressions of which the patient is aware and the emotions he is experiencing remain unchanged" (pp. 6–7). Beta elements can be changed to alpha elements by the containment of another's thinking mind; this he termed alpha function. The mother offers this through maternal reverie, the therapist through a thinking state of mind.

Once Dan and Caroline had evacuated their troubling experiences in this condensed form into the mind of the therapist, there was the sense that they then felt free to attack each other in a concrete way again. They became much more argumentative with each other, Caroline to justify having Tom in bed with them, and Dan wishing to move him into his own bed.

The therapist continued to contain and think about the panicky feelings, and managed to use the more neutral idea of co-sleeping (initially introduced by Caroline), as a concept to explain their different views of the problem, and this allowed the couple to engage in a different, gentler, way.

Unconsciously, the couple's anxiety had been held in the mind of the therapist, contained by her, and transformed into something that the couple could now take in, digest, and begin to think about, as the experience of the other. The intervention focused on the co-sleeping as the difference between them, rather than on other aspects of their relationship, such as jealousies or the lack of sex life, and this provided a way in to acknowledge the fact that the intimacy between them, and their couple relationship, was being put in jeopardy by Tom sleeping with them. They were both then able to talk together with the therapist about the difficulty of Caroline separating from Tom, and then to go back to the point at which the therapist experienced the panic in the room: the birth of their son, Tom. The therapist invited them to talk about the experience, which they admitted they had not done before.

Dan wept, as he said that Caroline nearly died from loss of blood. It was particularly poignant hearing that he had sat outside the operating theatre with his newborn baby son, not knowing if his wife was going to die, or whether she would have to have a hysterectomy. He was on his own, without a containing mind to help him make sense of the facts. Caroline was moved by his account, and talked about her physical weakness after the birth, and the difficulty in getting Tom to breastfeed over the subsequent months. She said she had not wanted a blood transfusion, although she should probably have had one, and, again, there was the feeling that she was on her own, trying to make a decision without the help and containment of another mind. There was also the idea that she might find it hard to accept help from professionals, as she had turned down the transfusion. Both Caroline and Dan had gone through the traumatic birth experience without the support and understanding they needed to make sense of it. "Many women . . . have felt frightened and traumatized by their experience and are fearful of another delivery" (Reid, 2011, p. 120).

The therapist was then able to collect up her observations, thoughts, and feelings, and to speak to them about the terrible experience that had left them both so traumatised that Caroline was unable to feel that she could separate from Tom. At the time of his birth, she probably felt she was dying, or that he was dying. Dan had thought she might die, and might have felt very guilty over her being the one to go through childbirth.

Hinshelwood says,

> It is the most intense emotions that need the greatest containing capacity. And a team of two is often quite small to provide that containing space for all the considerable intensity. Perhaps this is one reason why a marital couple at the core of a nuclear family is so intense and problematic. (2016, p. 55)

Although this was not explicit in the session, there was a sense that more of the role of the container of emotion within the couple had fallen on Dan, and his participating in a "bit of fun" was a sign that the burden had been shouldered by him for too long.

From the perspective of a child psychotherapist, the concerns for Tom in this situation would centre around the likelihood that he has not had much experience of his parents being a couple in his mind. He has grown to that of a school age child, with strong fantasies of being his mother's partner, as his occupation of his parent's bed has apparently left him feeling in control of his mother and father's intimacy, and the possibility of any further children.

Caroline observed that Dan is happiest when he is on his own with his son, and that he hates it when the three of them are together. Dan says it is the only time that Tom feels like his son, as though when the three of them are together, Dan cannot feel like a father, or a husband, as, in his mind, his son has become his wife's partner.

Tom has not had the full opportunity of experiencing being on the outside of his parents' relationship, and being able to mourn the loss of his exclusive bond with his mother. Being able to let go of the idealised relationship with his mother would be the beginning of his consideration of other relationships, and being able to view himself and others objectively.

As Britton (1989) has described,

> If the link between the parents perceived in love and hate can be tolerated in the child's mind, it provides him with the prototype for an object relationship of a third kind, in which he is a witness and not a participant. (p. 87)

Oedipal issues, combined with problems in establishing a good relationship with his mother from the beginning, when she was struggling to breastfeed him, could complicate Tom's ability to come to terms with change and loss as he develops.

In this one session, where so little is known about the couple, their past, their families of origin, or their individual psychologies, a huge landscape is uncovered, from a text message to a scene of birth and possible death, from a small piece of writing on a mobile phone to a scene of enduring pain at the beginning of life. I think that this session shows the capacity of the therapist to contain the feelings that they are all struggling with in different ways, and to create a landscape where there is meaning and connection across time, people, and events.

Oedipal dynamics and the "white heat" of the session
A clinical commentary for Daniel and Caroline

Brett Kahr

Many years ago, one of my former teachers, the distinguished child psychiatrist and psychoanalyst Dr Susanna Isaacs Elmhirst (1996), told me a lovely and little known story about two of *her* mentors, Dr Wilfred Bion, her former supervisor, and Dr Donald Winnicott, whom she succeeded as head of the psychology department at the Paddington Green Children's Hospital in London. Elmhirst reminisced about a meeting at the British Psychoanalytical Society when Winnicott discussed the intensity of undertaking psychoanalytical work and, in his characteristic literary fashion, he referred to the "white heat" of the consulting room as a revealing metaphor for what transpires therein. Although Winnicott and Bion rarely saw eye to eye, it seems that on this occasion Bion agreed with Winnicott wholeheartedly, and both men came to use this phrase—"white heat"—as an evocative descriptor of our work.

Commenting upon the intimate "white heat" experienced in the consulting room by a clinical colleague from the safe and faraway distance of one's study seems rather akin to being asked to speak about Laurence Olivier's performance as Hamlet simply on the basis of having read a theatre review of the play in one of the broadsheets. Without having seen the psychotherapist's facial expressions, without having heard the tone of her voice, without having observed the nods of her head, and without having absorbed the private and idiosyncratic atmosphere of the session, one can only describe oneself as hard-pressed to offer any reliable thoughts. Yet, in spite of the fact that my comments must derive solely from a brief summary of a preliminary consultation, I do know, none the less, that this colleague has undertaken an impressive piece of clinical work with the couple in question, and has managed, in the course of one initial session, to provide a space in which secrets could be revealed, tears could be shed, traumatic experiences could be unearthed, and a request granted for a second session in order to continue the process.

Clearly, the clinician in question has, indeed, survived what Bion and Winnicott referred to as the "white heat", and she has managed most skilfully to create a space for calm and creative reflection in which this decent but, nevertheless, troubled couple could begin to undertake some necessary psychological work.

Although one could offer views on many of the different aspects of this first seventy-five-minute consultation, I will focus my further thoughts upon the presence of one particular set of dynamics which, I will argue, remains crucial for our understanding: that is, the role of the Oedipus complex in the psychical life of both Caroline and Daniel.

From the very outset, the psychotherapist in question—whether consciously or, perhaps, unconsciously—has offered her readers a number of very revealing and intriguing clues that the marriage between Caroline and Daniel might be rather complex, strugglesome, and also, perhaps, a bit overcrowded. For instance, at the very outset, the clinician has taken the trouble to inform us that, "When I go to the waiting room my first impression is that the couple do not look as though they are together. They are sitting close, but look quite detached from each other. I only know that they are the couple booked in to see me since they are the only two people in the waiting room".

I must confess that when I read this initial description, I wondered why the psychotherapist took such pains to refer to Caroline and Daniel as "the only two people in the waiting room". After all, she could easily have begun the description of the session, more traditionally, after the couple had entered the consulting room. I do wonder whether, quite unconsciously, the psychotherapist sensed something important about being "the only two people", as if the presence of a *third* would be damning or dangerous in some way. Her sensitivity to the number of persons in view seems perhaps of some small significance.

I then found myself quite struck that when the psychotherapist greeted the couple, Caroline introduced herself by her full forename, whereas Daniel, by contrast, referred to himself in the diminutive, as "Dan". After this introduction, the psychotherapist then asked her new male patient, quite revealingly, "if he would like me to call him Dan or Daniel". This tiny detail caught my attention, and I began to wonder why the psychotherapist would use up precious time to clarify by what name the patient might wish to be addressed when he had *already*, quite *clearly*, selected the moniker "Dan". Although I cannot be certain, I did wonder whether the psychotherapist might have sensed, however unconsciously, that "Dan"—the shortened (indeed, *castrated*) form of "Daniel"—might not sit entirely comfortably with this gentleman.

Whether my preoccupation with these immensely tiny moments of clinical interaction—both of which took place in the waiting room, prior to the start of the first consultation—reveal anything of relevance we must leave to the author to decide for herself. But I wonder whether we already have some evidence of a couple struggling to function as a twosome in the presence of a third, and of a man struggling to feel fully potent.

Within a short while, we learn that Caroline and Daniel find themselves in great difficulty, in part, because they have a four-year-old son, "Tom", who still sleeps in the parental bed. As Daniel explains, "He should be in his own bed. He interferes with our sleep because he tosses and turns. We hardly ever have sex because he's there". Thus, as often unfolds in couple psychoanalytical work, we find ourselves instantly transported into the oedipal bedroom, and we become witnesses to the couple's challenge in sharing the space with a third person. In other words, the young son has intruded himself between the mother and the father, forging an unusually close alliance with Caroline, and rendering Daniel excluded and bereft.

In October 1897, Dr Sigmund Freud wrote to his colleague, Dr Wilhelm Fliess, about the universal preoccupation with the legend of Oedipus, underscoring that, "die griechische Sage greift einen Zwang auf, den jeder anerkennt, weil er dessen Existenz in sich verspürt hat" ("the Greek legend seizes on a compulsion which everyone recognises because he senses its existence within himself") (Masson, 1985, p. 272). Caroline, Daniel, and their son remain no exceptions to this fundamental bedrock of human psychology. The four-year-old boy desires to overthrow his annoying father so that he can enjoy more exclusive access to the mother. Similarly, Daniel, the father, feels castrated and overthrown by his own son—more of a "Dan" than a "Daniel"—and, like Laius from Greek legend, he resents the child and might even wish to rid himself of this annoying rival. Caroline, by contrast, enjoys the unconscious incestuous attentions of the son, and she uses her intimacy with her child as a means of soothing her own sense of woundedness, and as a weapon with which to torment her husband, whom she suspects of having some sort of extramarital affair.

In many respects, the dynamics of the case of Caroline and Daniel could not be more classical.

Couple psychoanalytical practitioners will be only too familiar with the challenge of triangulation in partners who have become parents. Indeed, Tavistock Relationships in London has developed quite a speciality, over many decades, in exploring the impact of such a struggle. Caroline experiences jealousy towards Daniel for having a girlfriend. Daniel experiences jealousy towards Tom for his extremely close relationship with his mother, and it would not be unreasonable to assume that Tom, the four-year-old son, might experience some jealousy towards his father for taking up too much space in the marital bed, which he longs to inhabit. In many respects, the drama of Caroline and Daniel absolutely epitomises classical psychoanalytical psychology and its emphasis on oedipal dynamics.

Caroline, the female partner, encapsulates the pain experienced by the family when she exclaims to Dan, the male partner, "Look, I know jealousy when I see it. You hate it when Tom wants my attention. I see the look on your face. You are only happy with him when you've got him on your own. You hate it when all three of us are together". This sort of expostulation underscores the extreme challenge experienced by every *twosome* who must, somehow, find a way to become a *threesome*.

The psychotherapist, to her great credit, perseveres in her attempts to understand this new couple who bombard her with accusations of jealousy and infidelity. Indeed, at one point, the clinician confesses privately, "I am flooded with a feeling of panic, and am shocked by the intensity of feelings. I cannot think. I want to get rid of the feeling, yet struggle to process it in some way". In other words, she has become fully immersed in the "white heat" of the session, and she finds herself overwhelmed by the oedipal dynamics contained herein, perhaps identifying unconsciously with the unwanted "third" party.

Happily, this skilled practitioner processes her experiences and recovers her fine mind, and then renders a series of very useful interpretations. First, she offers an observation that Daniel feels excluded from Caroline's intimate relationship with her son, and she emphasises "Dan wants to reclaim you". This comment helps Caroline to understand her husband's feeling of exclusion. After a "poignant silence", the couple begins to talk for the very first time about the fact that Caroline nearly died while giving birth to Tom, having begun to haemorrhage in the process. Heartbreakingly, Daniel sat outside the operating theatre at the hospital, holding his newborn baby son, fearing that his wife would soon be dead.

The psychotherapist then delivers a second interpretation: "It seems you both feel Tom's birth went terribly wrong. You were all traumatised and it sounds as though you haven't recovered since. The delivery, separation from your baby was so extremely difficult, traumatic, and it seems that separating from him since has become a problem". By interpreting the fear that separation might result in death—either Caroline's separation from her baby, or Daniel's separation from his wife—the psychotherapist has placed the idea of ruptured attachment quite helpfully on the agenda, ripe for further examination. This allows the couple to weep and to experience the sadness, rather than the aggression, which had characterised the earlier part of the session. As the seventy-five-minute meeting nears its conclusion, Caroline and Daniel request a further appointment.

The case of Caroline and Daniel illustrates the prevalence of oedipal dynamics in, perhaps, every human family. As Freud helped us to understand, each member of the family craves deep intimacy with his or her primary love-object, and when another stands in the way of that exclusivity—such as a father who prevents a little boy from having full access to the mother—everyone becomes murderous as a response.

As I scoured through this deftly written case, I found myself particularly absorbed by two further linguistic clues. At one point, Caroline, defending her wish to keep her four-year-old son in her bed, attempts a justification and she notes, "there are lots of cultures where the child sleeps with the parent". Later on, Daniel, in speaking of Caroline's near-death at the point of delivering her baby, explains, "They couldn't stop the bleeding, she had to be taken to theatre". Associating to these literary phrases, I found myself agreeing with Caroline that in lots of cultures, children do sleep with their parents, and, in particular, cultures such as ancient Greece in the time of Oedipus. I also found myself thinking about Daniel's reference to the "theatre". Although he spoke about the surgical operating theatre in the hospital, he also unwittingly described something of the outdoor theatre known to the ancient Greeks and, later, to Sigmund Freud— all about the drama of the young man, immortalised by Sophocles, who loved his mother and who killed his father. Unwittingly, Caroline and Daniel have taken us on a theatrical journey to ancient Greece . . . and the psychotherapist in question had certainly sensed that this might be the case.

The story of Oedipus has become archetypal, and we owe Freud a great debt of thanks for emphasising its importance in human psychology.

We also extend a warm appreciation to the highly competent couple psychotherapist for her ability to recognise these dynamics in the case of Caroline and Daniel. Indeed, one hopes that such an understanding will have permitted her to be of profound help and support to this troubled couple in the weeks and months that followed.

Some years ago, the noted British psychiatrist, Dr Peter Sainsbury, by no means a Freudian, confessed that, "I have always preferred dry facts to juicy theories" (quoted in Freeman, 1988, p. 165). Sainsbury devoted his professional life to the study of experimental psychopathology, in search of dry facts, and he never became a Freudian. However, for those of us who *have* derived inspiration from Freud, and who continue to do so, we salute the Viennese maestro for his capacity to have enjoyed juicy theories, and none more exciting and gripping and, also, of the greatest clinical inspiration than that inspired by *Oedipus Rex*.

Shared couple defences against anxiety
A clinical commentary for Daniel and Caroline

Monica Lanman

This story conveys the first part of what would clearly have to be a two-part consultation, since this first part is confined to the couple's recent and present situation. In a full consultation process, there would normally be some "triangulation", exploring what occurs in the room, what is going on in the couple's external life, and their early experience. Within that, the therapist can begin to develop hypotheses about why the couple are in difficulty, test those by making trial interpretations, and develop them as a result of the couple's responses. At this stage, my commentary is necessarily speculative, largely a matter of describing the tentative, associative ideas as they arise in my mind while reading the account. These would then need to be tested and modified by further exploration.

In this account, the therapist asks in the waiting room whether Daniel would like to be called Daniel or Dan, when he has just introduced himself as Dan, and then introduces herself a second time once they get into the consulting room. I wonder whether she might be responding to projected anxiety, perhaps that conveyed by the couple's having requested an urgent appointment. It seems as though she wants to reduce their, and perhaps her own, anxiety, and so ends up being a little over-solicitous. Such attempted anxiety reduction tells us something, possibly about the intensity of what the couple is experiencing and projecting.

The therapist notes how separate the partners appear when first encountered in the waiting room, although we are not told what she made of this. Once in the consulting room, the couple convey eagerness, talking of how convenient the place was to find. But the therapist feels the atmosphere is tense, increasingly so when they are silent in response to her invitation to tell her what brought them. She senses aggression from each to the other, and then Caroline tearfully blurts out that Dan has been having an affair.

Dan belittles the accusation, denying an affair, and claiming he has "just been having some fun". And then he throws in a retaliatory accusation with "what do you expect?" Caroline got her accusation in first, and Dan retaliates; attack seems to be a form of defence both use against what later emerges as a powerful shared anxiety. They are enacting in the room a pattern of fighting over painful experience (the more "paranoid–schizoid" state of mind, where things are either/or and threatening), rather than being able to be empathically thought about together ("depressive", where there is more room for doubt, empathy, and ambiguity). Even Dan's phone, bleeping with a message, seems to be a weapon in the fight (of course, we wonder whether the bleep was another message from his work "fun" partner).

The therapist opts to seek further information, asking what Dan meant by "What do you expect". Caroline answers, ending up accusing Dan of always having been jealous of their four-year-old son, Tom. Each claims to be the one with hurt feelings (as if it were either/or, rather than a more "depressive" both). The therapist asks more questions, having to do so because the couple are so engrossed in attacking each other that their wish for the therapist to understand seems to have been pushed aside. Fighting has displaced awareness of their dependency. The therapist asks for each partner's view, thus modelling the attention-giving they each need. Perhaps, her caution about commenting is partly a result of sensing the strength of the anxiety behind this defensiveness in both partners.

The couple describe how Caroline puts Tom to bed in their bed, and lets him stay there all night, claiming that he is frightened of the dark. She throws in two justifications for the behaviour, as if aware at some level that the first one is unconvincing (apparently, she never even tries to put Tom to bed in his own room). Dan says he feels Tom is only properly his son when he is alone with him.

At this point, I am wondering if Caroline is unconsciously using Tom to maintain a distance from Dan, and also thinking that she awards Tom a special position, always sharing his parents' evening and bed. I speculate that she is fearful of helping Tom to face any limits to his power to get what he wants, and that her fear might contribute to Tom's own fear of separation, as well as possibly to unconscious anxiety in him about his power to disrupt his parents' relationship. I also wonder which of these things might have resonance with Caroline's own early experience, and with Dan's.

It seems that each partner has difficulty managing the experience of being part of that underlying reality that all children have to navigate, a threesome. In this case, there are two heterosexual parents present, as in the classical theory of the Oedipus complex. However, post-Kleinian psychoanalytic work has shown how this theory applies to whatever "third party" begins to impinge on the experience of the baby, spoiling his illusion of receiving uninterrupted attention from the primary carer. The interruption could be the carer's job, or phone calls, or even just the carer's daydreaming and preoccupation about things other than the baby, which the baby has to tolerate. If the impingement is brief at first, and well enough managed, it is developmentally valuable, but if it is abrupt and severe, then extreme forms of defensiveness are likely to be provoked in the baby that can seriously damage development. The pain that awareness of such impingement brings can be intolerable, provoking denial, projection of blame, and omnipotent moves to assert control by clinging to the primary carer. The baby might sense the resentment this provokes, and this increases his terror of abandonment.

Extreme, primitive defences are an unconscious attempt to evade an experience that seems too much to bear, at the cost of denying and distorting psychic reality. Grier, in his Introduction to *Oedipus and the Couple* (2005b), highlights the defences of three couples in Sophocles' play, *Oedipus Rex*: there is Laius and Jocasta, who saw their infant son as such a threat to their relationship they tried to have him killed; there is the adoptive couple, the King and Queen of Corinth, who cannot acknowledge to Oedipus the reality of not being his birth parents; and there is the "tragic adult couple of Oedipus and Jocasta" who "turned a blind eye" (Steiner, 1985) to the clues, which they knew and denied, to the truth about their union. Three forms of turning away from difficult reality, which combine to bring about the very catastrophe they all tried to avoid.

Very often, when we see couples, we hear that their trouble began when the first baby arrived. Although, of course, there are all sorts of obvious strains imposed on anyone caring for a young child, couples often also convey their individual and joint lack of adequate negotiation of the oedipal situation for themselves originally, and, now, for their child. They have become stuck in some form of primitive defence against it that hurts all three. In our couple, Caroline wants to preserve a phantasy that all three are equal, and can stay there for ever, while Dan feels shut out from his rightful place, jealous, furious, and despairing. He appears to be taking revenge by turning to someone else. The couple's relationship and the child's development are in jeopardy. Neither parent seems able to create a comfortable form of threesome, where each party would have an appropriate place, facilitating the child's development, so he can gradually separate (we are told that Tom also has difficulty leaving Caroline when he goes to nursery). Each parent feels a special link with Tom, but in competition with each other. No wonder they looked so separate in the waiting room. They see each other as a threat to the security each desperately seeks. Caroline expresses this as Tom's fear (of separation), but her behaviour confirms that it is also her own fear, while increasing the likelihood that Dan will abandon her. Dan expresses his fear by attacking, and so endangering the relationship he feels excluded from. Each projects into the other hostility to the parental couple. Each identifies with the potentially excluded child, and, perhaps, seeks relief or revenge by evoking in the other the experience of being excluded.

In addition to their mutual attacks, the couple's very either/or statements about each other are clues to the primitive nature of the defences employed. Caroline: "I know you say to everyone, 'He's my son,' as though you are really proud of him, but really you're just jealous." Dan: "... when I'm alone with him it's different. It's the only time that he feels like my son." Perceptions are binary: you are either for me or against me; either you are hurting or I am; either you are wrong or I am; either my mother has abandoned me for ever and I will die, or she will never leave me. Nuance and degrees of disappointment and uncertainty are too sophisticated, too "adult"; indeed they are unbearable, when one is in this infantile state of mind (again "paranoid–schizoid" rather than "depressive").

The couple continue angrily, until the therapist makes her first interpretative comment, "I wonder if perhaps Dan wants to reclaim you and that he is saying he always feels he has to share you", and then they soften. Now they can respond more "depressively" to the therapist's capacity to reach the need of both. Soon, as a result of the therapist's sensitive use of her countertransference (an emotional surge inside herself in response to a question which the couple ignored), she is allowed to know more of their terror, the story of their traumatic experience of separation, when Caroline nearly died giving birth four years ago. Dan says, " I sat outside the theatre holding Tom, thinking, here I am with this beautiful new baby, and my wife is going to die. It was awful." Suddenly, his earlier statement about only feeling Tom is his son when he is alone with him is cast in a new light.

I think the therapist is right that the couple have not got over that traumatic introduction to being a threesome. It is associated with fear of death. Even though the wish to delay a second pregnancy is attributed to Caroline, perhaps both of them are afraid of it. I also wonder whether the couple might unconsciously blame the child for causing the danger they faced of nearly losing each other, through death. This could contribute to their difficulty in being firm with Tom, in moving him out of their bed, which might feel as if it would be done out of this unconscious anger. Again, this is expressed as Caroline's problem, but Dan is likely to be involved at some level, too. One of the principles of couple therapy is always to look for such shared unconscious ideas, which often appear to belong to just one partner (unconsciously projected by the other). Again, we might be seeing a primitive defence, whereby each uses the other as a repository for unwanted feelings.

The story we have indicates primitive defensive functioning in response to recent trauma. It leaves me speculating that part of the unconscious power of that trauma will turn out to lie in some kind of damaging early experience for each partner in negotiating the "oedipal situation" as children themselves.

Trauma, the first born, and the oedipal situation
A clinical commentary for Daniel and Caroline

Sara Leon

My comments about this first assessment session with the couple are drawn from my experience as a psychoanalytic couple psychotherapist and a psychoanalytic child psychotherapist. As no information about the couple's history is available, individually or as a couple, my initial thoughts are based on the clinical material, as it has been presented, which might well change shape and develop in the course of ongoing psychotherapy.

The therapist immediately creates a picture of sadness, as she describes the couple sitting alone in the waiting room, cloaked in an air of despair, with no spark of life or connection between them. Their request for an urgent appointment would have alerted the therapist to the possibility that something quite serious was going on. The way they were dressed and how they greeted the therapist further conveyed something of their states of mind. Caroline's anxious smile and casual dress might have suggested that she was in touch with more vulnerable feelings, while Daniel seemed a little more wary and self-protected in his well-cut suit, as if, perhaps, the couple's distress might be more located in Caroline.

There was eagerness to attend the appointment, as both expressed how easy the clinic was to find, suggesting there were no obstacles, physical or psychological, that got in the way of their reaching the appointment. However, when the therapist invited them to explain what had brought them, the atmosphere became tense and hostile.

Both members of the couple started the session from a position of attack and defence. Caroline wasted little time in accusing Daniel of having an affair with a female colleague, which he denied. Caroline, in turn, denied checking on him by reading the message on his mobile phone, communicating a sense she had read the text quite by chance, as he had been out of the room. This brief encounter raises many questions. Why was she so utterly convinced of his alleged affair? Why did she pick up his mobile phone and read his message(s)? Why was Daniel having "fun" conversations with a female colleague? If he was having an affair, why did he leave his mobile phone around for his wife to access it so easily? Also, even if Daniel were having an affair, what made this appointment so urgent, an urgency that seemed to engender a feeling of life and death?

Although we know little of the couple's past history, we do learn later in the session about the trauma surrounding the birth of their first born almost four years earlier, and that Caroline had almost died. Since this terrifying moment in time, they seemed to have lost a sense of being a couple, in every way. They could not talk about the birth experience, they have been unable to have sex, and they were struggling in parenting their first child together. It would seem that both were tangled in a web of trauma that gripped them so tightly they were unable to free themselves and each other. They might have feared that talking or having sex might lead to having another baby which, in their minds, might mean Caroline was at risk of dying. This was possibly the catastrophe they were both avoiding by letting Tom sleep in their bed. Although I think it is likely that this fear was shared by the couple, in the session, Daniel located this problem in Caroline. It was her fault they were not having sex, because she could not separate from Tom, and there was no sense that Daniel, as the father, might help mother and infant in the separation process.

The strength of Caroline's conviction about Daniel's possible affair might have also come from a sense of guilt about not having had sex for such a long time, and her assumption that Daniel was having his sexual needs met by someone else. Caroline might, therefore, have felt profoundly guilty about not feeling able to engage intimately in sexual activity, but also extremely enraged that she was the victim of circumstances. It would seem she projected her bad feelings into Daniel. Alternately, her unconscious and uncontained feelings might have left her feeling so persecuted and bad that she unconsciously felt she deserved to be punished by Daniel having an affair, and, ultimately, to be left and abandoned.

For his part, Daniel also suffered from the loss of a containing and rewarding couple relationship. Neither were able to talk about their experiences, and perhaps the only way, unwittingly or intuitively, that Daniel felt able to get through to Caroline was via his mobile phone. He was at work, partly in the world, and in touch with more ordinary life, which he wanted back in his relationship. What stopped him from really pursuing intimacy with his wife? Did he also feel guilty about what he had done in his mind, albeit unconsciously, and was he persecuted by a tormenting feeling that it was he who almost killed his wife? Is this what she unconsciously meant, when she accused him of doing something bad (having an affair), but really suggesting that he had almost killed her by giving her a baby? Thus, she could be seen to be punishing him for this by withholding sex.

It is also interesting to speculate about Daniel's alleged affair. Daniel claimed that it was only fun, though, consciously or unconsciously, he and his female colleague exchanged text messages that appeared to be somewhat more intimate than ordinary work emails. We know from the session that the couple had not found a way of communicating about the impenetrable darkness between them, and one could argue that, feeling desperate, Daniel was trying to get through to Caroline by "accidentally" leaving his mobile phone around for her to read. His message(s) might have been an SOS to Caroline via his colleague.

I think there is plenty in this brief session to suggest that the couple shared an unconscious fear of being abandoned. This fear kept them tightly together, and any degree of separation might well have been experienced at some level as life threatening. For example, they started a relationship with each other very quickly, and left no time before they got married and had a child, as if wanting to cement the relationship so securely that the other could not disappear. As a couple, it would appear that they had not been through the process of slowly getting to know each other and having the opportunity to develop their relationship on firm ground. In the same way, they had not been able to help their son to separate and sleep in his own bed or transfer to the nursery. Perhaps, in their minds, there was something dark and frightening about separation that predated their experience of childbirth. We are not told of their experiences growing up, but it would be reasonable to assume that neither had been helped developmentally to separate.

It is arguable that each separation we experience, starting from birth and weaning, and, in fact, all through our lives, is a preparation for our final separation of death, when we leave the world for the last time. So, if Caroline and Daniel had not processed the separations they encountered in ordinary developmental ways, to be faced with death at a point where they anticipated one of the most joyous moments of their lives must have been very frightening and devastating. They were left unable to put into words the terror they experienced around the birth of Tom, suggesting that both might have experienced some kind of difficulty while separating from their primary object at a very early, preverbal, stage in their lives. This could account for the fact that they were unable to come together and speak about their feelings: instead, both seemed to have felt alone in a dark place without words. Fortunately, with the help of the therapist, they began to articulate feelings and words, and this helped them to be in touch with their shared experience of terror. In turn, the shared awareness of what was, for both, unthinkable and unspeakable enabled them to reconnect in compassion.

Closely linked to the couple's shared difficulties in separation is the Oedipus complex, which was discovered by Freud (1924d) and has been recognised in psychoanalytic work as the central conflict in human development. Klein (1975d[1945]) thought that the oedipal situation began much earlier than Freud, when the infant begins the weaning process from the mother's breast and turns towards the father. This is the beginning of the triangular relationship. It is a complicated psychological organisation that is underpinned by the boy's attachment to the mother and the girl's attachment to the father. Likierman (2001) reminds us just how hard separating can be when the primary object is "invested with a fundamental life-giving significance and introjected to form the core of the ego . . . It develops to provide the foundation for hope, trust and goodness" (p. 119).

Put simply, working through oedipal longings means that the love and loss of the parent of the opposite sex is accepted, and the parents as a sexual couple are recognised. Britton (1989) claims that this successful negotiation of the Oedipus complex is inextricably linked to Klein's (1975d[1945]) concept of the depressive position. One cannot be resolved without the other, and these developments form the basis of good mental health, as the child slowly begins to accept this reality. Having secured a place for himself or herself in relation to the parental couple, the child is more likely to feel confident about his or her place in the world, and will have internalised a good template for all subsequent relationships. Britton (1998c) also reminds us that these developments are part of a never-ending process, and need to be renegotiated, to a certain extent, throughout life.

I think it is reasonable to assume that neither Caroline nor Daniel managed to negotiate and sufficiently work through the oedipal situation in their original families, considering that, after Tom's birth, which was complicated by trauma, neither appeared to have had the internal capacity and the belief that their relationship was robust enough to manage the introduction of a third. The fact that they could not speak about this again reinforces the possibility that their difficulties in the oedipal struggle were preverbal.

Another indication that this developmental phase did not go smoothly could be detected in Daniel's comment about "the beautiful nursery, every woman's dream", which had hardly been used. Perhaps, both Caroline and Daniel held an idealistic, as opposed to realistic, idea of what being a parent means; that having a baby entails both managing anxieties as well as the joys that are evoked in being a parent, and that, especially for a couple with their first child, having a newborn, the third, in their relationship is a momentous change.

What finally jolted the couple out of their trauma and propelled them into therapy was Caroline's fear of Daniel abandoning her for another woman in the workplace. Suddenly, the situation that they had tolerated for almost four years became urgent, and the couple sought help at last. The fact that they were ready to talk openly and honestly to the therapist enabled their anger and grievances to shift into more tender feelings, suggesting that this couple are committed to each other, and that there is hope that they will recover from this deadly state into a healthier couple state.

CHAPTER EIGHT

Greg and Lottie

The couple's general practitioner referred Greg (aged forty) and Lottie (aged thirty) for couple psychotherapy, as she was concerned that both members of the couple seemed unhappy, following their marriage eighteen months earlier. Lottie, in particular, had spoken to her about how difficult she was finding being married to Greg. The GP was also concerned that Lottie often spoke crossly about her two stepchildren, Selina and Alicia.

The GP mentioned that Greg had developed a reactive depression, following his first wife, Georgina's, death, four years earlier, and had been prescribed antidepressant medication, Citalopram 30 mg, by the psychiatrist he had seen at the time. He took this medication for nine months, before, with the support of his psychiatrist, he was slowly weaned off antidepressants; he saw a bereavement counsellor for approximately one year. He no longer sees the psychiatrist.

Greg's first wife developed an aggressive form of cancer, when she was thirty-five years of age, and died within six months of the diagnosis, four years ago. The couple had been married for ten years, and had two children. Selina, now ten years of age, was six at the time of her mother's death. Alicia, now seven years of age, was three when her mother died. Greg's mother and his late wife, Georgina's, mother had become good friends, and, when Georgina became ill, they immediately stepped in and looked after the children. Following Georgina's death, they continued to offer considerable support and practical help to Greg and the girls.

Greg and Lottie met about eighteen months after Georgina's death, at a quiz night arranged by the Rotary Club to raise funds for their local hospice. It was not long after Greg's counselling had ended. Lottie and Greg enjoyed each other's company, and soon started to see one another. Lottie thought Greg was a wonderful father, and felt sorry for the two little girls. She immediately said "yes", when he asked her to marry him, about a year later. The couple are living in the house that was Greg and Georgina's marital home, as Greg does not want to disrupt the children. Both Greg and Georgina's mothers thought the marriage was too soon, but, according to Greg, they have done their best to welcome Lottie and support her.

Both members of the couple work in finance. When Lottie met Greg, she had just returned from working in the USA for several years. The return to England coincided with the end of a fairly long-standing relationship, and Lottie has acknowledged that she was upset by this relationship coming to an end. Of particular note is the fact that, in Lottie's family of origin, there was a cot death of a baby boy, Matthew, prior to her birth. Soon after Lottie's birth, her mother conceived again, and gave birth to a son, Christopher. Lottie maintains that she "always felt like second best", and although she and her younger brother get on well, her relationship with her mother is strained. Her parents' marriage broke up, soon after the birth of her brother. Lottie has said her mother only stayed with her father long enough to have another son. After her parents separated, Lottie did not see much of her father, as he moved a considerable distance away. It was only when she reached her teenage years that she was able to establish a closer relationship with him.

Greg's parents are together, and he speaks of them getting on well. He has a younger brother and sister, and his family are close. When Greg and Lottie first met, she liked Greg's family, although she does find them a little formal. Greg has spoken of the family's considerable distress when his wife Georgina became ill, and died: "they all loved her so much".

The couple have been attending couple psychotherapy for two months. The focus of the work has been that Lottie feels she lives in Georgina's shadow, and that Selina hates her. She finds Alicia an easier child, but says that Selina often encourages Alicia to be difficult when she is with the two girls. Lottie does not think that Greg stands up for her when the girls are being "obnoxious". She says that she very much wants to conceive herself, but Greg is worried this will upset his daughters. Greg's view is that the girls have been through so much with their mother's death that they simply need continuity and stability.

Both members of the couple enjoy their work. Greg often has to travel abroad, but both have flexible work patterns, and the therapist has noted that, although there are considerable difficulties in the marriage, they form a good team when discussing work and in making arrangements for child care. The couple arrive on time and pay their invoice promptly.

Consulting room

The therapist lets the couple into the clinic when they press the buzzer. On this occasion, Greg is carrying an overnight bag and the therapist recalls that he was going to be away for two days this week, but thought he would be back in time for their session. They usually arrive together.

The therapist always thinks that they appear as a good-looking couple, who look right together. The couple sit in their usual chairs. Lottie looks strained and unhappy. As usual, the couple look smart: Greg is wearing a well-cut suit, and Lottie trousers and a stylish jacket. The therapist thinks that there does not seem to be any sense of warmth between the couple, and finds herself thinking that Greg has been away, and wondering if they have spoken to each other since his return. Greg is the first to speak.

Greg: I thought I was going to be late, as there was fog at the airport. In the end, we were only delayed about half an hour. I hate it when flights are delayed.

Lottie: Well, you might have rung me when you landed, so that I knew you would be able to get here.

Greg: I just rushed for the tube, there's no signal there. Lottie was ahead of me, when I came out of the station. [He turns to Lottie] How were the girls while I was away?

Lottie: [looks fed up] The girls were a nightmare! Well, Selina was. Alicia can be quite sweet when she's on her own, but then Selina makes sure that Alicia is upset. Last night, they said they didn't like the supper I made. They love that chicken breast in tomato sauce recipe that you make, but they said you do it differently, and then Selina said she didn't like to think they were eating chicken. She said they keep chickens at school, they give them all names, and Mrs Taffety is Alicia's favourite chicken. Then Alicia became upset, and wanted to know if we were eating Mrs Taffety. She didn't believe me when I said, of course not. Neither of them would eat it in the end. Then Selina said that Mummy only liked strawberry ice-cream, when she saw I'd bought that lovely chocolate ice-cream we had the other week. After supper, when I tried to help Alicia with her arithmetic homework, Selina assured me that they weren't taught to do it that way. Alicia ended up crying, because she thought the teacher would be cross that she had done it wrong, and then Selina blamed me that Alicia was crying.

Lottie begins to cry.

Therapist: That sounds difficult. Maybe you feel disappointed and angry, as well as sad.

Lottie: I did feel upset. I tried to make a nice evening for the girls, as Greg was away, and, then, it was all ruined. Selina hates me, it doesn't matter what I do!

Greg: [looks surprised] Well, I don't think that's the case. It's just that you are not her mother. Mum said the girls were great when she had them overnight on Wednesday. Do you think they were just a bit tired; it was Thursday night? Of course, Selina has netball on Thursday afternoon, she's always a bit scratchy, if her team doesn't win. Do you know if her team won?

Lottie: I don't pretend to be her mother, but I do try to look after her, and make sure she's all right! I sometimes wonder if your mother does wind them up a bit, when they stay with her, though.

Greg: That's ridiculous.

Lottie: Well, they *are* often even more upset with me when they've been staying with her. But that's not the point, you know the girls can be difficult with me, and you never support me. They always come first.

Greg: You know I worry about the girls all the time. Of course, I do. They've lost their mother, and they are having to get used to someone else. Alicia was very young when Georgina died, she doesn't remember her very well, but Selina does. She knows Lottie does things differently from her mother, and she's always taken care of her little sister. I know Georgina talked to her about taking care of Alicia before she died.

Therapist: That could be quite a burden for Selina.

There is quite a long pause.

Therapist:	I wonder how you feel, Lottie, about Greg saying, "How were the girls", at the start of the session, and then saying that "you are not their mother"?
Lottie:	I feel he's just being cruel. It's always about the girls. He knows I'd like us to have children of our own, and then he says that.
Therapist:	Perhaps there is a shared feeling that there is something very cruel and disturbing when anyone remembers that Lottie is not the children's biological mother. That could be for you, Greg, or Lottie, the girls, or even Greg's mother.
Lottie:	He's always telling me I'm not the girl's mother. Well, not in so many words, but he never backs me up. I never feel he supports me, or lets me set any rules. It can be a nightmare getting out of the house in the morning and getting the girls to bed. It's hopeless.

Lottie looks upset. Greg looks baffled.

Greg:	Well, Lottie isn't the girl's mother. She should understand that the girls miss their mother every single day of their lives. When they wake up in the morning, she's not there. When they come home from school, she's not there, and when they go to bed, she still isn't there. Lottie should understand, she should make allowances, not just criticise them.
Lottie:	I do understand it's hard for them, not that I ever felt that way about my own mother, she was never really there for me. I really try to make life nice for them. But you never support me. I just live in the shadow of this perfect dead woman. Perfect wife. Perfect mother. Her photographs are everywhere in the house. I know you're always looking at her with them.
Greg:	What do you expect me to do? Put all the photographs of the children's mother out of sight? Of course, they need photographs of her around the house.
Therapist:	I keep thinking about loss, and wondering whether you were both worried that you were going to miss your session today. Greg, you were worried the plane was late. Lottie, you weren't sure Greg was going to get here. A connection between you was not made . . .
Greg:	[interrupts, looking sulky] We always talked about it being hard for the girls. It wasn't that long after their mother died that we met.
Therapist:	Perhaps it's hard for all of you? Children often express the grief and rage that their parents cannot express.
Lottie:	You've changed so much. You really wanted us to get married.
Greg:	You don't think you have?
Therapist:	Greg, you talked about fog at the airport. I think it's almost as though there is fog in the room today. Perhaps around grief, but

also the guilt and anger that you feel about Georgina's death. Mourning someone who has been in your life for a long time is so hard, and I think you feel terribly guilty about moving on and having a life with Lottie. It's possible that you both feel disturbed about having to live with a shadow, in the fog.

Greg: [responds immediately] Yes, I had a great meeting, while I was away, and I thought Lottie would understand why I was so pleased about it. Then, I felt bad for Georgina. She didn't really understand my passion for finance; she was much more a people person. I like the way Lottie understands about my work.

Therapist: You seem to be talking about sharing something that is important. Suddenly having thought that you and Lottie do share something special, instead of just feeling persecuted by your marriage to her.

Lottie: Did you really think that, or are you just saying it?

Greg: [starts to cry quietly, tears stream down his face] Yes, I did.

Therapist: Greg, when someone dies, there can be enormous feelings of guilt, that you have life while the other person is dead. I think these feelings make you feel really bad about making a new life, and enjoying being with Lottie.

Greg: My parents and Georgina's mother thought it was too soon when Lottie and I got together, but it did feel like a new beginning, trying to put the past behind me, make a fresh start for all of us. Instead, so much of the time, I just feel haunted by what I've done. It's not fair on Lottie, I know she wants us to have a child.

Lottie: When you said about Greg feeling guilty that he was alive and that Georgina was dead, I knew exactly what you meant. I always felt that way about Matthew [brother who died in a cot death]. I always felt I had to pay the price somehow.

Greg: Lottie, that's awful, you've never said that before.

Therapist: No, but Lottie has talked about how hard she finds it living in your marital home, Greg. She has said she feels she lives in Georgina's shadow. I think it's similar to living in the shadow of a dead baby. The baby who is always in mother's mind.

Lottie: [nods] Yes, I've never felt as though I've come first. Daddy left soon after Christopher was born, so he wasn't around much for me when I was young. I know I can feel jealous of the relationship the girls have with Greg, especially when I feel excluded.

Therapist: You both seem to be struggling with living in the present, and not being overwhelmed by the shadows of the past.

Therapist: It's time to end now.

The couple say goodbye as they leave, and say they will see the therapist next week.

Anxieties and defences
A clinical commentary for Greg and Lottie

Susanna Abse

Introduction

In undertaking the task of responding to the case material of Greg and Lottie, I am reminded of the unpublished paper, written in 1983, by the American psychoanalyst, Robert Stoller. According to Kirsner (2001), who writes about this study in his paper on the future of psychoanalytic institutions, Stoller, while working at UCLA, filmed a session with a patient and then showed this session to twenty-seven professors of psychiatry. These professors could not agree on the issues, except to concur that the patient was "not elated"! Kirsner further noted that Stoller found,

> Experts disagree on their interpretations of what is happening at the moment, what has been happening during the course of the therapy, what happened in the patient's life that contributed to the problems and what should be said and done from moment to moment in a psychotherapy session in order for us to do our best work. (p. 198)

So, given this, I will now outline my thoughts about Greg and Lottie, with awareness that other clinicians might have different formulations, emphasis, and interpretations. I will try to elaborate my ideas sufficiently to ensure that readers who are less familiar with how psychotherapy works can see how I develop my thoughts, but the material is so rich, many other different strands could be teased out, all of which would have their parts to play in the overall dynamics.

In responding to this material, I have been asked to pay particular attention to the couple's anxieties and defences. By anxieties and defences, I mean, first, the things that worry and preoccupy them at an unconscious level, and, second, the unconscious strategies that they use to avoid coming into emotional contact with these worries. The lay reader might, quite rightly, ask how a therapist can know these things if they are unconscious? How can the therapist be sure that these issues are at play in someone's life? The simple answer is that we can never be sure, but we look for clues in the way the story is told, clues in the way the couple treat each other, clues in the way they relate to the therapist, and clues in the family history and the family stories that the couple tell. The therapist then synthesises these clues into an idea for the couple to think about. Quite often, the therapist gets it wrong, but, in hearing the therapist's ideas, new thoughts and new feelings can emerge which throw further light on what might be going on under the surface.

The story of Lottie and Greg involves dynamics that extend beyond the couple to include the children and their grandmothers. In reading their histories, it seems that overshadowing this family is the spectre of loss. Most centrally, we hear about the loss of Greg's wife, Georgina, but also, importantly, we learn about the loss of Lottie's baby brother Matthew, who died before her own birth. The couple, therefore, seem to share an experience of loss and perhaps that is, in part, what drew them to each other. Further, perhaps these losses have provoked complex, difficult feelings in both of them and I wonder if they have constructed this relationship to help manage and defend against these feelings.

My process

In the session material, I can hear Greg's anxiety about the children and his wish to make everything better for them. He is preoccupied with his daughters' distress and seems to want his new wife to be the ideal mother, who will alleviate their pain. We do not actually know how distressed the children are now, four years after their mother's death, but we do know that Greg is very concerned and protective towards them. In his mind, it seems that they are very fragile, must be sheltered from challenges such as a new baby, and that they need extra special, sensitive care. Given this, I began to wonder if his preoccupation with Selina and Alicia was one way in which he has defended himself against the enormity of his own loss. While, on the one hand, the death of Georgina is, of course, a devastating experience for them, it is now four years on and Greg's preoccupation with his girls' feelings seems a bit stuck, as though the loss had happened very recently. I am rather struck by the reference Selina makes to the ice-cream that her mother liked. Four years of dinner times have passed with, I presume, lots of ice-cream, so it makes me wonder whether this family can move on from the image of this dead mother; whether the children can let her go a bit, and enjoy whatever ice-cream they like best.

I also speculated that perhaps it has been hard for Greg to be fully in touch with all the complex feelings his wife's death has stirred up. He, the oldest child in his family, seems to be the "good guy", a "wonderful father", who dresses smartly and who simply wants to do the best by everyone. Yet, as we know, loss and grief engender complex feelings such as anger, irrational states of mind, and guilt. I wondered if, in an attempt to protect himself from some of these chaotic emotions, he had projected some of his own feelings of loss into his girls and he had been attempting to repair and manage these feelings by trying to make everything absolutely perfect for them. Perhaps, too, his own anger and resentment was being projected into Lottie, who, while at first having felt very sorry for her stepchildren, now finds herself frustrated and upset with both Greg and his elder daughter, Selina. But, I hear you ask, "What might Greg's anger and resentment be about?" Certainly, these kinds of feelings in the context of loss are not necessarily reasonable or rational, but it is one of the most common feelings that people experience when someone dies. Feelings can include a sense of betrayal or resentment towards the dead person, which can be confusing and difficult to acknowledge and can commonly be displaced on to others or turned into feelings of blame. So, while Greg is trying to be the perfect father, Lottie ends up with the feelings of anger at not being supported and not getting her needs met. All feelings, I would guess, that Greg could reasonably be expected to have himself. Here, we begin to see what Greg might be anxious and fearful of in himself, and how he tries to protect and defend himself against these feelings.

The therapist in the story, however, focuses on guilt. The therapist suggests, and Greg seems to concur, that marriage to Lottie was felt by some to have happened quite quickly. An indecent haste, perhaps? Greg also makes a connection to the feeling that, by marrying Lottie, he has betrayed Georgina; that by having a good life with Lottie, he would be turning his back on Georgina and the life he shared with her. He has the life. His dead first wife does not.

I then turned my attention to Lottie, and wondered how this links to her? As a couple therapist, I always try and understand the shared aspects of a couple's difficulties, and, although Greg and Lottie seem to be in different places, perhaps that is not quite the case. Indeed, Lottie echoes Greg when she says she felt she understood his feelings of guilt and had experienced this herself. Perhaps she wondered if her own life had depended on her brother's death. Would her mother have had her if she had not lost a child? These feelings, of course, would be largely unconscious, but perhaps they made her feel guilty, too. She has the life: Matthew, her dead older brother, does not.

I also did a bit of imagining. I began to think about Lottie's mother and the loss of her boy child, Matthew. In doing so, I was trying to understand what kind of infancy Lottie might have had. What kind of nurturing environment was Lottie born into? Lottie's mother must have missed and grieved for her baby son and I speculated that perhaps she had hoped to assuage that loss by having another child. Yet, in those circumstances, I wondered if, in having Lottie, her mother might have been beset by all sorts of complicated feelings. Would Lottie's mother have feared losing her, too? And if Lottie's mother is anxious, fearful, and, maybe, quite depressed, what kind of mother would that have made her? Would remembering the loss of Matthew have made her less emotionally present to her new infant? Lottie also wonders if her mother was disappointed that she was not a boy, and, if, perhaps, she had not been the perfect replacement for Matthew.

So, we might imagine that Lottie had a mother who was sad, anxious, and, therefore, not able to be very attentive to Lottie. Now, does this explain something? Does this give us some kind of clue why Lottie was so interested in Greg and his bereft daughters? Does she identify with their deprivation and their experience of having a missing mother? Does she want to make things better for the girls as a way of repairing her own experience? Did she also, unconsciously, imagine *this* time around she *could* be the perfect replacement—maybe not for Matthew, but for Georgina, and she could give these two little girls the experience of a mother who loved and nurtured them? In this way, I speculate she tries vicariously to meet her own needs via them, and attempts to repair her own experience of not having an attentive present mother around. Was trying to be the perfect mother to Selina and Alicia her way of managing her own painful feelings and defending herself against them?

These are the ideas that might imaginatively be in my head and I might be looking for clues to see if there is some evidence that I might be on the right track. I might put these thoughts gently to Lottie, to see if they make sense to her, or if they bring new thoughts and feelings to mind. Ideas such as these run along in my mind in the background and are spoken aloud when the time seems right, and this rightness is a bit mysterious and is to do with the therapist's emotional attunement to the patient.

Of course, the other aspect of Lottie's experience is being the outsider. Greg and the girls and, indeed, the grandmas, are all in agreement. She is the one who seems to be causing the trouble. She is the interloper; the unwanted one. These are real experiences in this family, but they are made more potent and powerful by the fact that they repeat her experience in childhood. Her mother had her and then, quickly, had her preferred child, Christopher, Lottie's younger brother. Then, she lost her father, too, by all accounts. So she is attuned already to feeling unwanted and unloved, and so the spectre of the ideal, preferred Georgina hangs heavy in front of her.

Conclusion

There are, of course, lots of other feelings and things at work in this family. Maybe there is quite a competition going on about who will replace Georgina and who will get the prize of being the most loving, good mother. Greg seems to want this position but, perhaps, so do the grandmothers, too.

The reader might well ask . . . so what? How do all these thoughts actually help the couple to be close again and to parent their children more collaboratively? And, indeed, move on as a couple themselves, leaving Georgina as an important memory, rather than a constant ghostly presence? Generally, psychoanalytic couple therapists believe that in opening up these ideas and helping the couple understand better the underlying drivers of their behaviour, couples can leave some of these unconscious anxieties and defensive behaviours behind and begin to create a more present, alive, and intimate relationship between them.

The fog and the shadows of the past
A clinical commentary for Greg and Lottie

Pierre Benghozi

The couple, Greg and Lottie, are presented in the context of psychoanalytic couple psychotherapy. The clinical material highlights the suffering of the entire family: the children, the couple, and the grandparents. Considering the distress in the family as a whole, family therapy would also have been an option. Perhaps, Greg's and Lottie's request for couple therapy is indicative both of their hopelessness that they would be able to work things through as a family, but also of their hope and desire to "become" a couple in their own right.

First, I would like to make a point about the intersubjective aspects involved in the selection and application of a particular psychoanalytic therapeutic modality. The choice of the modality by the patients, as well as by the therapist, is a co-construction. Before starting therapy, the patients have ideas, feelings, and unconscious sentiments about the therapist and the particular therapeutic modality, that is, pre-transference feelings. The therapist's feelings, the pre-countertransference, is an aspect of the therapeutic framework, and our desire to position ourselves, for example, as a couple therapist, a family therapist, or individual therapist. This dimension of an "already there" in the pre-transference and pre-countertransference is important in the foundation of the pact, or the unconscious therapeutic alliance, between the patient/s and the therapist/s.

Greg and Lottie are committed to their appointment, and hold on to the therapeutic framework, despite the difficulties they feel externally and internally that are pulling them apart. I call this alliance a structuring, or meshing, organising of the psychic links and the structuring of the genealogical containers (Benghozi, 1999).

In my conceptualisation of the structuring, de-structuring, and restructuring of the links, the psychic family and the psychic couple are seen as genealogical psychic containers that have a containing and transforming function: "transformation", in the sense of Bion (1959). Ideally, the choice of a psychotherapeutic modality with this couple should aim to provide functions that promote transformation both for Me, Ego-couple and Me, Ego-family (Benghozi, 1994, 1999, 2006, 2011a,b).

The couple therapy provides an opportunity for some differentiation of intergenerational boundaries. The couple link is a horizontal affiliate link, as is also the sibling link. It differentiates the generational level of the parents from that of the children. To listen to the couple is to welcome the intersubjective psychodynamics of the partners of the couple, it is to listen to the Me: Couple, Me: Ego-couple, the group couple, which I call the *grou-ple*: *couple as a group*. The links within the couple as a group are essentially an expression of a new unconscious pact of alliances that are created as the couple formed. The dynamic of the new object, the *grou-ple*, or the couple as a group, is analysed as a psychic group mental representation of the new couple's unconscious pact alliances and unconscious links with their families of origin (Benghozi, 2012).

In the situation presented, the family is reconstituted with Greg's marriage to Lottie, after the death of Georgina, his first wife, who was the mother of his two daughters. Lottie complains of not being supported by Greg, and that he only pays attention to his daughters' suffering. She says, "You never support me". At a first level, the conflict reflects the actuality of mourning, and the pain and anger around the unbearable replacement of the dead mother. Despite all Lottie's efforts to better assist the children through their bereavement, without wanting to take the place of their mother, she sees herself as unjustly rejected by the children, who are in alliance with their grandmothers. Lottie's complaint of Greg's lack of understanding and support places a risk not only on the newlyweds, but on the couple's link with the children and with the grandmothers. Everyone is holding on to the link with the deceased.

However, at another level, the clinical material illustrates perfectly what I have called "The paradox of the founding unconscious pact of the link of conjugal alliance" (Benghozi, 2012). My hypothesis is that the paradox of the founding unconscious pact manifests in the conjugal alliance. The conjugal link has a reparative function for the couple. It can promote a reciprocal rearrangement of the damages, "holes", "snags", "tears", in the mesh, or structuring and restructuring of the containers of the families (Benghozi, 2011a,b, 2012) of origin of each partner. The "holes" correspond to the deficits, due to the neglect or destructive interactions in the psychic elaboration of what is transmitted in intergenerational form and through generations. From this perspective, the founding paradox of the couple link, which will manifest itself at the intersubjective level in the actual couple, will contain the source of conflict of each of the individual partners. Yet, at the same time, paradoxically, the "holes", or deficits, are one of the aspects of the founding of the conjugal alliance, as well as the source that mobilises resistance to change. This can be formulated by the paradox: "I do not support the one you are, but if you were not (or not any more) the one you are, I would not be with you!" The "you" is, here, at once the singular subject but also the subject of the family/group.

The couple link constitutes the Me, Ego-couple, and the unconscious image of the body couple. It is an affiliate link, with a psychic economic function for the singular psyche and for the genealogical group of the partners' families of origin. The alliance pact is, according to Kaes (Kaes, 1995), an "unconscious alliance" between the "negatives", the unconscious transmitted and undeveloped hollow impressions that each partner of the couple has inherited.

The couple session testifies to this paradoxical founding alliance, and we can follow the work of reformulation of the affects experienced by the patients. It is this pact of unconscious alliance that can be described with the wonderful metaphor: the "shadows in the fog". "The fog" is an atmosphere of the conjugal and family group psychic climate. It is the actuality of being submerged in depression, a desperate state of anguish, shame, and guilt. The shadow of an idealised, irreplaceable dead person has an impact on the unconscious alliance pact that links Greg and Lottie. The partners' two families of origin of the couple are in mourning. There are shadows of Georgina's death and Lottie's brother's death.

Mourning, shame, guilt, and conflicts of loyalty concern all members of Greg's family. Everyone, the husband and father of the children, the children, the grandmother, the mother-in-law, all occupy, with the reorganisation of the mourning of Georgina, a function of maternal substitute. For Greg, the encounter with Lottie is a salvation for his depression, and he is the one who quickly proposes marriage.

Greg's marriage with Lottie is experienced in Greg's family as "too soon". It is a "treason" that Lottie, the new woman, should take from them the maternal place. Greg is struggling to sustain his desires and his adult choice to be in a relationship with Lottie. This is difficult in the face of what his daughters project on the couple. Children deal with their own guilt by attacking father's new object of love. He fears that assuming a position of firmness will increase his daughters' suffering. Yet, it is by being in touch with the experience of the loss of his late wife that he can work through his own guilt and shame, and allow and support his daughters to mourn, grow, and develop in clarifying "who is who". Since his new wife is not their mother, she cannot cancel out their mother's existence and the place she has in their history. The question is whether it will be possible to establish the link of conjugal alliance that will function as an organiser of a new intergenerational boundary in the meshing/structuring of the container of the reconstituted family.

It would seem that the new love story was a betrayal not only of the link to the dead mother, but also of the oedipal stakes in the father–daughter bond. How can the arrival of the new sibling, the birth of a child for a new couple be allowed? The therapist seems alone without a co-therapist, attentive to Greg's guilt and mourning and to Lottie's suffering at feeling relegated to second choice. Ideally, some work would also need to be done with the grandmothers to support the generational boundaries, so that each occupies their place without too much encroaching on the space of the others.

Lottie is part of the founding pact of the new family recomposition. It is a new alliance beyond Greg's relation with his family. Perhaps, it also serves a reparative function for her broken family, with her separated parents.

There is a ten-year age difference between the new spouses. Is it also the figure of "a wonderful father" that attracted her? Her father was absent, distant, just like Greg can be. Greg, potentially distant, could be the father of her child. Would he become this good father that she did not have, that she will finally possess? At the same time, this is what she holds against Greg—being possessed by his daughters.

Also, Greg, in not protecting her, is replicating the experience that Lottie had with her mother, who was not really there for her. She reactualises the experience of an injustice of not being able to rely on her mother, injustice she can feel when she tries to do the best for her husband's children, while they make her feel they cannot and will not rely on her. She feels jealous of Selina's and Alicia's relationship with their father, especially when she feels excluded. She has felt "like a second best" for her mother, after the death of her brother, Matthew, the baby boy. She cannot repair her parents' couple relationship after her brother's death.

In the covenant of conjugal alliance, she is continuing to live in shadow: in the shadow of a dead baby and in the shadow of a dead woman. Putting to work the alliance pact allows restructuring of the couple container, and co-creation of a new, neo-narrative couple content that could help the couple to work though the burden of mourning.

The question is how to invest in new shared objects, such as a new house, less inhabited by the phantom of Georgina's photographs, and the shadows of the past of Greg's and Lottie's families? How to invest a new family with a new baby? How to build a "new beginning to put the past behind"? We perceive this work of unfolding, elaborating paradox of the marriage conjugal pact in the course of therapy with Lottie's remark, "Did you really think that?" And Greg's, "You never said that before . . ."

In the alliance pact of transference, what happens after the fog?

Oedipal dynamics and the couple
A clinical commentary for Greg and Lottie

Peter Griffiths

In this commentary, I will be considering the oedipal dynamics as they appear in Greg and Lottie's couple story and session material. I will draw upon Kleinian and post-Kleinian theoretical development of the oedipal triangle, as a developmental dynamic in early infant development; a never fully resolved process, as described by Britton (1989, 1995) and Grier (2005a).

Mourning is part of negotiating the oedipal situation. Morgan (2005), however, suggests that negotiating the oedipal situation is not the same as resolving it. Difficulties in triangular situations, and in being part of a couple, emerge in different forms and, particularly, at times of stress. The vicissitudes of negotiating dependence, independence, inclusion, exclusion, issues of sexuality, intimacy, and procreation are all part of ordinary development. There is a necessity to do this sufficiently in infancy and adolescence, to develop and internalise what she would describe as a "creative couple state of mind". That is, a way of relating to oneself and the other, in order to later become a creative couple with an-other. For some individuals and some couples, this possibility is adversely affected by their earlier experiences. They might have received poor parenting, insufficient parental containment, or experienced difficult sibling relationships. Oedipal issues that remain insufficiently negotiated or traumatic can be reawakened and re-enacted in the couple relationship (Ruszczynski, 2005).

In the past and present histories of Lottie's and Greg's families of origin, oedipal shadows stand out as unwanted ghosts, and cast a shadow over their experience of each other. They are represented at multiple levels in the present, in the context of considerable separation and loss; unexpressed, and yet deeply felt, guilt, anger, and rejection.

Both Greg and Lottie have many unresolved issues regarding their previous relationships; indeed, it was the subject of the fund-raising event they attended when they met, the hospice having provided care to Georgina, Greg's late wife, who had died one year earlier. Greg had just finished seeing both his psychiatrist and bereavement counsellor, and had discontinued antidepressant medication. Had he still been in counselling, he might have been helped to think more about the reality of a new relationship that was likely to evoke guilt and sadness. Lottie had ended a long-term relationship in the USA. She was upset that this relationship had come to an end and conveyed that the separation and ending was not of her choosing. These were, for Lottie, real losses: the loss of a couple relationship and her home, thus echoing her earlier losses of childhood.

Lottie was, for her mother/parents, a penumbra baby (Reid, 2013), born in the shadow of a dead son. I wondered about feelings of unresolved grief in the mind of Lottie's mother. It is possible to imagine, because of her delight in her second son, that she was disappointed that Lottie was a daughter. Perhaps she felt regret that she could not welcome her. The father might have experienced similar feelings, or the couple might have mourned differently. They separated shortly after their third child was born.

Lottie seems to have experienced in her maternal object grief, distress, and anger, a lack of an affirmative maternal preoccupation that left her feeling uncontained and confused. Lottie spoke of always feeling she was second best, not good enough. Her mother favoured her brothers and she felt she lived in their shadow, as an unwanted child. Her father had also been jettisoned after her brother was born. She lost her father and, in her mind and intrapsychic life, her mother formed a relationship with her brother; the oedipal configuration had been formed. In her teenage years, Lottie perhaps achieved a late oedipal triumph of her own in reconnecting with her father and establishing a separate relationship with him, but an unresolved oedipal dynamic remained.

Lottie met in Greg, an older man who shared her world of work in finance, someone familiar and known. She thought Greg was a "wonderful father", relating to, and finding, the father she herself had not had. Greg, equally, found someone who shared his work interests, a feature he had not shared with Georgina. In Greg's extended family, Lottie perhaps found the family she herself had not had: three live siblings, two loving parents, a family that got on well, and a parental couple that had remained together.

Lottie, in saying "yes" to marriage, one year into their relationship, suggests a couple/marital fit (Ruszczynski, 2005) propelled and underpinned for both by a shared unconscious phantasy of their rescuing each other from the experience of separation and loss, grief, guilt, anger, and fears of abandonment, loneliness, and melancholia. Lottie needed Greg and needed to be wanted by Greg. He could equally sense in Lottie her early experience of loss and, in this relationship, she could be a "wanted" replacement. Greg, still mourning, longed to be loved, and wanted a replacement wife and mother. The relationship was perhaps set up to repeat, to manage, and to work through unresolved early and later conflicts, anxieties, and losses (Bannister & Pincus, 1965, Hewison, 2014).

The sense of idyllic couple fit before the marriage soon dissipated after it, as Lottie, living in the context of Georgina's unmourned death, found herself in a dynamically similar relationship to that of her own family of origin, that of loss, idealisation, dejection, and denigration. A number of intergenerational oedipal triangles, with reverberating dynamics, ricochet within all these contemporary relationships.

Greg lost Georgina, but, equally, in meeting and marrying Lottie, lost his own mother and mother-in-law as surrogate mothers to his girls, and as partners to himself (his father is not mentioned). Thus, Lottie additionally represents to the girls the loss of their grandmothers, as she has replaced them.

Lottie is unwanted by Selina, who, in her own way, had gained her father, at the expense of her mother's death, at the age of six years. One wonders how much either of the two girls were enabled to mourn the loss of their mother, in the context of a depressed father. Selina's own fear of the loss of her father, having gained him and the guilt that accompanies this, is demonstrated both in her hatred of Lottie and in how she propels her younger sister to "act out" her anger and "act up" in Lottie's presence. Lottie's more benign experience of Alicia might mask an identification with a young girl who lost her mother at about the time Lottie lost her own.

Thus, Lottie, the replacement wife, daughter-in-law, and stepmother, is latently, and less manifestly, unwanted by many of Greg's family, with so many echoes of her own experience of entry into her birth family: unwanted by her mother in the shadow of her dead brother. She lives with this experience in her mind and in reality, within Greg and Georgina's family home, redolent with memories, a home that cannot be changed, which needs to remain as a mausoleum.

There is no reference to the couple's sex life in the vignette, but I would imagine it is limited (Grier, 2005c), as is their psychic intercourse. Lottie's own wish to have children with Greg is thwarted by both his wish not to upset his daughters and, equally, by the memory of his dead wife and the guilt he still feels. Lottie might also be ambivalent at the prospect of a child, welcoming and fearing identification with her own mother. They are trapped in unmourned loss and a re-enactment of an earlier primitive experience that is thwarting any developmental impetus for them to become a creative couple. Indeed, such a prospect seems to risk disaster and overwhelming internal recriminations for both.

As the session begins, with the couple arriving physically and psychologically separate, the themes of exclusion and abandonment seem present. The therapist finds herself thinking about Greg and his absence, and I wonder how Lottie experiences the female therapist in relation to Greg.

Greg, in asking "how were the girls?", excludes any consideration of Lottie, who already has experienced being left in the dark as to Greg's whereabouts. She is not related to in his mind, seemingly prior to the session or within it, as he largely communicates directly with the therapist. Lottie also addresses the therapist, but as if not expecting to be heard, or to have her experience empathised with, perhaps reflecting her experience of her own mother. Both are seeking care, but relating to the therapist separately.

That the girls "were a nightmare" speaks to Lottie's conscious and unconscious experience. Neither girl would receive Lottie's nurture. Indeed, Lottie could not get it right, she was not Georgina, she was equally not Greg, who was away; after all, it was his recipe that was not right.

Lottie's claim that "Selina hates me, it doesn't matter what I do", in many ways speaks to the place Selina represents transferentially for Lottie, in the role of her mother, who favoured her brother. Lottie is having to experience and manage both the rejection and hatred of a stepdaughter, but, unconsciously, the resonance is with her own internal mother.

Greg cannot acknowledge the hatred in Selina, his own absence contributing to this, or his own anger and hatred. Greg contributes to Lottie's sense of marginalisation and alienation through his preoccupation with Selina, ignoring Lottie's distress and adding to it by invoking how happy the girls were with his mother. Greg admits "I worry about the girls all the time", they are having to get used to "someone else", and he appeals again to the therapist, ignoring Lottie.

For Selina, in looking after her little sister, there is quite a burden, but also the unspoken wish/perceived expectation to look after her father and replace her mother, which she will feel guilt about. As the therapist suggests, there is a shared feeling, a family interpretation of something very cruel and disturbing for everyone. While Lottie feels hopeless, Greg continues to talk to the therapist, as if Lottie is not there, speaking about the girls' loss of their mother, but, within this, his own loss of his wife. Lottie responds in relation to her own experience of living not just in the shadow of a perfect dead woman, but intrapsychically in the presence of a perfect dead son.

There is still, in Greg, a denial of the existence of his torn feelings towards Georgina, as he complains, "What do you expect me to do? Put all the photographs of the children's mother out of sight?" Should he forget her/deny her?

While the therapist tries to make an interpretation that addresses both loss and separation, Greg interrupts and brings it back to "their original meeting", initially idealised, but now associated with guilt, regret, and anger.

In the "fog" that might have separated them, the therapist manages to make a couple-centred interpretation (Morgan, 2014a) that connects them. It makes conscious the unconscious connections that they dynamically share in their past and present histories, and which trouble and infuse their present relationship. Its containing mutative quality enables Greg to talk to the shadow of guilt at experiencing something new and hopeful in his thoughts about Lottie and of sadness and loss. He can express his feeling of being haunted by Georgina, but equally by his own and Georgina's parents.

This link with the therapist helps, as it enables Lottie to feel connected and heard and makes a link with Greg's experience and that of her own, when she felt excluded and rejected by her mother (and father).

The therapist provides a model of a third position thus linking the couple to a more depressive couple state of mind, which, over time, they might internalise with ongoing therapy. As the therapist points out, they, both individually and as a couple, are struggling to live in the present and not be overwhelmed by shadows of the past. I have, thus, tried to focus on the oedipal dynamics as they reverberate across the generations and within the couple's relationship.

Containment and the couple
A clinical commentary for Greg and Lottie

Patsy Ryz

After reading Greg and Lottie's story, I drew a genogram, as this always helps me in my thinking. I found myself starting by drawing Greg, Georgina, and their two girls. This struck me as significant, given the presenting problem, which is described in terms of Lottie feeling she lives in Georgina's shadow, something that is later reframed by the therapist as a shared problem. "It's possible that you both feel disturbed about having to live with a shadow, in the fog."

The therapist's reframing marks an important point in the session, where the therapist addresses the latent content of the material. She does not shy away from talking about the cruel reality of Georgina's death and its impact on the couple relationship, as reflected in Greg and Lottie's struggle to establish themselves as a new, creative couple (Morgan, 2001, 2005), who are alive and have a future together; a couple who can exist beyond the fog and the shadow of death.

The therapist's intervention leads to a shift in the session, enabling a more depressive atmosphere (Klein, 1975f[1952]), in which Greg and Lottie are able to connect in a less persecuted and more benign state of mind. Something difficult and painful has been processed, detoxified, and understood, giving the couple an experience of containment (Bion, 1962, 1967c[1962a]).

I had a number of associations to the material. I was interested in how Greg and Lottie met. (". . . a quiz night arranged by the Rotary Club to raise funds for their local hospice"). We are not told whether Georgina had been a patient there, but it might reasonably be assumed that she had been. Be that as it may, meeting at such an event provides a very particular context to the start of Greg and Lottie's relationship. One might say it very literally begins in the shadow of death, thus setting the scene for what is yet to unfold between them. It is not difficult to imagine what might have drawn Greg to such an event, but what drew Lottie there? Perhaps a pre-existing preoccupation with loss, connected to her childhood experience as a "replacement child" (Cain & Cain, 1964), following her brother Matthew's cot death.

We are told that "Lottie thought Greg was a wonderful father, and felt sorry for the two little girls". Why was this so attractive to Lottie? I wondered about oedipal issues; a phantasy that she would treat Greg better than her father was treated by her mother, who "only stayed with her father long enough to have another son". The replacement child theme re-emerges here. There is an experience of a mother preoccupied with a dead baby, and a sense of a mother whose loss can only be ameliorated by the birth of another baby boy. So, Lottie's sense of being second best relates not just to being a replacement baby for Matthew, but also to being a very poor and inadequate replacement by virtue of her gender. Reid (2003) vividly describes replacement children "feeling that they could not be as important to their mother as the dead baby".

My thoughts then turned to rescue phantasies linked to reparative drives connected to guilt about murderous urges towards mother and her baby boys (Reid, 2003). Lottie's childhood experience of feeling squeezed in between a cot death and another baby suggests inadequate containment; a mother preoccupied with two baby boys, one alive and one dead, leaving little or no space for Lottie's own needs to be met. According to Reid (2003) Bourne and Lewis (1984) refer to replacement children's "Life-long sense of nameless guilt as if living in someone else's shoes" (p. 31) and Reid (2003) suggests that when the death of a sibling precedes the child's birth, it is "perceived as a living entity within the [mother's] inner world and within the mother–child relationship" (pp. 208–209).

At another level, the fact that the marriage ended soon after her brother's birth suggests that Lottie grew up with an unhelpful model of couple functioning; a relationship that was not able to function as a resource or container (Colman, 1993); it could not survive the cot death.

Given the timing of the breakup, and Lottie's ideas about this, one might speculate that Lottie felt deprived of father by mother, as if, in phantasy, mother chooses baby over father. Echoes of this childhood experience are likely to have a particular resonance for Lottie in the current situation, where Selina and Alicia are seen as prioritised over her couple and co-parental relationship with Greg.

And what of Greg's unconscious choice of Lottie? The fact that they met not long after his bereavement counselling had ended seems significant. I wondered about a phantasy that the bereavement had also ended, and he was free to move on. This is supported by Greg's reference to feeling that getting together with Lottie "was like a new beginning; trying to put the past behind me, make a fresh start for all of us".

But mourning is a long and complicated process, involving many different and, at times, contradictory feelings, including the paradox of needing to let go of the loved, lost object, in order to be able to reintroject it and move on (Freud, 1917e).

Greg feels "haunted" by what he's done. What *has* he done? The therapist suggests that "survivor's guilt" prevents him from "making a new life, and enjoying being with Lottie". This resonates with Lottie, who "always felt . . . [she] had to pay the price somehow" . . . (for the cot death). I wonder whether, in phantasy, they respectively share feelings of responsibility for these deaths. For Lottie, it is as if her very existence is predicated on Matthew's cot death. For Greg, it is as if it was not the cancer, but the act of getting together with Lottie that killed Georgina. I think these unconscious phantasies might go some way towards explaining the problems that this newly reconstituted family is experiencing.

The difficulties appear to hinge on the issue of difference, as if no one is to notice the very obvious fact that Lottie is not Georgina, and that to do so, as mentioned by the therapist, is cruel.

Greg notices he can share things with Lottie that he would not have been able to share with Georgina, but immediately cannot bear knowing this. He also cannot bear noticing that a visit to maternal grandmother stirs up difficult feelings in the children, who, then, "are often even more upset with [Lottie]", particularly when she does things differently to Georgina. Is there a phantasy that if only Lottie did everything the same as Georgina, the latter's loss would be counterbalanced or wiped out? Is Georgina's loss to be permanently enshrined by keeping everything exactly the same? The material regarding Selina taking care of Alicia, which seems partly equated with keeping everything the same, supports this idea. The therapist's comment about how burdensome this might be for Selina alerts us to Greg's passivity. In allowing Selina to take on this responsibility, he relinquishes his place alongside Lottie in the new parental relationship.

I was interested in the supper material, which encompasses issues of difference, loss, and murderousness. With Greg away, Lottie prepares a recipe the children like, but they complain that Greg does it differently, thus communicating that they miss him and notice the difference caused by his absence. Selina's reference to the chickens kept at school stirs up anxiety and distress in Alicia and in Lottie, who is unconsciously implicated in something aggressive and murderous. Even "that lovely chocolate ice-cream" is tainted by Georgina's shadow, because "mummy only liked strawberry ice-cream". This is another communication about difference and loss. The girls miss Georgina, and will not allow Lottie to do anything right.

Perhaps, if Greg were more able to take his place alongside Lottie, thus presenting the girls with a united parental couple, Lottie might, in turn, be more able to hear the distress behind Selina's hostile attacks. But, instead, she just feels persecuted. "Selina hates me. It doesn't matter what I do."

The relationship between Lottie and Selina is complicated. At times, it is difficult to disentangle what belongs to whom. Selina's understandable anger at the loss of her mother is appropriate. Lottie is an easy target, given her long-standing predisposition for feeling second-best. It might also be that Greg, still reeling from Georgina's death, is experienced as a more fragile object, who needs to be protected from Selina's rage, not only at Georgina's death, but at Greg getting together with Lottie.

Selina is a handy receptacle for Lottie's projections. Her attacks on Lottie can be understood as expressing Selina's own feelings, as well as Lottie's own infantile, murderous rage towards her mother and siblings.

I was interested in the therapist's comment that "children often express the grief and rage that their parents cannot express". I agree with this, and would take it further. Children's behaviour and communications can reflect a couple's own infantile needs, and can become a focus in the work, offering hope for change. This brings to mind the interface between work with couples and work with parents. Greg and Lottie are on the cusp of this interface as Selina's difficulties are symptomatic of an issue in the couple relationship. The GP understood this, and opted for referral to couple therapy, rather than Child and Adolescent Mental Health Services. But, as a child psychotherapist, I have often experienced situations in which the couple's difficulties are very firmly lodged in the child, who, then, becomes the identified patient. In such circumstances, addressing the couple issues can be problematic, because the parents have not signed up for couple work, and the therapist might feel she does not have permission or expertise to venture into that area. Further complications emerge when the parents' difficulties have been internalised, and the child also needs help in his/her own right.

When it is the other way around and material about the children is brought to couple therapy sessions, interesting technical issues arise. What is the function of such material? Is it defensive or developmental? Is it possible to venture into parent work without going off task? This partly depends on how the primary task (Bion, 1961) is defined. If it is seen in terms of facilitating growth and development in the couple relationship, then, surely, attending to the parental couple can be seen as part of the work. However, in such cases, as with Bion's binocular vision (1965), it is essential that the therapist keeps in mind both the couple as couple (that is, the couple relationship) and the couple as parents (that is, the parental couple), as well as the way each has impacts on the other.

In conclusion, I return to Greg's and Lottie's struggles to establish themselves as a new, creative couple. Their struggle takes place within the context of unresolved mourning. The latter is part of the couple fit (Ruszczynski, 1993). We know little of Greg's individual history, and, therefore, cannot know whether his difficulties with the mourning process are rooted in childhood experience. Although his position seems more straightforward than Lottie's, his choice of Lottie is interesting. They seem to have been drawn together by death, but perhaps also by the hope of leaving these shadows behind. The therapy then becomes a lifeline, offering the possibility of creating a different kind of future, away from the shadows, and free from a preoccupation with death. The therapist's capacity for containment will be a crucial part of such an endeavour.

EPILOGUE

And so we leave our "Couple stories". If Marco and Rosa, Peter and Helen, Caroline and Dan, and Greg and Lottie continue in their couple psychotherapy, changes might occur, but we cannot know the outcome of the work or the future of their lives. What this book highlights are moments in the emotional life of a couple and the stories they bring, and yet, alongside these, they also bring their "untold" stories—their deepest misunderstandings, hopes, fears, and desires.

REFERENCES

Balfour, A. (2005). The couple, their marriage, and Oedipus: or problems come in twos and threes. In: F. Grier (Ed.), *Oedipus and the Couple* (pp. 49–71). London: Karnac.

Balfour, A. (2016). Transference and enactment in the "oedipal setting" of couple psychotherapy. In: A. Novakovic (Ed.), *Couple Dynamics: Psychoanalytic Perspectives in Work with the Individual, the Couple, and the Group* (pp. 59–83). London: Karnac.

Bannister, K., & Pincus, L. (1965). *Shared Phantasy in Marital Problems*. London: Institute of Marital Studies.

Benghozi, P. (1994). Porte la honte et maillage des contenants généalogiques familiaux et communautaires en thérapie familiale. Le groupe familial en psychothérapie. *Revue de Psychothérapie Psychanalytique de Groupe*, 22: 81–94.

Benghozi, P. (1999). *Adolescence et Sexualité—Liens et Maillage—Réseau*. Paris: L'Harmattan.

Benghozi, P. (2006). Pré-contre-transfert, cadre et dispositif. In: Diversité des psychothérapies psychanalytiques de groupe. *Revue de Psychothérapie Psychanalytique de Groupe*, 47: 25–29.

Benghozi, P. (2011a). The mythic narrative neo-container in psychoanalytical family therapy. Shame and treason as heritage. In: A. Nicolo, P. Benghozi, & D. Lucarelli (Eds.), *Families in Transformation* (pp. 41–63) London: Karnac.

Benghozi, P. (2011b). Anamorphosis, sloughing of containers, and family psychical transformations. In: A. Nicolo, P. Benghozi, & D. Lucarelli (Eds.), *Families in Transformation* (pp. 199–217). London: Karnac.

Benghozi, P. (2012). Paradoxalité du pacte d'alliance conjugal et remaillage réciproque des contenants généalogique familiaux : le grouple. *Revue de Psychothérapie Psychanalytique de Groupe, 58*: 105–120.

Bergman, I. (1988). *The Magic Lantern*. London: Hamish Hamilton Penguin.

Berkowitz, D. (2011). Maternal instincts, biological clocks, and soccer moms: gay men's parenting and family narratives. *Symbolic Interaction, 34*(4): 514–535.

Bion, W. R. (1959). Attacks on linking. *International Journal of Psychoanalysis, 40*: 308–315.

Bion, W. R. (1961). *Experiences in Groups and Other Papers*. London: Karnac.

Bion, W. R. (1962). *Learning from Experience*. London: Heinemann.

Bion, W. R. (1963). *Elements of Psycho-analysis*. London: Heinemann.

Bion, W. R. (1965). *Transformations*. London: William Heinemann [reprinted London: Karnac, 1984; reprinted in *Seven Servants*, 1977].

Bion, W. R. (1967a). Differentiation between the psychotic and the non-psychotic part of the personality. In: *Second Thoughts* (pp. 43–64), London: Heinemann [reprinted London: Maresfield Library & Karnac, 1990].

Bion, W. R. (1967b). Notes on memory and desire. *Psychoanalytic Forum, 2*: 271–286.

Bion, W. R. (1967c)[1962a]. A theory of thinking. In: *Second Thoughts* (pp. 110–119). London: Heinemann.

Bion, W. R. (1970). *Attention and Interpretation*. London: Tavistock.

Bléandonu, G. (1994). *Wilfred Bion: His Life and Works 1897–1979*. London: Free Association Books.

Bollas, C. (1991). *The Shadow of the Object: Psychoanalysis of the Unthought Known*. London: Free Association Books.

Boswell, J. (2001). The Oedipus complex. In: C. Bronstein (Ed.), *Kleinian Theory—A Contemporary Perspective* (pp. 77–92). London: Whurr.

Bott Spillius, E., Milton, J., Garvey, P., Couve, C., & Steiner, D. (2011). *The New Dictionary of Kleinian Thought*. London: Routledge.

Bourne, S., & Lewis, E. (1984). Pregnancy after stillbirth or neonatal death. *Lancet, ii*: 31–33.

Britton, R. (1985). The Oedipus complex and the depressive position. *Sigmund Freud House Bulletin, Vienna, 9*: 7–12.

Britton, R. (1989). The missing link: parental sexuality in the Oedipus complex. In: J. Steiner (Ed.), *The Oedipus Complex Today: Clinical Implications* (pp. 83–101). London: Karnac.

Britton, R. (1995). Foreword. In: S. Ruszczynski & J. Fisher (Eds.), *Intrusiveness and Intimacy in the Couple* (pp. xi–xiii). London: Karnac.

Britton, R. (1998a). Before and after the depressive position: Ps(n)→D(n)→Ps(n+1). In: *Belief and Imagination: Explorations in Psychoanalysis* (pp. 69–81). London: Routledge.

Britton, R. (1998b). Subjectivity, objectivity and triangular space. In: *Belief and Imagination: Explorations in Psychoanalysis* (pp. 41–58). London: Routledge.

Britton, R. (1998c). *Belief and Imagination: Explorations in Psychoanalysis*. London: Routledge.

Britton, R. (2003). *Sex, Death, and the Superego: Experiences in Psychoanalysis*. London: Karnac.

Britton, R., & Steiner, J. (1994). Interpretation: selected fact or overvalued idea? *International Journal of Psychoanalysis, 75*: 1069–1078.

Cain, A., & Cain, B. (1964). On replacing a child. *Journal of the American Academy of Child Psychiatry, 3*: 443–456.

Clarke, J. (2016). Revisiting the crossroads: can Oedipus take a gay turn in the 21st C? *Psychoanalytic Psychotherapy, 30*(3): 256–283.

Cleavely, E. (1991). Relationships: interaction, defences, and transformation. In: S. Ruszczynski (Ed.), *Psychotherapy with Couples. Theory and Practice at the Tavistock Institute of Marital Studies* (pp. 55–69). London: Karnac.

Cleavely, E. (1993). Relationships: interaction, defences, and transformation. In: S. Ruszcynski (Ed.), *Psychotherapy with Couples. Theory and Practice at the Tavistock Institute of Marital Studies* (pp. 55–69). London: Karnac.

Clulow, C. (1982). *To Have and to Hold: Marriage, the First Baby and Preparing Couples for Parenthood*. Aberdeen: Aberdeen University Press.

Colman, W. (1993). Marriage as a psychological container. In: S. Ruszczynski (Ed.), *Psychotherapy with Couples: Theory and Practice at the Tavistock Institute of Marital Studies* (pp. 70–96). London: Karnac.

Cudmore, L., & Judd, D. (2001). Traumatic loss in the couple. In: C. Clulow (Ed.), *Adult Attachment and Couple Psychotherapy: the Secure Base in Practice and Research* (pp. 152–170). London: Brunner-Routledge.

Dicks, H. V. (1993)[1967]. *Marital Tensions. Clinical Studies Towards a Psychological Theory of Interaction*. London: Karnac.

Dylan, B. (2006). Rollin' and Tumblin'. *Modern Times*. Columbia Records.

Elmhirst, S. I. (1996). Personal communication, 25th January.

Ezriel, H. (1952). Notes on psychoanalytic group therapy II: interpretation and research. *Psychiatry, 15*: 19–126.

Feldman, M. (1989). The Oedipus complex: manifestations in the inner world and the therapeutic situation. In: J. Steiner (Ed.), *The Oedipus Complex Today: Clinical Implications* (pp. 103–128). London: Karnac.

Feldman, T. (2014). From container to claustrum: projective identification in couples. *Couple and Family Psychoanalysis*, 4(2): 136–154.

Fisher, J. (1999). *The Uninvited Guest. Emerging from Narcissism Towards Marriage.* London: Karnac.

Freeman, H. (1988). In conversation with Peter Sainsbury. *Bulletin of the Royal College of Psychiatrists*, 12, 162–168.

Freud, S. (1897). Extracts from the Fliess papers. Letter 71. *S. E., 1*: 263–265. London: Hogarth Press.

Freud, S. (1900a). *The Interpretation of Dreams. S. E., 4–5.* London: Hogarth Press.

Freud, S, (1905d). *Three Essays on the Theory of Sexuality. S. E., 7*: 125–245. London: Hogarth Press.

Freud, S. (1909b). *Analysis of a Phobia in a Five-year-old Boy. S. E., 10*: 3–149. London: Hogarth.

Freud, S. (1912d). On the universal tendency to debasement in the sphere of love. *S. E., 11*: 177–190. London: Hogarth.

Freud, S. (1917e). Mourning and melancholia. *S. E., 14*: 239–258. London: Hogarth.

Freud, S. (1923b). *The Ego and the Id. S. E., 19*: 3–66. London: Hogarth.

Freud, S. (1924d). The dissolution of the Oedipus complex. *S. E., 19*: 173–182. London: Hogarth.

Freud, S. (1930a). *Civilization and Its Discontents. S. E., 21*: 50–145. London: Hogarth.

Green, P. (1968). Love that Burns. *Mr. Wonderful.* London: Blue Horizon.

Grier, F. (Ed.) (2005a). *Oedipus and the Couple.* London: Karnac.

Grier, F. (2005b). Introduction. In: F. Grier (Ed.), *Oedipus and the Couple* (pp. 1–8). London: Karnac.

Grier, F. (2005c). No sex couples, catastrophic change, and the primal scene. In: F. Grier (Ed.), *Oedipus and the Couple* (pp. 201–220). London: Karnac.

Grotstein, J. S. (2008). What is love? In: J. Pickering, *Being in Love. Therapeutic Pathways through Psychological Obstacles to Love* (pp. ix–xii). Hove: Routledge.

Grotstein, J. S. (2009). Projective *trans*identification. In: *". . . But at the Same Time and on Another Level . . .": Psychoanalytic Theory and Technique in the Kleinian/Bionian Mode* (pp. 286–301). London: Karnac.

Halton, W., & Sprince, J. (2016). Oscillating images: perceptions of couples in organizations. In: A. Novakovic (Ed.), *Couple Dynamics:*

Psychoanalytic Perspective in Work with the Individual, the Couple, and the Group (pp. 145–164). London: Karnac.

Hertzmann, L. (2011). Lesbian and gay relationships: when internalised homophobia gets in the way of couple creativity. *Psychoanalytic Psychotherapy*, 25: 346–360.

Hertzmann L. (2015). Objecting to the object. Encountering the internal parental couple relationship for lesbian and gay couples. In: A. Lemma & P. E. Lynch (Eds.), *Sexualities: Contemporary Psychoanalytic Perspectives* (pp. 156–175). London: Routledge.

Hewison, D. (2007). The power of theory and research: the psychotherapist's aids to thinking about the couple. In: M. Ludlam & V. Nyberg (Eds.), *Couple Attachments: Theoretical and Clinical Studies* (pp. 171–188). London: Karnac.

Hewison, D. (2014). Shared unconscious phantasy in couples. In: D. E. Scharff & J. Savege Scharff (Eds.), *Psychoanalytic Couple Therapy: Foundations of Theory and Practice* (pp. 158–169). London: Karnac.

Hinshelwood, R. D. (1989). Splitting. In: *A Dictionary of Kleinian Thought* (pp. 417–419). London: Free Association Books.

Hinshelwood, R. D. (1994). *Clinical Klein*. London: Free Association Books.

Hinshelwood, R. D. (2016). Couples and primitive processes. In: A. Novakovic (Ed.), *Couple Dynamics: Psychoanalytic Perspectives in Work with the Individual, the Couple, and the Group* (pp. 43–58). London: Karnac.

Jaques, E. (1988)[1965]. Death and the mid–life crisis. In: E. Bott Spillius (Ed.), *Melanie Klein Today: Developments in Theory and Practice: Volume 2: Mainly Practice* (pp. 226–248). London: Routledge.

Johns, M. (1996). Why are three-person relationships difficult? In: C. Clulow (Ed.), *Partners Becoming Parents* (pp. 44–54). London: Sheldon.

Jones, E. (1961). *The Life and Work of Sigmund Freud*. London: Penguin.

Joseph, B. (1985). Transference: the total situation. In: E. Bott Spillius & M. Feldman (Eds.), *Psychic Equilibrium and Psychic Change: Selected Papers of Betty Joseph* (pp. 156–167). London: Routledge, 1989.

Joseph, B. (1989). Projective identification: some clinical aspects. In: M. Feldman & E. Bott Spillius (Eds.), *Psychic Equilibrium & Psychic Change: Selected Papers of Betty Joseph* (pp. 98–111). London: Tavistock/Routledge.

Josephs, L. (2006). The impulse to infidelity and Oedipal splitting. *International Journal of Psychoanalysis*, 87: 423–437.

Jung, C. G. (1954)[1925]. Marriage as a psychological relationship. In: *The Development of Personality. C. W.*, 17: para. 324–345. London: Routledge and Kegan Paul.

Jung, C. G. (1963). Mysterium coniunctionis: an inquiry into the separation and synthesis of psychic opposites in alchemy. *C. W., 14* (2nd edn). London: Routledge & Kegan Paul.

Kaës, R. (1995). *Le groupe et le sujet du groupe*. Paris: Dunod.

Kernberg, O. (1995a). *Love Relations: Normality and Pathology*. New Haven, CT: Yale University Press.

Kernberg, O. (1995b). Aggression, love, and the couple. In: *Love Relations: Normality and Pathology* (pp. 81–96). New Haven, CT: Yale University Press.

Kirsner, D. (2001). The future of psychoanalytic institutes. *Psychoanalytic Psychology*, 18: 195–212.

Klein, M. (1928). Early stages of the Oedipus conflict. *International Journal of Psychoanalysis*, 9: 167–180.

Klein, M. (1952). Notes on some schizoid mechanisms. In: M. Klein, P. Heimann, S. Isaacs, & J. Riviere (Eds.), *Developments in Psycho-analysis* (pp. 292–320). London: Hogarth Press.

Klein, M. (1975a)[1927]. Criminal tendencies in normal children. In: *The Writings of Melanie Klein Volume 1: Love, Guilt and Reparation and Other Works 1921–1945* (pp. 170–185). London: Hogarth Press.

Klein, M. (1975b). Love, guilt and reparation. In: *The Writings of Melanie Klein Volume 1: Love, Guilt and Reparation and Other Works 1921–1945* (pp. 306–343). London: Hogarth Press, 1975 [reprinted London: Karnac, 1993].

Klein, M. (1975c). Mourning and its relation to manic–depressive states. In: *The Writings of Melanie Klein Volume 1: Love, Guilt and Reparation and Other Works 1921–1945* (pp. 344–369). London: Hogarth Press, 1975 [reprinted London: Karnac, 1993].

Klein, M. (1975d). The Oedipus complex in the light of earlier anxieties. In: *The Writings of Melanie Klein Volume 1: Love, Guilt and Reparation and Other Works 1921–1945* (pp. 370–419). London: Hogarth Press, 1975 [reprinted London: Karnac, 1993].

Klein, M. (1975e). Notes on some schizoid mechanisms. In: *The Writings of Melanie Klein Volume 3: Envy and Gratitude and Other Works 1946–1963* (pp. 1–24). London: Hogarth Press, 1975. [Reprinted London: Karnac, 1993.]

Klein, M. (1975f). The origins of transference. In: *The Writings of Melanie Klein Volume 3: Envy and Gratitude and Other Works 1946–1963* (pp. 48–56). London: Hogarth Press [reprinted London: Karnac, 1993].

Klein, M. (1975g). Envy and gratitude. In: *The Writings of Melanie Klein Volume 3: Envy and Gratitude and Other Works 1946–1963* (pp. 176–235). London: Hogarth Press [reprinted London: Karnac, 1993].

Klein, M. (1975h). Our adult world and its roots in infancy. In: *The Writings of Melanie Klein Volume 3: Envy and Gratitude and Other Works 1946–1963* (pp. 247–263). London: Hogarth Press [reprinted London: Karnac, 1993].

Klein, M. (1975i). On the sense of loneliness. In: *The Writings of Melanie Klein Volume 3: Envy and Gratitude and Other Works 1946–1963* (pp. 300–317). London: Hogarth Press [reprinted London: Karnac, 1993].

Lanman, M. (2005). The painful truth. In: F. Grier (Ed.), *Oedipus and the Couple* (pp. 141–162). London: Karnac.

Likierman, M. (2001). *Melanie Klein: Her Work in Context*. London: Continuum.

Likierman, M. (2015). "So unattainable": two accounts of envy. In: *Melanie Klein: Her Work in Context* (pp. 172–191). London. Bloomsbury.

Little, M. (1966). Transference in borderline states. *International Journal of Psychoanalysis, 47*: 476–485.

Lynch, P. (2015). Intimacy and shame in gay male sexuality. In: A. Lemma & P. Lynch (Eds.), *Sexualities: Contemporary Psychoanalytic Perspectives* (pp. 138–156). London: Routledge.

Lyons, A., & Mattinson, J. (1993). Individuation in marriage. In: S. Ruszczynski (Ed.), *Psychotherapy with Couples: Theory and Practice at the Tavistock Institute* (pp. 104–125). London: Karnac.

Marvell, A. (1681). To His Coy Mistress. Available at: www.poets.org/poets org/poem/his-coy-mistress.

Masson, J. M. (Ed.) (1985). *The Complete Letters of Sigmund Freud to Wilhelm Fliess: 1887–1904*, L. Newman, M. Loring, & J. M. Masson (Trans.) (pp. 270–273). Cambridge, MA: Belknap Press of Harvard University Press.

McCann, D. (2014). Responding to needs of same-sex couples. In: D. E. Scharff & J. Savege-Scarff (Eds.), *Psychoanalytic Couple Therapy* (pp. 81–91). London: Karnac.

McDougall, J. (1986). *Theatres of the Mind: Illusion and Truth on the Psychoanalytic Stage*. London: Free Association Books.

Meltzer, D. (1986). The psychoanalytic process: twenty years on, the setting of the analytic encounter and the gathering of the transference. In: A. Hahn (Ed.), *Sincerity and Other Works: Collected Papers of Donald Meltzer* (pp. 551–556). London: Karnac.

Meltzer, D. (1992). *The Claustrum: An Investigation of Claustrophobic Phenomena*. Strathtay, Perthshire: Clunie Press.

Morgan, M. (1995). The projective gridlock: a form of projective identification in couple relationships. In: S. Ruszczynski & J. Fisher (Eds.), *Intrusiveness and Intimacy in the Couple* (pp. 33–48). London: Karnac.

Morgan, M. (2001). First contacts—the therapist's "couple state of mind" as a factor in the containment of couples seen for consultation. In: F. Grier (Ed.), *Brief Encounters with Couples: Some Analytic Perspectives* (pp. 17–32). London: Karnac.

Morgan, M. (2005). On being able to be a couple: the importance of a "creative couple" in psychic life. In: F. Grier (Ed.), *Oedipus and the Couple* (pp. 9–30). London: Karnac.

Morgan, M. (2010). Unbeliefs about being a couple. *fort da, 16*(1): 56–63.

Morgan, M. (2012). How couples work with parenting issues. In: A. Balfour, M. Morgan, & C. Vincent (Eds.), *How Couple Relationships Shape Our World* (pp. 71–83). London: Karnac.

Morgan, M. (2014a). The couple state of mind and some aspects of the setting in couple psychotherapy. In: D. Scharff & J. Savege Scharff (Eds.), *Psychoanalytic Couple Psychotherapy* (pp. 125–130). London: Karnac.

Morgan, M. (2014b). What do we mean by containment? (unpublished paper).

Morgan, M., & Stokoe, P. (2014). Curiosity. *Couple and Family Psychoanalysis, 4*(1): 42–55.

Nathans, S. (2012). Infidelity as a manic defence. *Journal of Couple and Family Psychoanalysis, 2*(2): 165–181.

Novakovic, A. (2016). The quarrelling couple: the couple's unconscious relations and enactments. In: A. Novakovic (Ed.), *Couple Dynamics: Psychoanalytic Perspectives in work with the Individual, the Couple, and the Group* (pp. 85–105). London: Karnac.

Nyberg, V. (2005). Shadows of the parental couple: oedipal themes in Bergman's *Fanny and Alexander*. In: F. Grier (Ed.), *Oedipus and the Couple* (pp. 101–120). London: Karnac.

Ogden, T. (1979). On projective identification. *International Journal of Psychoanalysis, 60*: 357–373.

Person, E. (1988). *Dreams of Love and Fateful Encounters: The Power of Romantic Passion*. New York: W. W. Norton (reprinted Arlington, VA: American Psychiatric Publishing, 2007).

Phillips, A. (1996). *Monogamy*. London: Faber and Faber.

Proust, M. (2002)[1919]. *In the Shadow of Young Girls in Flower*. London: Alan Lane, Penguin.

Quinodoz, D. (2009). Growing old: a psychoanalyst's point of view. *International Journal of Psychoanalysis, 45*: 332–337.

Reid, M. (2003). Clinical research: the inner world of the mother and her new baby—born in the shadow of death. *Journal of Child Psychotherapy, 29*(2): 207–226.

Reid, M. (2011). The impact of traumatic delivery on the mother–infant relationship. *International Journal of Infant Observation and its Applications*, 14(2): 117–128.
Reid, M. (2013). Parenting the next child in the shadow of death. In: E. Quagliata (Ed.), *Becoming Parents and Overcoming Obstacles* (pp. 61–77). London: Karnac.
Rey, J. H. (1988). That which patients bring to analysis. *International Journal of Psychoanalysis*, 69: 457–470.
Rosenfeld, H. R. (1983). Primitive object relations and mechanisms. *International Journal of Psychoanalysis*, 64: 261–267.
Ruszczynski, S. (1993). Thinking about and working with couples. In: S. Ruszczynski (Ed.), *Psychotherapy with Couples* (pp. 197–217). London: Karnac.
Ruszczynski, S. (1995). Narcissistic object relating. In: S. Ruszczynski & J. Fisher (Eds.), *Intrusiveness and Intimacy in the Couple* (pp. 13–32). London: Karnac.
Ruszczynski, S. (2005). Reflective space in the intimate couple relationship: "the marital triangle". In: F. Grier (Ed.), *Oedipus and the Couple* (pp. 31–47). London: Karnac.
Scharff, J. (1992). Projective and introjective identification, love and the internal couple. In: *Projective and Introjective Identification and the Use of the Therapist's Self* (pp. 133–157). Englewood Cliffs, NJ: Jason Aronson.
Segal, H. (1984). Joseph Conrad and the mid-life crisis. *International Review of Psycho-Analysis*, 11: 3–9.
Segal, H. (1988a). Phantasy. In: *Introduction to the Work of Melanie Klein* (pp. 11–23). London: Karnac.
Segal, H. (1988b). The paranoid–schizoid position. In: *Introduction to the Work of Melanie Klein* (pp. 24–38). London: Karnac.
Smith, E. E. (2014). Masters of love. *The Atlantic,* June 12. Available at: www.theatlantic.com/health/archive/2014/06/happily–ever–after/372573/.
Sorenson, P. B. (1997). Thoughts on the containing process from the perspective of infant–mother relations. In: S. Reid (Ed.), *Developments in Infant Observation* (pp. 113–122). London: Brunner Routledge.
Spillius, E. (2007a). Kleinian thought: overview and personal view. In: *Encounters with Melanie Klein: Selected Papers of Elizabeth Spillius* (pp. 25–62). Hove: Routledge.
Spillius, E. (2007b). Varieties of envious experience. In: *Encounters with Melanie Klein: Selected Papers of Elizabeth Spillius* (pp. 140–162). Hove: Routledge.

Steiner, J. (1985). Turning a blind eye: the cover up for Oedipus. *International Review of Psychoanalysis*, 12: 161–172.

Steiner, J. (1988). Interplay between pathological organizations and the paranoid–schizoid and depressive positions. In: E. Bott Spillius (Ed.), *Melanie Klein Today: Developments in Theory and Practice: Volume 1: Mainly Theory* (pp. 324–342). London: Routledge.

Steiner, J. (1992). The equilibrium between the paranoid–schizoid and depressive positions. In: R. Anderson (Ed.), *Clinical Lectures on Klein and Bion* (pp. 46–58). London: Routledge.

Stoller, R. (1983). Judging psychotherapy. Unpublished manuscript.

Swift, G. (2016). *Mothering Sunday*. London: Scribner.

Tarsh, H., & Bollinghaus, E. (1999). Shared unconscious phantasy: reality or illusion. *Sexual and Marital Therapy*, 14: 123–136.

Tseng, W.-S., Chang, S. C., & Nishisono, M. (Eds.) (2005). *Asian Culture and Psychotherapy: Implications for East and West*. Honolulu: University of Hawaii Press.

Westcott, B. (2017). Essence of group analysis. Unpublished paper.

Willi, J. (1984). The concept of collusion: a combined systemic–psychodynamic approach to marital therapy. *Family Process*, 23: 177–185.

Winnicott, D. W. (1984). Primary maternal preoccupation. In: *Through Paediatrics to Psychoanalysis: Collected Papers* (pp. 300–305). London: Karnac.

Winnicott, D. W. (1960). The theory of the parent–infant relationship. In: *The Maturational Processes and the Facilitating Environment* (pp. 37–55). London: Hogarth Press.

Wollheim, R. (1984). *The Thread of Life*. Cambridge, MA: Harvard University Press.

Woodhouse, D. (1990). The Tavistock Institute of Marital Studies: evolution of a marital agency. In: C. Clulow (Ed.), *Marriage: Disillusion and Hope* (pp. 69–119). London: Karnac.

Zavattini, G. C., Bianchini, B., Capello, M., Dallanegra, L., Lupinacci, M. A., Monguzzi, F., and Vitalini, L. (2015). *Talking with Couples. Psychoanalytic Psychotherapy of the Couple Relationship*. London: Karnac & The Harris Meltzer Trust.

Zepf, S., Zepf, F., Ullrich, B., & Seel, D. (2016). *Oedipus and the Oedipus Complex: A Revision*. London: Karnac.

Zinner, J. (1988). Projective identification is a key to resolving marital conflict. Unpublished paper.

INDEX

abandonment, 6–7, 29, 37, 97, 103, 111, 132, 160, 187–188
affect(ive), 109, 182
  balance, 93
  dysregulation, 93, 95
    negative, 93
  experience, 95
  hotspot, 93
  information, 93
  negative, 93
  positive, 93
  regulation, 93
  theme, 93
aggression, 7, 19, 21, 42–43, 48, 104, 122–123, 142, 156, 158, 193
anger, 6, 8, 15, 20, 22, 57, 64, 77, 87, 93, 98, 102, 104, 108–109, 132, 143, 145, 167, 172, 174, 177, 181, 185–189, 193 see also: unconscious
anxiety, 3–4, 7, 10, 13, 17, 20, 23, 29, 38, 43, 49, 55, 59–60, 62, 67, 72, 77, 94, 103–104, 111, 121, 124, 129–130, 138, 141, 147, 149, 158–159, 167, 175–178, 187, 193
  see also: unconscious
  acute, 133
  basic, 111
  depressive, 4
  distressing, 31
  disturbing, 122
  frenzy of, 15
  infant's, 49–50
  main, 5, 9
  oedipal, 38, 122
  paranoid, 16, 24
    -schizoid, 4
  persecutory, 5–6, 15, 19
  projected, 59, 158
  primitive, 29, 30, 129
  reduction, 158
  related, 5
  shared, 159
  situations, 5
  surge of, 13
attachment, 98, 103, 108, 110, 166

attenuated, 110
enormous, 110
intense, 109
primary, 103–104
    figure, 92
    ruptured, 156

Balfour, A., 28, 37
Bannister, K., 187
behaviour, 52, 65, 68, 95, 97, 106, 119, 124, 159, 161, 179, 193
    defensive, 179
    evocative, 50
    patterns, 55
    regressive, 37
    unexpected, 63
Benghozi, P., 180–181
Bergman, I., 35
Berkowitz, D., 29
Bianchini, B., 80
Bion, W. R., 5, 10, 31, 49–50, 52, 56, 60, 66, 68–70, 73, 76, 78–81, 97, 126–127, 149, 152–153, 180, 190, 194
Bléandonu, G., 70
Bollas, C., 51
Bollinghaus, E., 38
Boswell, J., 30
Bott Spillius, E., 50
Bourne, S., 191
Britton, R., 9–10, 29–34, 36, 45, 51, 102, 127, 136, 139, 151, 166, 185

Cain, A., 190
Cain, B., 190
Capello, M., 80
case studies
    Daniel and *Caroline*, 141–167, 195
    Don and *Carol*, 71–72, 77, 81
    Erica and *Mona*, 42–43
    Greg and *Lottie*, 169–195
    Marco and *Rosa*, 85–111, 195
    Peter and *Helen*, 113–140, 195
    Sade and *Errol*, 76–77, 81
    Ted and *Tania*, 39–40
Chang, S. C., 44

Clarke, J., 44
Cleavely, E., 51, 53, 80
Clulow, C., 39
Colman, W., 52, 79–81, 191
complex *see also*: Oedipus
    Don Juan, 42
    Electra, 25
    Ganesh, 44
    parent–child, 44
conscious(ness), 17, 27, 53, 65, 73, 75, 77, 80, 84, 91, 127, 137, 147, 153–154, 165 *see also*: unconscious
    choice of partner, 53
    container, 58
    continuous, 73
    drives, 75
    elements, 100
    emergence of, 73
    experience, 188
    fantasy, 134
    forms, 70
    illusions, 34
    imaginings, 23
    implication, 74
    impression, 18
    intent, 91
    level, 7, 17
    love, 74
    partial, 73
    pre-, 26
    preoccupations, 11
    reflections, 37
    relations, xxiii
    thought, 133
    wishes, 75
containment, xxiii, 6, 15, 31, 49, 53, 56, 81, 94–95, 98, 147, 149–150, 190, 194 *see also*: conscious, object, unconscious
    flexible, 56
    importance of, 30
    inadequate, 191
    individual, 79
    limited, 50
    maternal, 32

    parental, 185
    process of, 49
    psychic, 37
    self-, 73
couples, xix–xx, xxiii–xxiv, 3, 23, 27,
    36–37, 39, 41–42, 44, 47, 53, 57,
    59–60, 62, 66, 73, 80–81, 93, 100,
    103, 120, 123, 128, 130, 135–137,
    160, 179, 185, 193 *see also*:
    depression, ego, phantasy,
    sexual, unconscious
    inner, 137
    narcissistic, 59
    "no sex", 129
    same-sex, xx
Couve, C., 50
Cudmore, L., 57

Dallanegra, L., 80
depression, 57, 63, 70, 102, 104, 115,
    129, 159, 161, 178, 182 *see also*:
    anxiety
    atmosphere, 190
    concern, 17, 23
    couple, 189
    father, 187
    functioning, 131
    guilt, 22
    mother, 43
    partner, 63
    position, xxiii, 3–4, 8–10, 13–14,
        16–23, 29, 31, 56, 71, 129, 132,
        166
    psychotic, 9
    reactive, 169
    state of mind, 11
    undiagnosed, 43
development(al) (*passim*)
    aspects, 10
    capacity, 38
    changes, 122
    child, 6, 18, 28, 161
    constant, xix
    difficulties, 123
    dynamic, 85
    early, 4, 7–8, 48–50, 77

emotional, 97, 133
expansions, 73
failure, 33
Freudian, 25
healthy, xix
human, 68, 166
hurdles, 37
impetus, 188
individual, 107
infant, 185
interpersonal, 102
journeys, 135, 139
mental, 9
normal, 32–33, 50
pathway, 42
phase, 167
possibilities, 44, 106
potential, 102, 140
process, 28, 66
psychic, 20, 55–57, 66
psychological, 41, 68, 75
relationship, 80
significant, xxiv, 49
social, 41
spectrum, 41
trigger points, 28
understanding of, xxi
Dicks, H. V., 54, 75
Dylan, B., 127

ego, 48, 54, 57, 166
    -couple, 181–182
    -family, 181
Elmhirst, S. I., 152
envy, 5, 7–8, 10, 19, 21, 28, 31, 38, 49,
    69, 86, 105–106, 108, 133
    oedipal, 35
    primitive, 130
Ezriel, H., 111

fantasy, 23, 31, 50, 121, 132, 147, 150
    see also: conscious, unconscious
    narrative, 132
    object, 92
Feldman, M., 29, 52
Fisher, J., 55, 60–61

Freeman, H., 157
Freud, S., 8, 25–29, 32, 35–37, 41, 44–45, 80, 121, 139, 154, 156–157, 166, 192 *see also*: development

Garvey, P., 50
generosity, 9, 15, 18, 20–23, 62, 128, 140
Green, P., 128, 152
grief, 10, 118, 140, 173, 177, 186–187, 193
  healing, 21
Grier, F., 129, 160, 185, 187
Grotstein, J. S., 5, 65
guilt, 9–10, 20, 22, 72, 117, 126, 147, 150, 165, 174, 177, 182–183, 185–189, 191 *see also*: depression, unconscious
  feelings, 34–35, 174, 178
  nameless, 191
  persecutory, 9, 12, 19
  profound, 164
  -ridden, 34
  sense of, 35, 164
  shadow of, 189
  survivor's, 192

Halton, W., 18–19, 24
hate, 4, 10, 15, 18, 21–23, 36, 64, 116, 143, 151, 155, 171
  -filled, 99
Hertzmann, L., 44
Hewison, D., 6, 44, 187
Hinshelwood, R. D., 4, 8, 150

instinct(ual), 65, 74–75, 79
intervention, 76, 95, 99–100, 109, 125, 139–140, 149, 190
introjection, xxi, 4–5, 49–51, 55, 58, 67–68, 80, 166, 192

Jaques, E., 10, 21
jealousy, 7, 25, 27, 38, 88, 93, 143, 148–149, 155, 159, 161, 174, 184
  oedipal, 130
Johns, M., 37

Jones, E., 27
Joseph, B., 56, 131
Josephs, L., 42
Judd, D., 57
Jung, C. G., 66, 73–75, 77, 79–81

Kaës, R., 182
Kernberg, O., 22, 43
Kirsner, D., 175
Klein, M., 3–5, 7–9, 11, 18, 21–23, 29–32, 47–50, 52, 54, 66–69, 80, 139, 160, 166, 185, 190

Lanman, M., 35
Lewis, E., 191
Likierman, M., 7, 166
Little, M., 58
love, 4, 10, 18–23, 25, 36, 38, 41, 45, 53, 64, 70, 74, 86, 92, 96, 98–99, 111, 125, 128, 151, 157, 166, 170, 178, 187 *see also*: conscious, object
  absence of, 15
  illicit, 127
  missing, 98
  mother's, 35
  nourishing, 18
  passionate, 98
  -relationships, 11
  -less, 41
  simple, 74
  un-, 179
Lupinacci, M. A., 80
Lynch, P., 44
Lyons, A., 58

Marvell, A., 127
Masson, J. M., 25, 154
Mattinson, J., 58
McCann, D., 29
McDougall, J., 99
Meltzer, D., 52, 60–62, 80
Milton, J., 50
Monguzzi, F., 80
Morgan, M., 6, 20–21, 28, 40, 42–43, 47, 61, 63, 71, 106, 132, 136, 138, 185, 189–190

mourning, 9–10, 21–23, 34, 41, 57, 86, 92, 102, 125, 128, 132, 139, 151, 174, 181–188, 192, 194
  effective, 134
  importance of, 9
  unresolved, 102, 194

narcissistic, 47, 55–56, 61, 104, 106, 109 *see also*: couples
  fit, 60
  object, 60
  personality, 102, 108
  relationship, 47, 51
  structure, 56
Nathans, S., 28–29, 41
Nishisono, M., 44
Novakovic, A., 17, 55
Nyberg, V., 9, 35

object, 6–7, 12–14, 17, 23, 30, 41, 48, 50–52, 54–57, 59–60, 62, 123
  see also: fantasy, narcissistic, split, unconscious
  containing, 49
  fragile, 193
  good, 6–7
  inner, 60, 127
  internal, 48, 54, 58
  lost, 192
  loved, 7, 32, 156, 183
  maternal, 31, 94, 186
  new, 181
  oedipal, 42
  of desire, 32, 42
  of projection, 67
  parental, 42
  part-, 23, 54
  primary, 166
  psychic, 20
  relations, 3, 17, 23, 32, 36, 54, 56, 60, 107, 137, 151
    aggressive, 48
    internal, 63
    primary, 55
  shared, 184
  unknown, 11–13

untrustworthy, 49
whole, 24
oedipal *see also*: anxiety, envy, jealousy, object, unconscious
  bedroom, 154
  configuration, 45, 186
  conflict, 27, 42, 120
  constellation, 102
  difficulties, 132
  dilemmas, 25, 46
  disillusionment, 14
  divide, 122
  drama, 27
  dynamics, xxiii, 20, 155–156, 185–186, 189
  experience, 45
  feelings, 28–29, 35–36, 41, 45
  framework, 45
  hurdles, 137
  issues, 38, 151, 185, 191
  illusions, 30, 33–34
  longings, 43, 45, 166
  manifestations, 34
  phantasies, 8, 38
  preoccupations, 12
  reality, 33
  rejection, 44
  relationships, 135
  resolution, 35
  setting, 37
  shadows, 185
  situation, 9, 18, 29–34, 42, 160, 162, 166–167, 185
  spectrum, 36
  stakes, 183
  strivings, 45
  struggle, 13, 34, 38, 122, 167
  tensions, 36
  themes, 34, 104
  triangle, 25, 31–35, 42, 139–140, 185, 187
  triumph, 186
  victory, 137
Oedipus, 26, 30, 44, 157, 160
  complex, xxi, 8–9, 20, 25–36, 44–45, 106, 153, 160, 166

legend, 154
myth, 25–27, 44, 139
theory, 26
Ogden, T., 50, 58

paranoid, 24, 104 *see also*: anxiety
  defences, 5
  experience, 13
  fear, 17, 23
  –schizoid
    function, 131
    level, 7
    position, xxiii, 3–6, 8–10, 18–19, 21–23, 67, 71, 132
    state, 8, 11–13, 81, 159, 161
    universe, 48
Person, E., 42
phantasy, 4–5, 9–14, 17–20, 23, 27, 30, 33–34, 38, 42, 47, 51–52, 60–62, 66–68, 132, 139, 161, 191–192
  see also: oedipal, unconscious
  child's, 41
  couple, 19–20, 37, 39
  defensive, 30
  erotised, 45
  human, 26
  internal, 68
  intrapsychic, 5
  mother, 42
  persecutory, 12, 19
  primitive, 48
  projective, 50–51
  relationship, 42
  unrealistic, 29
  world, 9
Phillips, A., 135
Pincus, L., 187
projection, 4–5, 7, 12–13, 23, 48, 50–51, 53–54, 56–60, 62–63, 66–67, 69, 72, 75, 80, 106, 130–131, 133, 158, 160, 193
  see also: anxiety, unconscious
  archetypal, 79
  child's, 19
  experiences, 50
  hostile, 43
  intrusive, 60–61
projective *see also*: phantasy
  gridlock, 43, 47, 60
  identification, xxi, xxiii, 5–7, 13, 47–64, 66–71, 75, 78–80, 111, 140
  processes, 51, 56, 59, 66–67
  system, 42–43, 47, 52–57, 59, 62–63
Proust, M., 3, 11–12, 16–18
psychoanalytic, 133
  concepts, xxiii–xxiv, 53
  couple therapists, xxiv, 135, 137, 179
  field, 68
  formulation, xxi
  frame, 120
  gift, 47
  ideas, xxiii
  institutions, 175
  lens, xxi
  literature, 28
  model, 101
  parlance, 25
  perspective, 127
  practitioners, 155
  psychology, 155
  psychotherapy, 65, 85, 91, 101, 113, 163, 180
  school, 29
  theory, xxi, 25, 27, 29, 69
  therapeutic modality, 180
  thinking, 28, 65, 80
  understanding, 25, 29, 41
  ways of working, xxiv
  work, 120, 152, 154, 160, 166
  writers, 29

Quinodoz, D., 123

Reid, M., 150, 186, 191
rejection, 7, 22, 27, 39, 56, 103–106, 181, 185, 188–189 *see also*: oedipal
Rey, J. H., 127
Rosenfeld, H. R., 54
Ruszczynski, S., 55, 102, 135, 185–186, 194

Scharff, J., 58
Seel, D., 45
Segal, H., 4, 6, 15, 123
self, 4–9, 23, 33, 48–49, 53–54, 56, 58–59, 63, 67–68 *see also*: containment
  -analysis, 25
  -assured, 59
  bad, 48
  beautiful, 102
  -denying, 140
  -destructive, 9
  good, 48
  -protective, 102, 163
  -recognition, 134
  -reflection, 133
  sense of, 57, 60–61, 67, 74, 102
  -sufficient, 121, 140
sexual(ity), 19, 41, 80, 121–124, 134, 164, 185 *see also*: unconscious
  activity, 164
  adult, 37
  attraction, 53
  couple, 14, 122–124, 166
  desire, 41, 44
  difficulties, 132
  expression, 29
  feelings, 45
  hetero-, 29, 71, 80, 107, 160
  identity, 44–45
  infantile, 37
  inhibition, 133
  intercourse, 31
  life, 75, 119, 148–149
  non-, 138
  parental, 30
  practices, xx
  relationship, 31–32, 36, 40–41, 101, 128, 132
  satisfaction, 40
Smith, E. E., 128
Sorenson, P. B., 147
Spillius, E., 4, 7
splitting, 4–6, 12–13, 31, 38–39, 41–42, 48, 55–56, 63, 67, 69, 72, 78, 94, 123, 133

  -object triangulation, 42
Sprince, J., 18–19, 24
Steiner, D., 50
Steiner, J., 9–10, 127, 160
Stokoe, P., 136
Stoller, R., 175
subject(ive), 5–10, 13, 20–22, 48, 51, 57, 62–63, 66, 74, 78, 115, 134
  belief, 30
  cultural, 44
  experience, 35
  inter, 17, 65, 180–182
  singular, 182
Swift, G., 118, 127, 132, 134
symbol(-ic), 35, 67, 131, 134, 139
  excitement, 130
  formation, 62
  meaning, 126
  reparation, 126
  representations, 27, 36, 42
  story, 125

Tarsh, H., 38
Tavistock Relationships, 53, 57, 79, 155
transference, xx, 53, 109–111, 120, 136, 184, 188
  counter-, xx, 84, 95, 111, 124, 133, 147, 161
  maternal, 148
  pre-, 180
  sibling, 107
Tseng, W.-S., 44

Ullrich, B., 45
unconscious(ness) (*passim*) *see also*: conscious
  agreement, 63
  alliance, 182
    pact of, 181–182
    therapeutic, 180
  anger, 162
  anxieties, 42–43, 159, 179
  arrangement, 57
  artificially, 74
  attraction, 102

belief, 20, 139
blame, 162
choice of partner, 48, 53–54, 63, 101
collusion, 43
communication, xxi, 65
complementariness, 54
conflicts, 40
construction, 98
contained, 58–59, 147
couple fit, 48
driven, 102
dynamics, 12, 17
   couple, 47
elements, 100
engagement, 17
expectations, 37, 43
experience, 52, 188
factors, 53
fantasies, 134
fear, 132, 165
feelings, 132
   of hate, 21
   sexual, 45
forces, 59
forms, 70
function, 80
guilt, 35, 40
   sense of, 35
identification, 18, 155
identity, 75
image, 182
imagination, 69
immersion, 127
implication, 74
impression, 18
incestuous
   attentions, 155
   longings, 40
invitation, 93
level, 6, 17, 175

links, 181
material, 69
metaphor, 131
minds, 21
motivation, 20, 74, 101
need, 38
objects, 17, 55
oedipal strivings, 45
organisation, xx
parental, 45
phantasy, 4–5, 42, 48–50, 52–54, 59, 134, 186, 192
   couple, 37
   nature of, 23
   omnipotent, 52
preoccupations, 11, 124
projection, 45, 162
recognition, 63, 80
relations, xxiii, 17, 53, 55, 74
representation, 4, 12
   mental, 4, 23
rivalrous attack, 43
sentiments, 180
shame, 130
strategies, 175
system, 53, 62

Vitalini, L., 80

Westcott, B., 22
Willi, J., 55
Winnicott, D. W., 68–69, 102, 152–153
Wollheim, R., 100
Woodhouse, D., 56

Zavattini, G. C., 80
Zepf, F., 45
Zepf, S., 45
Zinner, J., 60

Printed in Great Britain
by Amazon